Changing Architectural Ed

Higher education in the built environment is under pressure to change in order to cope with increasing student numbers in the face of diminishing resources, to meet the demands of an evolving construction industry and to prepare students more explicitly for their working lives and changes in society—in short, to foster a new professionalism.

This book examines and discusses contemporary architectural education through a series of case studies that illustrate how educators have responded to the need for change. In particular, there is a focus on the potential of design studio teaching to enhance attitudes and skills in communication and teamworking and to prepare students for lifelong learning.

Changing Architectural Education is written by teachers of architecture for teachers, and it

- gives an up-to-date account of research on learning and its implications for architecture,
- provides a source of practical ideas to enhance design-studio teaching,
- suggests strategies for improving assessment practices,
- illustrates ways of supporting change across a whole school of architecture.

This book brings together contributions from those working in the fields of architectural education, architectural practice and educational research both in the UK and the USA. The writers are at the leading edge of educational development and they describe how they, and their schools of architecture, have been responding to the professional challenges.

David Nicol has been working in the field of educational development, both nationally and internationally, for over twenty years. He is now at the Centre for Academic Practice at the University of Strathclyde, Scotland, where he works in partnership with academic departments and faculties on educational improvement projects. He is also a consultant on higher education to a number of universities and he has published widely in this area.

Simon Pilling is an architect with broad experience both in practice and in education as a design studio tutor. Particularly concerned with the role of the architect in contemporary society, he has served on national committees addressing this topic. Now working as a freelance consultant, he coordinated the HEFC-funded teaching and learning project 'Clients and Users in Design Education' (CUDE).

Changing Architectural Education

Towards a new professionalism

Edited by David Nicol and Simon Pilling

London and New York

First published 2000
by Spon Press
11 New Fetter Lane, London EC4P 4EE

Simultaneously published in the USA and Canada
by Spon Press
29 West 35th Street, New York, NY 10001

Spon Press is an imprint of the Taylor & Francis Group

Typeset in Frutiger by Keyword Publishing Services Ltd
Printed and bound in Great Britain by Biddles Ltd, Guildford and King's Lynn

British Library Cataloguing in Publication Data
A catalogue record for this book is available from the British Library

Library of Congress Cataloguing in Publication Data
Changing architectural education: towards a new professionalism/edited by David
Nicol and Simon Pilling.
   p.cm.
 Includes bibliographical references and index.
 1. Architecture – Study and teaching. I. Nicol, David, 1950– II. Pilling, Simon, 1952–

NA2000 C48 2000
720'.71–dc21

                                                                            00-023887

ISBN 0-419-25920-1

Contents

List of figures   viii
List of tables   ix
List of contributors   x
Preface   xiii
Foreword by Robin Nicholson   xv

1 Architectural education and the profession:
   preparing for the future   1
   DAVID NICOL AND SIMON PILLING

2 The changing context of professional practice   27
   JOHN WORTHINGTON

SECTION 1
**Communication: developing sensitivity to the
needs of users and clients**   41

3 Architectural assumptions and environmental
   discrimination: the case for more inclusive design
   in schools of architecture   43
   RUTH MORROW

4 Seeing the world through another person's eyes   49
   ROBERT BROWN AND DENITZA MOREAU YATES

5 Social practice: design education and everyday life   58
   CHRISTOPHER JARRETT

6 The degree laboratory: the work of Unit Six at the
   Bartlett School, University College London   71
   NICK CALLICOTT AND BOB SHEIL

7 Introducing clients and users to the studio project: a case study of a 'live' project 77
RACHEL SARA

8 The development of group-working skills and role play in the first-year architecture course 84
JUDITH TORRINGTON

9 The 'real' client and the 'unreal' project: a diploma case study 93
PRUE CHILES

10 Reviewing the review: an account of a research investigation of the 'crit' 100
MARGARET WILKIN

11 Introducing alternative formats for the design project review: a case study 108
TIM BRINDLEY, CHARLES DOIDGE AND ROSS WILLMOTT

SECTION 2
Collaboration: developing teamworking skills for professional practice 117

12 Habits and habitats: interdisciplinary collaboration in a community architecture studio 119
KATERINA RÜEDI

13 Is working together working? 128
JAKI HOWES

14 Developing skills with people: a vital part of architectural education 137
ANGELA FISHER

15 Achieving richness and diversity: combining architecture and planning at UWE, Bristol 145
SANDRA MANLEY AND JIM CLAYDON

16 Integrated architectural design: issues and models 155
STIRLING HOWIESON

17 Interdisciplinary working in built environment education 165
GERARD WOOD

SECTION 3
Lifelong learning: developing independence in learning 177

18 Learning in practice: a retreat, an opportunity
or an imperative? 179
JUDITH V. FARREN BRADLEY

19 The role of personal development plans and learning
contracts in self-directed student learning 191
DEREK COTTRELL

20 Establishing and managing a student learning contract:
a diploma in architecture case study 201
HELENA WEBSTER

21 The student-led 'crit' as a learning device 211
ROSIE WHITE

SECTION 4
**A new professionalism: embedding change
in schools of architecture** 221

22 Delight in transgression: shifting boundaries
in architectural education 223
LEONIE MILLINER

23 Schools and practice in the United States 232
ROBERT GUTMAN

24 The design studio as a vehicle for change:
the 'Portsmouth Model' 241
WENDY POTTS

25 Embedding change: a case study of the CUDE experience 252
GEORGE HENDERSON

26 The 'crit' as a ritualised legitimation procedure in
architectural education 259
HANNAH VOWLES

27 Preparation and support of part-time teachers: designing
a tutor training programme fit for architects 265
NICHOLAS WEAVER, DAVE O'REILLY AND MARY CADDICK

28 Evaluation and feedback in architectural education 274
JOHN COWAN

Appendix Workshop plans: teamwork 284

Figures

2.1	Education for diversity	28
2.2	High-value services are increasingly outside the core of the design and construction process	30
2.3	Different competences required to optimise the workplace	32
2.4	The components of intellectual capital	35
2.5	Evolution of a practice's intellectual property—DEGW	36
2.6	Distribution of competency and roles	38
8.1	Students' initial self-assessment of strengths and weaknesses	85
15.1	Award Structure Diagram: BA (Hons) Architecture and Planning	150
17.1	The Kolb learning cycle as a developmental spiral	171
20.1	Example of completed two-year plan—the formalised student learning contract	205
21.1	Student feedback: increasing participation	213
21.2	Student feedback: improving presentation	214
21.3	Student feedback: constructive criticism	215
21.4	Tutor feedback: increasing participation	216
21.5	Tutor feedback: improving presentation	216
21.6	Tutor feedback: constructive criticism	217

Tables

2.1   Redefining the professional service   32
2.2   Change in the distribution of total costs for a
       typical office building   33
11.1 Alternative formats for design project reviews   109
11.2 Alternative review formats selected for first-year
       students   111
11.3 Alternative review formats selected for second-year
       students   111
20.1 Graduate diploma in architecture 1998: course
       components and subjects offered in each
       component   202
20.2 Diploma in architecture: examples of common
       course routes leading to DipArch and Dip/MA
       alternative route   203
20.3 Structure of the learning contract module, as
       defined in the *Staff Diploma Guidelines* manual   210

Contributors

Tim Brindley is Director of Postgraduate Studies in the Leicester School of Architecture, De Montfort University UK. He was the project leader for the Design Project Reviews study, and is developing computer-based teaching and learning for De Montfort's Electronic Campus programme.

Robert Brown is an associate with Levitt Bernstein Architects and tutors at the Universities of East London and Westminster UK.

Mary Caddick, a fine artist with a background in art education and art psychotherapy, is the Course Tutor of the Tutor Training programme at the School of Architecture at the University of East London UK.

Nick Callicott is a partner in the architectural practice sixteen* (makers) and teaches at the Bartlett school University College London UK.

Prue Chiles is an architect and diploma course coordinator at the School of Architecture at the University of Sheffield UK.

Jim Claydon is the Head of the School of Planning and Architecture at the University of the West of England, Bristol UK.

Derek Cottrell is Head of Hull School of Architecture, University of Lincolnshire and Humberside UK.

John Cowan is a Senior research fellow at Perth College, University of the Highlands and Island Project UK.

Charles Doidge is Undergraduate Course Leader at Leicester School of Architecture, De Montfort University UK.

Judith V. Farren Bradley is Principal Lecturer and Course Director in Professional Practice at Kingston University UK, Sector Chair for Part 3 and CPD with the RIBA Review of Education, member of the RIBA Part 3 Review Task Force, and the QAA subject benchmarking group.

Angela Fisher is an education consultant and coordinator of the CUDE project at the School of Architecture, University of Sheffield UK.

Robert Gutman is Professor of Sociology Emeritus at Rutgers University and currently is Lecturer in Architecture at Princeton University USA.

George Henderson is Head of School and Professor of Architecture at The Leicester School of Architecture, De Montfort University UK, President of the Commonwealth Association of Architecture and was RIBA Vice President for Education between 1996 and 1998.

Jaki Howes is course leader of BA(Hons) Architecture and leader of the TIME-IT Project at Leeds Metropolitan University UK.

Stirling Howieson is a Chartered Architect and Director of Studies in Building Design Engineering at the University of Strathclyde UK.

Christopher Jarrett is Assistant Professor of Architecture Georgia Institute of Technology, Atlanta, Georgia, USA.

Sandra Manley is a planner and senior lecturer and led the team that developed a new degree in architecture and planning at the University of the West of England, Bristol UK.

Leonie Milliner is RIBA Director of Education UK.

Ruth Morrow coordinated a project based in the School of Architecture, University College Dublin, Eire, to develop the awareness and design skills needed to achieve inclusive access to the built environment.

David Nicol is based at the Centre for Academic Practice at the University of Strathclyde UK and has been working in the field of educational development, both nationally and internationally, for over twenty years.

Robin Nicholson is a director of Edward Cullinan Architects, chairman of the Construction Industry Council and board member of the Movement for Innovation.

Dave O'Reilly is Head of Research in Educational Development at the University of East London UK and works on the Tutor Training programme within the Department of Architecture.

Simon Pilling is an architect and overall coordinator of the HEFC-funded teaching and learning project 'Clients and Users in Design Education' (CUDE).

Wendy Potts is Head of the School of Architecture at the University of Portsmouth UK. Member of Standing Conference of Heads of Schools of Architecture-Steering Committee, Joint Validation Panel Executive Committee, RIBA Overseas Advisory Group, ARB European Advisory Group and elected UK representative of European Association for Architectural Education.

Katerina Rüedi is Director of and Professor at the School of Architecture at the University of Illinois at Chicago USA, teaching architectural design, architectural theory and professional practice.

Rachel Sara is a PhD student and studio design tutor, at the School of Architecture, University of Sheffield UK.

Bob Sheil is a partner in the architectural practice sixteen* (makers) and teaches at the Bartlett school University College London UK.

Judith Torrington is an architect in private practice and part-time visiting first year tutor at the School of Architecture, University of Sheffield UK.

Hannah Vowles trained as an architect and works as an artist. She is a founding partner of ART in RUINS collaborative art practice and a senior lecturer at the Birmingham School of Architecture, University of Central England UK.

Nicholas Weaver is Deputy Head of Architecture, Reader in Education Development and works on the Tutor Training Course at the University of East London UK.

Helena Webster is an architect and currently chair of the diploma course in Architecture at Oxford Brookes University UK.

Rosie White is a PhD student and studio design tutor, at the School of Architecture, University of Sheffield UK.

Margaret Wilkin is an educational researcher based at Homerton College, Cambridge UK.

Ross Willmott is a member of the Centre for Education Technology and Development at De Montfort University UK, and coordinator of the CUDE project at the Leicester School of Architecture.

Gerard Wood is a Principal Lecturer in the School of the Built Environment at Leeds Metropolitan University UK. His subject specialisms include Interdisciplinary Studies across a range of undergraduate courses and Project Management at both undergraduate and postgraduate levels.

John Worthington is a founder partner at DEGW, visiting professor in Briefing & Building Performance at the University of Sheffield, CUDE Project Director, and former professor of architecture at the Institute of Advanced Architectural Studies at the University of York UK.

Denitza Moreau Yates is a designer at Fraser Brown McKenna Architects and a part-time tutor at the University of East London UK.

Preface

In April 1999 an international conference—Changing Architectural Education: Society's Call for a New Professionalism—was hosted at De Montfort University, Leicester, UK. Attended by over 70 full- and part-time educationalists/practitioners and students from the UK, mainland Europe and the USA, its aim was to share experiences in innovative studio teaching methods. The underlying theme of the two days was the changing context of practice and the need to reflect this in the expectations of architectural education and its approach to teaching and learning. Two further goals underpinned the conference: to create a forum for the often 'unheard voices' of architectural education—part-time tutors drawn from architectural practice, and student graduates; and to focus on the processes of architectural education—looking at how students learn, rather than just what they learn.

Over the course of two days the conference participants heard 42 presentations from part-time teachers, full-time academics, heads of schools, students and representatives of the professional institute—the Royal Institute of British Architects. The main focus of the presentations was innovation in teaching and learning in architectural education—the scope was wide ranging. Some contributors described innovations in design studio teaching that centred on community, interdisciplinary and client-based projects. Others described how the review process, or crit, had been developed to make it more participative and a better vehicle for learning. Others described how teaching had been restructured across whole schools of architecture in support of better learning, or how to prepare tutors to teach in the design studio. In all the presentations there was attention to ways of improving students' acquisition of skills—in design, teamworking and communication—and to the development of independence in learning. The participants showed a determination to bring a new professionalism to the delivery of architectural education—to effect change based on a radical rethink of the context for which students are being educated and the skills they will require.

The origins of this book lie in that conference, an event made possible by a grant received from the Higher Education Funding Council for England (HEFCE) for a three-year teaching development programme: Clients and Users in Design Education (CUDE). Since reference is extensively made throughout the book to this acronym, it would seem appropriate briefly to explain the initiative here.

In 1996 the HEFCE created a Fund for the Development of Teaching and Learning (FDTL), for which bids were invited from university departments across all subjects to catalogue and disseminate good teaching practice. The CUDE project was one such funded programme. Its goal was to bring a greater understanding of clients, users and cross-disciplinary working into design education, using the design studio as its primary vehicle. Undertaken at the former Institute of Advanced Architectural Studies at the University of York, in association with the Universities of Sheffield and De Montfort at Leicester, the programme was aimed at enhancing students' skills in listening, communication and teamwork, in the context of a collaborative rather than a confrontational approach to learning. These themes are developed throughout the book.

This is a snapshot of architectural education at the end of a decade that has seen dramatic changes in professional practice. It is hoped that this book will act as a prompt for reflection and stimulate a broader debate.

DAVID NICOL AND SIMON PILLING

Foreword

Robin Nicholson CBE

The Clients and Users in Design Education (CUDE) process gives me real hope that tomorrow's architects will have a greater chance to be more effective as conceivers and coordinators of the built environment.

CUDE has brought together a number of educators who are questioning our traditional practices in education and are 'trying to do it completely differently' as Sir John Egan (1998) would put it. A programme of sharing ideas in particular fields has begun.

We should not, however, underestimate the enormity of achieving the necessary cultural change in the ever more competitive higher education industry, which, like the design professions themselves, is struggling to deal with nineteenth-century professional models. It is even more difficult when the promoters of the status quo can point to the very real success of the British architectural elite in the world marketplace. If we can be so successful, should we not just do what we do a great deal better?

There is no doubt, that we already operate in a global economy, although a great deal of the work we do is and will continue to be at a very small scale—for example, 80 per cent of European construction enterprises employ fewer than 10 people. But the rules of the game have changed, again. After a devastating 20-year assault by the crusaders of the free market and the collapse of institutionalised socialism, we can begin to see the way towards understanding the needs and opportunities of the knowledge-based society that so many commentators have been trying to clarify for us for so long.

Few truly 'heard' the messages contained in the *Strategic Study of the Profession*, published by the Royal Institute of British Architects (RIBA, 1992, 1993, 1995), where for the first time the institute asked our clients what they really thought of the service we gave them. In his Introduction to Phase 2 of the study (*Clients and Architects*, October 1993) the then RIBA president, Frank Duffy, spoke of the 'need to be prepared to devote as much design imagination to managing their [architects'] relations with clients as they devote to crafting their clients' buildings', a subject that in his words is the 'one single, critically important relationship that rivets the attention day by day, week by week, of all practising architects.'

Surely we now have to overthrow the received myth that, as architects, we lead the design process by right and that we can do it on our own. Rather there is lurking in the interstices of our culture a radical belief in cooperation, that the whole (team) is greater than the sum of its parts, or as Charles Leadbetter (1999) puts it, 'An ethic of collaboration is central to knowledge-creating societies. In order to create we must collaborate.'

One of the most heartening aspects of this publication is the, albeit small, number of green shoots of courses with overlapping professional subject areas such as architecture with planning. This is just a beginning in the refocusing of the industry's formations.

To collaborate requires mutual respect—one of the radical concepts in Egan's programme for change that pleasantly surprised me as being so central to this forthright industrialist's ideas. Immediately, this highlights a major issue in our education—a process that traditionally leads us to demand respect for the architect with little or no mutuality. If that was ever sustainable, it certainly ceased to be so during the 1970s, when the pattern of authority right around the world was changed irrevocably and since which we, and it could be argued the professions in their traditional form, have been progressively marginalised.

The central role of design in our education is of course vital to the nurture of our unique 'core' skills and our central contribution to society. But, I would contend, educating all students of architecture towards achieving the goal of 'signature architect'—in my day Frank Lloyd Wright, and perhaps today Zaha Hadid—does not help the 95 per cent who will not begin to achieve that level of invention coupled with a necessarily ruthless approach to implementation.

The UK weekly newspaper for architects—*Building Design*—recently published a review of the 'top 100 architectural students'. It revealed the continuing strength of this myth, through the stated desire of 98 per cent of them to have their own office within 10 years. It is this myth that lies at the heart of our malaise because it allows architecture to be self-justifying and above criticism, except occasionally from other architects. It is ironic that our knowledge-based society demands heroes and the design industries readily provide the necessarily unconventional heroes.

Recognising the dysfunctionality of our fragmented industry, the Construction Industry Council was formed in 1988 to begin to bring together the disparate parts, with a strong belief in the central role that education could play in bringing about change. In 1993 the CIC published *Crossing Boundaries*, jointly written by a chartered builder (John Andrews, Professor of Construction at the Bartlett) and a chartered architect (Sir Andrew Derbyshire, Chairman of the RMJM).

Its remit was to find and support areas of commonality in our formation and to introduce the idea of continuing professional development (CPD) for all.

Although many of its recommendations have been implemented—and the present volume can properly claim to be part of its heritage—there remains considerable personal and institutional opposition to change. When the CIC was formed it was difficult to get senior members of the RIBA, the Institute of Structural Engineers, the Royal Institute of Chartered Surveyors and the Chartered Institute of Builders to sit on the same committee—let alone work together for a common purpose. Ten years later, that working together has engendered a greater mutual respect between the institutions (the CIC now has 51 member institutions, representing over 350 000 professionals in construction in over 19 000 firms).

Today, more than ever before, resistance to change is not an option. Many universities are undertaking a radical managerial churn that is leading schools of architecture into faculties of varying constituents—many of whom feel threatened by falling numbers and therefore try, disastrously, to hinder change. I believe that initiatives such as CUDE must be welcomed as a major contribution by our profession to the future of the construction industry.

Accepting that we are part of an industry is a precondition for change. The CIC holds an annual Heads of Schools (of all construction disciplines) Conference, and in 2000 it will be considering the consequences of *Rethinking Construction* for education. Sir John Egan's report (Egan 1998) demands that we shake off our inward-looking culture and become client-focused.

In this, he wants better value with a greater predictability of cost, time and quality. He identifies the elimination of waste, such as competitive tendering, as being critical for major clients, not just as a one-off exercise but as the start of a process of continuous improvement.

The challenges for education are significant. Traditionally we have thought of ourselves as being 'the client's friend' in an adversarial culture. The latter is undeniable, the former increasingly anachronistic. How are we to educate ourselves to run alliances of professionals and specialists to deliver branded products at a small scale? While we are good at selling our concepts to other architects, we have developed a secret code that few others understand. We are frequently seen as poor listeners and, accordingly, not very client-focused. To what extent does our current education system promote such a situation and how can it redress the perceived shortcomings?

The Movement for Innovation has been charged with implementing the targets set in *Rethinking Construction* (Egan 1998). This is an initiative founded on a programme of demonstration projects (in excess of £3 billion across the whole industry), which, once their performance has been measured, will provide the information and the beginnings of the knowledge base of a new collaborative industry. Our schools need to draw on this knowledge, and we need to become part of a completely different industry. It demands structured feedback and an understanding of the consequences for design of whole-life costing, which has for too long been missing from the process. The programme is rich and the rewards huge, but it requires us to review our role—in the words of Egan (ibid.), to effect 'a change of style, culture and process, not just a series of mechanistic activities.'

How we choose as a profession to position ourselves is up to us, but the vanguard of tomorrow's quality design is being formed now and needs us to develop the greater understanding of our clients that they rightly have come to expect. I commend this book, not as a finished product, but as the next step in a continuing process of educational collaboration that is essential if architects are to play a leading part in the formation of tomorrow's environment.

References

Andrew, John and Derbyshire, Sir Andrew (1998) *Crossing Boundaries: A Report on the State of Commonality in Education and Training for the Construction Professions*. London: CIC.

Egan, Sir John (1998) *Rethinking Construction*. London: Department of the Environment, Transport and the Regions.

Leadbetter, Charles (1999) *Living on air*. London: Viking.

RIBA, (1992) Strategic Study of the Profession: Phase 1: Strategic Overview, London: RIBA.

RIBA, (1993) Strategic Study of the Profession: Phase 2: Clients and Architects, London: RIBA.

RIBA, (1995) Strategic Study of the Profession: Phases 3 and 4: The Way Forward, London: RIBA.

1 Architectural education and the profession

Preparing for the future

David Nicol and Simon Pilling

Introduction

Over the last 10 years numerous reports and studies have described how changes in society and in the construction industry are impacting on architecture and the other construction professions. A need has been identified for greater client sensitivity and responsiveness to user needs in construction and for more effective cross-disciplinary teamwork amongst industry professionals. Also, nowadays, not all architecture students go into mainstream architecture when they leave formal study: an increasing number are embarking on careers that only have a marginal connection with the construction industry. And as a result of changes in society, technological advances and the rapid growth in information, those entering a profession are likely to have to update their knowledge and skills many times over a lifetime. All this is calling on architects to become more skilled in the human dimensions of professional practice and more adaptable, flexible and versatile over the span of their professional careers. Architectural education must respond to these changes: it must enable students to develop the skills, strategies and attitudes needed for professional practice and it must lay the foundation for continuous learning throughout life.

This book presents a broad range of innovative educational responses to the needs of architectural graduates. This chapter provides the background to the rest of the book and is divided into four sections. Section 1 identifies the pressures for change in the UK construction industry and the architectural profession. Section 2 highlights issues of concern in architectural education in relation to preparation for professional practice. Section 3 discusses how learning and teaching within architecture could be realigned to meet the challenges posed by professional practice. Section 4 explains the scope and organisation of the other chapters in the book.

1   Pressures for change in the construction industry

The Latham and Egan reports

Reports in the UK published over the last decade have examined the construction industry in the context of changes in society, and have made recommendations for radical change in industry practices. Two reports in particular stand out: *Constructing the Team* (Latham 1994) and *Rethinking Construction* (Egan 1998).

The Latham Report (Latham 1994) was jointly commissioned by the government and the construction industry with the 'invaluable participation of clients'. The remit of the report was to review the procurement and contractual arrangements in the UK construction industry, with a particular focus on 'the processes by which clients' requirements are established and presented'. Latham saw clients as the driving force of the construction industry and the goal was 'to help clients obtain the high quality projects to which they aspire'. The report is principally concerned with the fragmentation of the construction industry, adversarial relationships and short-termism brought about by a 'lowest-price wins' approach. The answer put forward was partnering between customers and industry (based on providing best value, not lowest cost) and between the constituent parts of the industry. The main conclusion of the report was that, above all, better industry performance requires teamwork, and that achieving this would require much rethinking within the construction industry.

The Egan Report (Egan 1998) was the result of work by a construction task force set up by the UK deputy prime minister 'against a background of deep concern in the industry and among its clients that the construction industry was under-achieving, both in terms of meeting its own needs and those of its clients'. The report focused on the scope for improving the quality and efficiency of UK construction. It cited the findings of a British Property Federation survey of major clients, carried out in 1997, which found that 'more than a third of major clients are dissatisfied with consultants' performance in coordinating teams'. It concluded by identifying the need for 'a change of style, culture and process' within the construction industry and identified five 'drivers' of necessary change:

- Committed leadership.
- A focus on the customer.
- Integrated processes and teams.
- A quality-driven agenda.
- Commitment to people.

The Egan Report recognised that the achievement of these drivers would be inextricably linked to training. The whole industry would have to educate its workforce, not only in the necessary technical skills and knowledge, but also in the culture of teamwork. With particular regard to the professional designer, the report suggested that 'the high standards of professional competence in their training and development needed to be matched by a more practical understanding of the needs of clients and of the industry generally'.

It is clear from the nature of these reports that clients are becoming increasingly knowledgeable and demanding in their dealings with the construction industry and architects. The traditional client/architect/contractor relationship has changed radically. Clients are no longer content to rely on the architect as primary adviser. Even one-off clients are more demanding and knowledgeable than in the past, and many clients, both one-off and regular, wish to be more involved in making design decisions. In addition, team working is increasingly demanded within and across built environment disciplines, as clients and users call for better industry performance and more integrated construction services. Both these trends demand that architects acquire a broader range of people and communication skills.

The public image of architecture and architects

Over the same time period as these reports, and since, there has also been increasing scrutiny of the architectural profession by the general public and building users. Demographic developments such as the ageing population, new patterns of work and leisure, technological changes and society's demand for a more sustainable environment are leading the public to demand that architects develop a wider repertoire of design responses to the built environment. As a result there have been calls in the media, and elsewhere, for architects to demonstrate greater sensitivity in their designs to the needs of building users and society, and for them to communicate more clearly the meaning behind their work. Not only must architects develop interpersonal skills in relationship to clients and other professionals, but they must also become better at listening and responding to, and communicating with, building users and the public. In addition they must become more effective advocates of the contribution that they make to the quality of the built environment and to society.

The architectural profession and its education

In parallel with the Latham and Egan Reports, the construction professions and their associated professional institutes have been reviewing their changing role in society, the expectations of that society and the implications for the aspects of the education system that they validate. For architecture, the Burton Report—the findings and recommendations of a Royal Institute of British Architects (RIBA) steering group on architectural education (RIBA 1992)—set an agenda for change. Its recommendations were to be extensively developed in the RIBA's subsequent additions to the *Strategic Study of the Profession* (RIBA 1992, 1993, 1995).

In Phase 2 clients and architects reported that:

> the gap between clients' needs and the service provided by architects is much larger than we could have anticipated ... and seems to be growing ... it demands radical action, if market forces are not to diminish further the status and role of the architect, and the architects' ability to influence the built environment.

The study indicated that architects were generally not seen as good listeners, communicators or team players. Clients believed that these shortcomings reflected the architects' attitudes, beliefs and training, and concluded that urgent and radical steps should be taken to

> Re-examine what the educational process ought to achieve from a client perspective and reinforce elements which address client needs without threatening the "magic" which clients look to architecture to provide.

Another research study at around the same time drew similar conclusions. Lawson and Pilling (1996) sought to discover what relationship existed between the services that architects provide and those desired and valued by clients. The researchers interviewed both clients (from large institutional organisations) and architects. One area of questioning was the extent to which the client is involved with and understands the design process. Typical responses from clients to this issue were:

> Architects don't explain their services well ... part of it is protectionism. In general architects are not good at putting over what they do, there is an inbuilt arrogance within the profession that makes them difficult to approach.
>
> They've [architects] got a vision in their head which we can't see, it might be a fantastic vision and they might be able to draw it down in time and have a contractor produce it, but it's no good if we can't see it.

It was clear from this study that not only clients but also architects themselves were aware of the problem. Typical responses from architects were:

> The single thing which is most important is that the form of presentation used is one the client is able to read and understand.
>
> I make an absolute point about talking in lay person's language ... a famous ex-president of the RIBA went on about 'dynamic contextualism' on television. What ... does it mean? I don't know what it means and lay people are left absolutely clueless after remarks like that.

However the architect must be able to do more than clearly describe the benefits of a good design to clients. Communication is not just about effective description: equally important is listening to clients and negotiating and facilitating the processes of building design. Much of the frustration that architects and clients experience in design stems, according to Lawson and Pilling (1996), from a failure to engage with the client. They recommended that schools of architecture 'should engender a more client-centred approach in the educational process and develop the necessary skills of listening, extracting the brief, negotiating agreements, making presentations and managing client relationships'.

The RIBA obviously has a role to play in promoting the development of communication and teamworking in schools of architecture. In the recent *Review of Architectural Education* (Stansfield Smith 1999) the RIBA made some radical recommendations in this regard. The following extract from that review is central to the concerns of this book:

> The hothouse climate of architectural education can be extraordinarily productive. Among other things, architects learn sophisticated spatial ordering systems which, as a way of thinking, can and are applied to many situations whether real, virtual, technical or cultural. But it can also encourage the idea that architectural discourse is esoteric by nature and therefore of limited use for communication purposes. Such a tendency isolates architecture from its public and its procurers and diminishes the vitality of the discourse itself. Architecture needs to flourish as a language to engage its public, to generate the demand for architecture and qualities it represents.

Stansfield Smith (1999) concludes that the key to a successful architectural profession is not only that profession's ability to represent quality and deliver high standards, but also its ability to represent the values and aspirations of the society it serves. Many of the authors in this book have been closely associated with this wide-ranging review and their chapters resonate with most of the concerns expressed in the final report.

The rapid growth in knowledge

Over and above the necessary technical and interpersonal skills, there are other skills that architects must possess. The rapid pace at which knowledge is growing means that they, like all other professionals, need to develop strategies to deal with new information that may be relevant to their professional development. There are two aspects to this. It is essential that architects, as part of their training, have learned how to learn, so that they can keep up to date as the industry and the profession change. But also, because of the sheer volume of new information and the range of media by which this is made available, architects need expertise in accessing, identifying, evaluating and prioritising information. All this implies a high degree of autonomy and flexibility in learning throughout life.

2   Issues of concern in architectural education

The reports and studies quoted above clearly have implications for the nature of architectural education. Design education, as undertaken in the schools of architecture, appears to be preparing students for models of practice that are no longer in full accord with the current professional context. But what is it about design education that is not supportive of the needs of professional practice?

Architecture is a multidisciplinary field of study that draws on the arts, sciences and social sciences. There are five areas of study in the UK architecture syllabus (Part 1 and Part 2) as well as a practical training requirement (Royal Institute of British Architects and Architects Registration Board 1997). The five areas are: architectural design; the cultural context of architecture; environmental design, constructional and architectural technologies; communication skills; professional studies and management. However, the most important part of architectural education in terms of curriculum focus and time spent by students is architectural design. It is in the design studio that students are expected to bring together knowledge from the different disciplines to inform the development of their architectural designs.

The design studio offers the potential to provide a multifaceted and enriching learning experience. One inherent educational strength in studio teaching is the implicit commitment to 'experiential learning' or 'learning by doing'. Donald Schön (1987), in his work *Educating the Reflective Practitioner*, describes design studio teaching in architecture as a 'practicum'—a setting designed for the task of learning a practice. In a context that approximates a practice world, students learn by doing, by undertaking projects that simulate and simplify practice. Schön calls this a 'virtual world', relatively free of the pressures, distractions and risks of the real world, to which it nevertheless refers. 'It could therefore be seen to stand in an intermediate space between the practice world, the lay world of ordinary life, and the esoteric world of the academy' (Schön 1987).

However, and crucially, Schön goes on to observe that the virtual world of the studio becomes a collective world in its own right, with its own mix of materials, tools, languages and appreciations. For the student it embodies particular ways of seeing, thinking and doing that tend, over time, to assert themselves with increasing authority. It is this feature of the studio which is seen to hold both the strength and, potentially, the greatest weakness of architectural education as a preparation for practice (Cuff 1991).

Communication and teamwork

Isolation of the design studio

Architecture in practice is a participative process involving communication with many stakeholders in design: clients, users, other architects, engineers, specialist consultants, construction managers, statutory authorities and so on. However the schools, through both their formal structures and their more informal socialisation processes, may not be fully preparing students in the skills needed for participative practice. Dana Cuff (1991), in her work *Architecture: the Story of Practice*, proposes that the inward focusing of the design studio, where students work long hours at the drawing board, results in students becoming isolated from the outside world, knowing only how to talk to other architects.

Primacy of the individual

In the construction industry it is well-established that effective architectural practices, in terms of both design quality and business, tend to be associated with a culture of teamwork and collaboration. Moreover, many of those responsible for teaching in the built-environment disciplines are committed to developing these skills in students (see Chapter 17 by Wood of this book). However the design studio in schools of architecture still remains primarily geared towards developing individual star architects as unique and gifted designers, rather than preparing team players. This is what Cuff (1991) terms 'the primacy of the individual', which is an inevitable consequence of the principal social relationship in a school of architecture—that between studio tutor and student. In contrast, she refers to the reality of the architect's role in practice as that of 'translator', employing design— the art of architecture—to mediate between human function and the final form. Worthington develops this proposition further in Chapter 2 of this book, where he describes the role of the designer in practice as that of an 'integrator', drawing together people, process and place in order to create a coherent working environment. In professional practice, skills in managing interpersonal relationships enrich and extend the boundaries of design thinking rather than constrain them.

The familiar model of architectural education seems unlikely to foster in students a positive attitude towards collaboration—what Egan (1998) calls the crucial 'culture of teamwork'—while it remains primarily geared to developing individual stars rather than preparing team players.

Communication and interpersonal skills are not
systematically developed or assessed

Design studio learning embraces numerous forms of representation— visual, verbal, tactile, written—and is therefore rich in communication potential. It also sometimes involves students working in groups, and so it is arguably rich in teamworking potential. Yet in schools of architecture there is usually little *systematic* development or assessment of communication and interpersonal skills. Even though in practice architects need to be able to communicate concepts to different audiences (for example specialist engineers, clients, the public), it is not common for students to gain experience in tailoring their presentations to these different groups, or for this ability to be assessed. More importantly, the skills required for two-way communication, as against mere presentation, are even less likely to be purposefully developed and assessed. Furthermore, group-working on designs in schools is normally restricted to the early research stage of a project, with the final design invariably produced and assessed on an individual and competitive basis. Hence assessment processes in schools do not specifically encourage students to share and develop their ideas with each other.

The main form of assessment in architectural education is the review or 'crit'. The traditional structure of this has been criticised. It has been argued that the review lays the foundations for an adversarial relationship between presenter and listener, which is then taken forward into the professional's dealings with non-architects (Boyer and Mitgang 1996). The review has also been criticised for being the breeding ground of architectural jargon (Cuff 1991). In Chapter 10 Wilkin reports the results of a recent study of students' and tutors' views about the effectiveness of the review in relation to the development of communication skills.

Brief-building is unrelated to design in practice

Brief-building in practice is a wide-ranging process that relies on the architect putting him- or herself in the shoes of the client while negotiating and analysing requirements in a context of regular discussions. Yet design briefs in architectural education typically grow from a tutor' s construct, and any subsequent analysis of the brief is invariably carried out by the student as a form of private research. Insufficient attention is thus paid to the human interactive skills (for example listening, questioning, negotiating, explaining) needed to delve into a client's aspirations, values and concerns. In this can be seen the roots of client observations of architects such as the following:

> Almost the sole reason for the architect being mistrusted [is that] they will take a brief off somebody and go away and produce something which is not quite right ... they have not understood the real aims of the project and what has gone on before they have come on board (Lawson and Pilling 1996).

For the practising architect, brief-building and design proposals are parallel activities—the former not being completed until the latter is finalised and agreed with the client. Problem and solution emerge together rather than one necessarily preceding the other—the design in parallel with the brief. This raises an issue: does the academic environment promote a belief in students that these acts are serial—firstly create (or receive) a 'finished' brief and then design a proposal. The question of brief development, both its subject and its manner, is a recurrent theme in this book.

Design as product rather than process

Architectural design has been defined as 'the intelligent and directed use of physical resources to achieve what users, clients and society really need—as opposed to what they may demand—now and in the future' (Duffy 1995). This relies on developing in students a particular way of design thinking:

> Architects, compared to most disciplines, and certainly to every other discipline in the construction industry, are distinguished by

deploying two extremely powerful and characteristic ways of thinking:

- we invent
- we use our skills to relate what we invent to the aspirations of those who use our buildings

It is the combination in action of these two special ways of thinking ... that ultimately adds up to what we mean by architectural knowledge (ibid.).

The architect's role is to provide a medium in which these different aspects of design come together. These ways of thinking are not practised in isolation but are performed within a multidisciplinary context. According to Stansfield Smith (1999) 'there is a dynamic equivalence between the skills needed to develop a design proposal and the skills needed to realise a design proposal—from identifying the possibility to post occupancy evaluation'.

In schools of architecture priority is given to 'design as product'— in terms of visual and graphic output—rather than to design as a dynamic and interactive process. The educational emphasis in the design studio is primarily on the student's models and drawings. This is most clearly reflected in the conduct and focus of assessment through tutor feedback and reviews. Students are not usually rewarded explicitly for their analysis of user or client needs unless they result in a creative addition to the conceptual design proposal—even though a great deal of analytical thinking may have been undertaken by the students. In Chapter 3, Morrow goes further and argues that 'students typically come to understand analysis in an oppositional relationship to design', and that this has negative repercussions on the range of social forms that emerge in their designs. Jarrett (Chapter 5) reinforces this view when he notes that urban design projects in schools are not about 'cultivating a sense of place and belonging', rather they are conceived as art objects, 'disconnected from life on the streets'.

A further example of the emphasis on product is the tradition in architectural education that students assemble, during their undergraduate years, a tangible product in the form of a portfolio of work that they can take to the marketplace (and to prospective employers) as a demonstration of their 'artistic' ability.

Difficulty in achieving a skills balance through studio learning

Earlier in this section the syllabus for architecture in the UK was outlined (RIBA and ARB, Parts 1 and 2). In that syllabus it would appear that professional skills are already included under the subject headings 'Communication Skills' and 'Professional and Management Studies', and it is assumed that students will acquire these skills through their design studio work. However two points are worth making here. Firstly, achieving a balance across a number of skills areas (both inter-personal and technical) in the design studio context is exceedingly difficult. At the very least it requires careful planning. Secondly, it is noteworthy that within the prescribed syllabus (particularly Part 1) communication skills are primarily described in terms of the ability to present to others rather than as a two-way interactive process. This might be one reason why some key skills for professional prac-tice—such as listening to others (for example clients, other team mem-bers), questioning and negotiation—are not sufficiently developed in the undergraduate years.

Lifelong learning

Another challenge for architectural education is to prepare students for a changing profession where knowledge is growing at a rapid rate and the needs of the construction industry and society are continu-ously evolving. For this students will need to acquire skills and atti-tudes that are transferable across contexts and permit continuous and lifelong learning. In this changing context, architecture students do not just need to learn about architecture and acquire design skills; they must also learn how to learn, learn how to manage and take responsibility for their own learning throughout life. They must know how to identify the existence of new information, access it and judge if it is good and useful. And they must be able to develop and agree success criteria for their own working, alone and with cli-ents (and with the rest of the team), and be able to monitor and evaluate achievements against those criteria.

Lack of structure for the development of self-responsibility in learning

The studio environment, where students work independently on a design project in relative freedom, would seem to be an ideal situation in which to develop these lifelong learning skills. But the potential of that environment for the development of self-reliance in learning is not always fully realised, for a number of reasons. Firstly, few studio programmes are consciously structured to lead students from depen-dence to independence in learning during the undergraduate years, and it is notoriously difficult to strike a good balance between giving students responsibility and providing systematic instruction and guid-ance. Secondly, not all design tutors agree that teaching students

transferable skills such as communication, groupwork and management of learning is their responsibility (or they may not feel confident
about or have sufficient expertise in teaching these skills). Thirdly, it is
not yet common to provide students with regular opportunities to
reflect on their own learning, and in particular to monitor and evaluate their own processes of working, even though regular reflection,
self-monitoring and self-evaluation are crucial to the development of
self-responsibility. Some of these points can be illustrated by examining the way in which assessment, including the architectural review or
crit, is organised in schools of architecture.

Students often have little sense of control over their own learning

For many students the review fosters anxiety and defensiveness rather
than communication and dialogue, and the research literature identifies this is an area of particular concern in architectural education
(Boyer and Mitgang 1996; Wilkin 1999). Students are not usually
involved in deciding the manner in which they will be reviewed. The
criteria by which their designs will be judged are often implicit rather
than explicit and appear to students as mysterious and subjective.
At the review, students are not usually asked to reflect on and evaluate
their own designs before this is done by their tutors and outside critics.
Many students do not participate fully in the review because of fear of
being exposed.

   All these factors could result in students having little sense of control over their learning; and taken together they could easily encourage a dependency culture where tutors and critics are seen as the only
true arbiters of good design. At the very least, students should be
helped to develop an understanding and ownership of the criteria
and standards against which their work will be judged. This would
enable them to direct their own learning and to work knowingly in
directions that will be valued by tutors.

Few opportunities to appraise the processes of learning

The development of autonomy in learning requires that students learn
not only how to judge their own design output (product) while learning, but also how to evaluate and improve upon their own learning
(processes) from one design project to the next. More specifically,
students need regular opportunities to step back from design project
activities in order to analyse and evaluate how they learned through
those activities and to provide for their own feedback and performance judgements. The more learning becomes self-regulated in this
way, the more students will assume control over their own learning

and the less they will be dependent on tutor support. Structuring opportunities for this kind of self-regulation facilitates in students the transfer of acquired knowledge and skills to new design tasks and problems.

The learning climate in schools of architecture

The knowledge, attitudes, skills and values that architectural students acquire during their undergraduate years are formed as much by the social culture of the school and the manner of teaching and learning in that school, as by the specific formal content of their courses. For example Vowles (Chapter 26) examines how the hidden social rituals in the architectural review influence both what and how students learn and what attitudes and skills they carry forward into architectural practice. There is currently a perceived gulf between the learning in architecture schools and the realities of professional life. In order to bridge that gulf and to meet the challenges posed by practice and lifelong learning, it may be necessary to reexamine not only the educational processes but also the relationships that exist in the schools amongst learners, and between learners and teachers. The learning climate may have to be realigned around different relationships—those more relevant to the future profession, and in particular those that emphasise the importance of communication, collaboration and self-reliance.

Summary: the challenges for education

From the foregoing discussion it is possible to identify the key challenges for architectural education. Firstly, students should develop more effective communication and interpersonal skills, so that they are better able to appreciate, understand, engage with and respond to the needs of clients and users. Secondly, students should acquire a foundation in teamworking in order to prepare them for the cross-disciplinary working relationships that characterise professional life. Thirdly, there is the challenge of preparing students for a changing society where knowledge is growing at a rapid rate and the needs of society and the construction industry are continuously evolving. For this students will need to acquire skills and attitudes that are transferable across contexts and enable continuous lifelong learning. They need to learn how to learn in order to be able to manage their ongoing learning in relation to their future goals. Lastly, learning environments in schools of architecture should be realigned to encourage a more collaborative and supportive culture so that students develop sensitivity to others and a sense of community, as well as independence of thought.

3   Meeting the challenges: a view from higher education research and practice

Section 2 of this chapter identified some challenges from practice that confront architectural education. This section discusses how to meet those challenges. It identifies the learning and development processes that should be elicited in students in order to facilitate the development of attitudes and skills for professional practice.

Five key principles of effective learning and their processes are considered:

- Learning is an active rather than a passive process.
- Reflection on learning develops wisdom or artistry in practice.
- Collaborative learning enhances individual learning.
- Authentic learning tasks develop professional competencies.
- Self- and peer assessment develop skills for lifelong learning.

The arguments in this section draw on the research on learning and teaching in higher education over the last 10 years (e.g. Biggs 1999; Nicol 1997; Ramsden 1992) including research on learning for the professions—medical, legal, architectural. This research has significantly increased our understanding of how students learn and how teaching can be better organised so that deep and relevant learning takes place (see Nicol 1997 for a concise review of the research on learning in higher education).

Learning is an active process

Research on learning in higher education shows that 'what the student does is actually more important in determining learning than what the teacher does' (Shuell 1986). For effective learning to occur, students have to interact actively with new information and new experiences in order to own them and make them personally meaningful. They do this by actively constructing and reconstructing information input—by modifying, revising and extending it, relating ideas to each other and to what they already know—in an effort to make personal sense of it. This *constructivist* view places the student at the centre of the learning relationship as far as knowledge and skill acquisition are concerned. Rather than try to do the job on behalf of the students, the teachers' task is to make learning (for understanding) possible, to *facilitate* learning. Their role is not just to impart the important facts and concepts in the discipline but also, more importantly, 'to help bridge the gap between the structures of the discipline and the structures in the students' minds' (McKeachie 1992). For this the teacher must engage students in active dialogue around learning and with learning materials. A repertoire of tasks and strategies are needed that will facilitate and involve students in active processing (for example discussion, debate, questioning, explaining) so that they transform, translate and own the learning as personal knowledge.

Design projects in the architectural studio are central to the learning environment in schools of architecture. Through design studio projects students acquire knowledge, develop skills and explore appropriate professional, social and cultural attitudes. The design studio acts as a micro-environment for the development of professional competence. As noted earlier, a characteristic feature of the architectural design studio is its learning methods, which are rooted in 'experiential learning' or learning by doing. This is fortunate because, as we have just explained, this kind of active learning is an important principle for learning generally (Biggs 1999) and for the development of professional skills (Weil and McGill 1989).

Therefore, if we wish students to learn to design—to integrate knowledge from different domains in their conceptual designs—we should set design tasks that explicitly call for this kind of active integration. While this is what is usually intended to take place in the design studio, it might be possible to refine and extend the method to other aspects of learning. For example if we want students to learn to communicate their ideas to clients and users, or to learn to negotiate a brief, then we need to set learning tasks that encourage them actively to engage in communication or brief-building activities. It would be much less helpful merely to provide them with lecture information about users and clients, and about how typical negotiations proceed.

Reflection on learning develops wisdom or artistry in practice

While active learning is a necessary condition for the development of personal understanding it is not sufficient on its own, according to learning research (Brockbank and McGill 1998; Boud, Keogh and Walker 1985). To develop understanding from experience requires students consciously and systematically to reflect on the experiences that result from action. Critical reflection is a process of analysing and evaluating personal experience, and making sense and generalising from that experience so that future learning is more skilful and better informed. Reflection is a way of linking together theory and practical experience so that both inform each other.

The book by Schön (1987) mentioned earlier has had a resounding effect on all areas of education because it identified the importance of reflection for professional practice. Schön analysed the demands of professional practice and showed that in practice most real-world problems are, by nature, messy, ill-defined, uncertain and invariably unique; and that solutions to these problems call on the integration and use of knowledge from many different domains. He showed that mastery in these 'indeterminate zones of practice' cannot be achieved through the rigorous application of scientific knowledge. Instead expert professionals resolve the dilemmas of practice through a continuous process of reflection in and on action. They use reflection to discern patterns in the complexity of practice situations, to identify critical factors and to ask further questions before resuming action. Over time this reflective activity becomes a natural part of the thinking of professionals and becomes a habit of mind. Schön used the concept of the 'reflective practitioner' to characterise such professionals.

While some aspects of Schön's writings have been criticised (for example Eraut 1994) most researchers now agree about the benefits of cultivating critical reflection in students in their undergraduate years in order to help them develop more productive thinking and the 'wisdom' or 'artistry' needed for practice. Researchers such as Kolb (1984) and Cowan (1998) have shown how learning can be enhanced when it is organised around cycles of learning activity and reflection. Cowan (1998) distinguishes three different types of reflection that can contribute to learning and development: students can reflect before they engage in activity (that is, reflection for action); they can reflect while in activity (reflection in action), for example by monitoring the activity as it is happening; or they can reflect after an activity (reflection on action) and before going on the next activity. Each of these three types of reflection helps develop deeper and more elaborated knowledge and skills. Some examples of reflection in architecture may clarify this idea.

Imagine that a group of students have been asked to carry out a site analysis. Before going to the site they might be asked to spend some time, either alone or in groups, identifying the goals to be achieved when visiting the site, the questions they might ask about that site in relation to the needs of the users of the proposed building and how they will carry out their analyses (reflection for action). While on the actual site, the students might record in a journal their initial impressions of the site, how they go about analysing and interpreting the site in terms of user needs, and the answers to the questions they had identified beforehand, plus any unexpected observations and new questions that emerge (reflection in action). Upon their return to the studio the students might—either alone or in groups—re-examine the scope and relevance of their original questions, and they might evaluate their methods of carrying out a site analysis and how successful they were in meeting their original goals (reflection on action). All this would be done in order to analyse, summarise and extract generalisations about the processes of learning *for future use*—for example about problem formulation, the strategies of site analysis or how to make design decisions. By consciously reflecting on experiences, doing is given a meaning beyond the activity itself, and knowledge and skills are better assimilated and more easily transferred across contexts.

There are many descriptions in this book of reflection being used to improve learning, although not all writers use this term. For example Torrington (Chapter 8) has used reflective activities to develop in students the questioning skills needed to negotiate a design brief with clients. She asked students in groups to devise questions to ask clients when they met them, and to reflect on their likely effectiveness (reflection for action). Then, after their meeting with the clients the students reflected back on (reflection on action) and evaluated the success of their questioning strategies. The concept of reflection is also relevant to Farren Bradley's discussion in Chapter 18 about the need for architecture students to integrate their learning from formal academic study with that from supervised practical experience.

Where the focus of reflection is on the processes of learning itself—the how of learning (ways of thinking) rather than the what of learning—this not only develops expertise in the subject but also helps students to take control of their own learning and become self-regulated learners. They learn how to learn and how to manage their own learning—a necessary lifelong learning skill in a knowledge-rich and rapidly changing society. Cottrell (Chapter 19) and Webster (Chapter 20) discuss some aspects of this kind of reflection.

While the idea of reflection is not new to architectural education there is a need to plan for it in the design of courses. Boud, an authority in this area, notes that 'the activity of reflection is so familiar that, as teachers or trainers, we often overlook it in formal learning situations' (Boud *et al.* 1985).

Collaborative learning enhances individual learning

In schools of architecture there has always been some use of peer group discussion and interaction around design projects. This can now be judged a valuable feature of architectural education, given the large body of research evidence showing that interaction and discussion in student groups positively enhances individual learning. Research in education has clearly demonstrated the benefits of collaborative and cooperative learning arrangements for the development of students' critical thinking (for example Qin, Johnston and Johnston 1995) and for the development of self-concepts, social skills, personal responsibility, values and attitudes. Group learning gives students practice in thinking and explaining, it increases learner activity, it exposes students to multiple perspectives that help develop more robust and elaborated thinking, it provides opportunities for scaffold-ing (students supporting each others' learning), and it often results in students teaching each other, which is as profitable for the teacher as it is for the students being taught.

There are two other reasons for increasing the amount of group-work in courses for the architecture profession. Firstly, group discus-sion on learning tasks increases the focus of students on the processes of learning—for example when they discuss how best to carry out a task or procedure (see Nicol, Kane and Wainwright 1994). Thus group discussion extends and amplifies the potential of reflection for learn-ing. Secondly, groupwork makes it possible to focus the learning of students specifically on the processes of communication and interac-tion within groups. Thus group learning could serve as an important vehicle (or laboratory) for the initial development of the attitudes, communication and teamworking skills regarded as so important for architectural practice. Where group learning occurs in an inter- or cross-disciplinary setting there is additional value. Architecture stu-dents could learn how to communicate and take the perspectives of other construction disciplines, and how they might work together to solve design problems.

Many of the educational projects described in this book involve collaborative learning. For example Callicott and Sheil (Chapter 6) show how group processes can be utilised to enable students to explore how their designs communicate with others. Rüedi (Chapter 12) describes a community project in which students of architecture and planning work together on a design project and learn about the dif-ferent skills of each discipline in relation to design, and about the different ways that disciplines communicate with clients. Similarly Howes (Chapter 13) describes her experiences in setting up and imple-menting a series of design projects, centred on the use of new tech-nology, in which students worked in multidisciplinary teams. Manley and Claydon (Chapter 15) and Howieson (Chapter 16) describe inter-disciplinary undergraduate degree courses that were specifically developed to enable students from different construction disciplines to learn and work together in teams on design projects.

It is vital for students to be prepared for groupwork if it is to be an effective vehicle for the learning of professional skills and attitudes (Jaques 1991; Matthews 1996), and that there is progressive develop-ment of these skills during the undergraduate years. Furthermore, group tasks centred on design projects must be carefully crafted so that there is a genuine shared inquiry and all participants are active and their contributions are valued (Jaques 1991). Fisher (Chapter 14) provides essential advice on how to plan and structure group learning for the development of communication and teamworking skills. When effectively implemented, collaboration in learning not only helps develop important skills for life and for professional practice, it also helps lay the foundation for the building of communities in schools of architecture.

Authentic learning tasks develop professional competencies

What kinds of learning task are best used to prepare students for architectural practice? Ideally, students' learning processes should be embedded in authentic physical and social contexts that represent, as far as possible, 'real life' practice situations. If we wish students to learn the social art of design in practice, it is better that they negotiate a brief with a real client than receive a typed brief from the course tutor. Similarly, learning about the needs of building users is better achieved by having students go into the community to talk with users than by having them infer the needs of users while at the drawing board.

However these arrangements are not always possible (or even practicable) in design studio projects. Real clients are in short supply and the number of students working on a design project is likely to be large. In this case the skills that are to be developed and the tasks employed should, as far as possible, be relevant to real life contexts and, more importantly, be perceived to be relevant by students. For example students could practice in pairs the questions they might ask a client who is commissioning a building. The client might be imaginary but the questioning skills being developed are relevant to an authentic situation. This was part of the strategy used by Sara (Chapter 7) in her project. Another example comes from Brown and Yates (Chapter 4), where students learnt about how children experience their school environment by visiting a school and, together with the children, mutually analysing, comparing and discussing differences in their values, perceptions and language in relation to that space.

There are three points in favour of the above arguments. First, authentic and relevant tasks help develop skills that are valid in relation to professional practice. Second, students learn from context (and perceived context) as much as from the task itself (Lave and Wenger 1991). So it is important to use tasks and contexts that are relevant to practice. Third, when the learning is perceived as relevant to real life situations, students are highly motivated to learn.

Authentic learning contexts and tasks have to be structured for maximum effectiveness. Complex tasks may have to be simplified and their components sequenced for pedagogic purposes, as noted by Chiles (Chapter 9), who had students interact with real clients from a large and complex regeneration project. The degree of structure will depend on the experience and academic level of the students: in general first year-students will require more structure than students in later years. Finally, for maximum transferability of skills across contexts, learning environments should provide extensive opportunities for students to practice the same skills in different combinations and for a range of different tasks and situations.

Self- and peer assessment develops skills for lifelong learning

Assessment is arguably the most significant influence on learning and on the development of professional abilities in schools of architecture. As Crooks (1988) notes, assessment 'guides [students'] judgement of what is important to learn, affects their motivation and self-perceptions of competence, structures their approaches to and timing of personal study ... and affects the development of enduring learning strategies and skills'.

If students are to be prepared for practice and develop life-long learning skills, then assessment that depends on the traditional review or crit should be re-examined. As well as assessing the product of learning (the conceptual design outcomes), assessment should also focus on interpersonal processes that characterise design in practice. For example some assessment tasks might focus on the student's ability to explain or present a design to different audiences (for example client, user, construction manager), rather than just to tutors. Other tasks might assess students' ability to listen and learn from the perspectives of others. Still others might assess students' ability to negotiate and develop a design with another party in the context of realistic constraints using, for example, role play. In addition, all students could be assessed on how well they contribute to a team project. Brindley, Doidge and Willmott (Chapter 11) make a number of valuable suggestions for widening the scope of the traditional review.

Just as important as reviewing traditional models of assessment is the need to increase the use of self- and peer assessment in schools of architecture. Self-assessment is related to the earlier discussion about reflection on learning. It is a form of reflection on past action. It goes beyond the analysis of past experience to include the making of judgements about one's own achievements (see Boud 1995). The idea is to help students learn how to construct and agree criteria and standards of good performance, and then to encourage them to use these regularly to assess the strengths and weaknesses of their work and decide how to make improvements. Ideally students should engage in self-assessment before receiving feedback from tutors. Peer and tutor assessment can, however, be integrated to enhance and support such self-assessment processes, especially in the early undergraduate years. By engaging in self-assessment, students learn to notice and correct weaknesses in their work, and over time they become more autonomous in managing their own learning. These changes in assessment will, however, highlight the need for criteria and standards of judgement to become less mysterious and more explicit and discussible in schools of architecture.

Self- and peer assessment taken together are also vital strategies for structuring an increase in students' involvement in the review or crit. Instead of tutors doing all the work, students themselves acquire the 'tools' to evaluate their own designs. Self-assessment, supported by peer processes, has great potential to enhance the traditional review or crit so that it becomes a positive vehicle for learning, rather than a source of concern. White (Chapter 21) describes the organisation and benefits of a student-led and peer-supported crit. Self- and peer assessment are vital skills for future professional practice and for the development of life-long learning, especially in a society where knowledge is growing at a rapid rate and professionals must continually evaluate the worth of new information and monitor their own and others' performance.

Embedding change across schools of architecture

In order for the changes described above to have a significant effect in schools of architecture, attention will also have to be paid to the learning climate in the schools. Research in higher education on the social context of learning stresses that learning is 'situated' in the contexts of schools, departments and institutions, and that students learn as much from the context as from their interactions with subject knowledge (Lave and Wenger 1991). What and how they learn is strongly influenced by how they interpret the social context and, in particular, how they perceive and act out their relationships with their teachers and other students (Stefani and Nicol 1997).

Studio tutors who plan to set up learning situations to encourage student reflection, independence and collaboration will undoubtedly have to refine or develop their own skills and reflect on how they work out in teaching practice. This will require schools to create frameworks and opportunities to support the learning and development of architecture tutors, and this is already happening in some schools. For example Weaver, O'Reilly and Caddick (Chapter 27) describe a preparation and support programme for new tutors that utilises the same kinds of reflective processes, group sharing and discussion of experiences (in this case teaching experiences) that were advocated above to support learning by students. If tutors do introduce such changes to their teaching practices, they will need to devise ways to obtain feedback from students about these changes as they occur, and to evaluate them and make informed improvements. Cowan (Chapter 28) provides some valuable advice on how this might be done.

The adequacy of systems for supporting, monitoring and evaluating the quality of teaching is particularly important at present. The quality of study programmes, of teaching in architecture (as in all disciplines) and of internal quality-assurance procedures subject to much greater scrutiny than in the past by agencies concerned with the standard of performance of graduates going into the professions (for example the Quality Divisions of the Higher Education Funding Councils). Also, as a result of the findings of a national committee of inquiry into higher education (Dearing 1997), most higher education institutions are in the process of setting up procedures and programmes that will enable higher education teachers to acquire a qualification in teaching; and an Institute of Teaching and Learning has recently been formed to accredit professional programmes devised by institutions (see Utley 1999).

As well as helping teachers to develop their teaching abilities there is also a need to cultivate in schools of architecture learning environments and attitudes that are consistent with and reinforce the professional skills that we wish to develop in students. Purposeful attention to the building of 'learning communities' would help this, as would the promotion in schools of strategies and values that foster learning alliances and dialogue within and amongst students and staff. Potts (Chapter 24) outlines one approach to the creation of a supportive learning climate at the school level. She describes how an entire school was reorganised so that each design studio comprised students from all years (undergraduate and postgraduate) so as to encourage collaboration in learning and mentoring both within and across the years. Henderson (Chapter 25) discusses the progress made and the difficulties encountered in another school when it changed its strategy to give more importance to the development of professional skills in students.

On a wider front, there is also a need for schools of architecture to develop scholarly partnerships with professional practices. This could be beneficial to both parties. New opportunities could be created to enrich students' academic studies with work experience in the early undergraduate years; and the period in practice after the undergraduate degree could be more effectively integrated into the educational programme of schools. Architectural practices could in turn benefit from research carried out by schools on their behalf, and from the updating programmes that schools could provide for them. Gutman (Chapter 23) discusses the value of school-practice partnerships in the United States. Finally, the professional body for architecture (the RIBA) has an important part to play in promoting positive changes in the education programmes of schools through its formal validation procedures and more informal processes. This is explored by Milliner in Chapter 22.

4   The chapters in the book: scope and organisation

Up to this point we have described how changes in society, the construction industry and the architectural profession are leading to a reassessment of how architects are educated, and we have suggested how architectural education might address these changes. In this section we describe the scope and organisation of the other chapters of the book, and show how the contents relate to the professional context and to the educational challenges.

In Chapter 2 Worthington provides some additional background that is relevant to the whole book. He offers a wide-ranging analysis of the changing nature of professional practice and explores the implications of these changes for education.

The majority of the 26 chapters that follow Worthington's describe educational projects or initiatives carried out by architectural educators (or practitioner-educators) to enhance students' acquisition of professional skills. These chapters could be classified as case studies of educational change. They describe how architectural educators have responded to the perceived demands of professional practice, and they explain the outcomes of these responses and the issues that were faced along the way. In some cases the writers provide an evaluation of the success of the project or initiative, based on data collected, for example, from students and/or teachers. In other cases there is little hard evaluative data but the writers still try to give an idea of what worked well and what was problematic. Each writer tries to provide enough information to give others wishing to make similar changes to their courses or studio practices some idea of the important issues that might have to be addressed. The rest of the chapters take the form of discussions or essays rather than case study descriptions of educational change. Nonetheless they complement the other chapters. The writers provide a range of perspectives on issues in architectural education that relate to professional practice, and they analyse and point to ways in which educators might address these issues.

Chapters 3–28 are organised into four sections. Those in Section 1 concentrate on the development of students' professional skills in relation to clients and building users. The central theme in this section is communication, but in the widest sense of the term—that is, not just presenting but also listening, empathising, perspective-taking, questioning and so on. The common focus of the chapters in Section 2 is on the development of teamworking skills for professional practice, including cross-disciplinary teamworking. As might be expected there is considerable overlap between the chapters in Sections 1 and 2, given that communication is essential to effective teamwork and that in many construction projects clients are part of the team.

The theme of Section 3 is the development of skills for life-long learning. The chapters in this section include case study examples of educational initiatives aimed at developing students' ability to manage and monitor their own learning—to learn how to learn. It should be noted, however, that the development of life-long learning skills was also a goal of many of the other initiatives described in the book.

Section 4 focuses on the wider context of change—at the level of the school and beyond rather than at the studio or course level. Again there are both case studies and general discussions, and the topics include educational change across a whole school, teacher training and support, and the role of the RIBA in promoting the development of professional skills in schools of architecture.

Conclusion

There is considerable interest in schools of architecture in extending the boundaries of architectural education. This book is one expression of that interest. It is hoped that the range of perspectives presented here will contribute usefully to the ongoing debate on this subject and will offer some valuable insights into this fascinating field, which exerts such a profound influence on all our lives.

References

Biggs, J. (1999) *Teaching for Quality Learning*. Buckingham: Society for Research into Higher Education and Open University Press.

Boud, D. (1995) *Enhancing Learning Through Self Assessment*. London: Kogan Page.

Boud, D., Keogh, R. and Walker, D. (1985) 'What is Reflection in Learning?', in D. Boud, R. Keogh and D. Walker (eds), *Reflection: Turning Experience into Learning*. London: Kogan Page.

Boyer, E. L. and Mitgang, L. D. (1996) *Building Community: A New Future for Architectural Education*. Princeton, NJ: The Carnegie Foundation for the Enhancement of Teaching.

Brockbank, A. and McGill, I. (1998) *Facilitating Reflective Learning in Higher Education*. Buckingham: Society for Research into Higher Education and Open University Press.

Burton, R. (1992) *Report of the Steering Group on Architectural Education*. London: RIBA.

Cowan, J. (1998) *On Becoming an Innovative University Teacher: Reflection in Action*. Buckingham: Society for Research into Higher Education and Open University Press.

Crooks, J. T. (1998) 'The Impact of Classroom Evaluation Practices on Students', *Review of Educational Research*, 58(4), pp. 438–81.

Cuff, D. (1991) *Architecture: the Story of Practice*. Cambridge, Mass.: MIT Press.

Dearing, R. F. (1997) *Higher Education in a Learning Society*, report of the National Committee of Inquiry into Higher Education (the Dearing Report). London: HMSO.

Duffy, F. (1992) *Strategic Study of the Profession: Phase 1: Strategic Overview*. London: RIBA.

Duffy, F. (1995) Strategic Study of the Profession: Phases 3 and 4: The Way Forward, London: RIBA.

Egan, Sir John (1998) *Rethinking Construction: The Report of the Construction Task Force*, as the Egan Report. Department of Environment, Transport and the Regions. London.

Eraut, M. (1994) *Developing Professional Knowledge and Competence*. London: The Falmer Press.

Jaques, D. (1991) *Learning in Groups*. London: Kogan Page.

Kolb, D. A. (1984) *Experiential Learning: Experience as the Source of Learning and Development*. Englewood Cliffs, NJ: Prentice-Hall.

Latham, Sir Michael (1994) *Constructing the Team: Final Report of the Government/Industry Review of Procurement and Contractual Arrangements in the UK*. London: HMSO.

Lave, J. and Wenger, E. (1991) *Situated Learning: Legitimate Peripheral Participation*. New York: Cambridge University Press.

Lawson, B. and Pilling, S. (1996) 'The Cost and Value of Design', *Architectural Research Quarterly*, 1(4), pp. 82–9.

Matthews, R. S. (1996) 'Collaborative Learning: Creating Knowledge with Students', in R. J. Menges and M. Weimer, *Teaching on Solid Ground*. Francisco: Jossey-Bass.

McKeachie, W. J. (1992) 'Recent Research on University Teaching and Learning: Implications for Practice and Future Research', *Academic Medicine*, 67(10), pp. 548–71.

Nicol, D. J. (1997) *Research on Learning and Higher Education Teaching*, UCoSDA Briefing Paper 45. Universities' and Colleges' Staff Development Agency, Sheffield.

Nicol, D. J., Kane, K. and Wainwright, C. (1994) 'Improving Laboratory Learning through Group Work and Structured Reflection and Discussion', *Education and Training Technology International*, 31(4), pp. 152–68.

Qin, Z., Johnston, D. W. and Johnston, R. T. (1995) 'Cooperative versus Competitive Efforts in Problem Solving', *Review of Educational Research*, 65(2), pp. 129–43.

Ramsden, P. (1992) *Learning to Teach in Higher Education*. London: Routledge.

Royal Institute of British Architects (1992) *Strategic Study of the Profession— Phase 1: Strategic Overview*. London: RIBA Publications.

Royal Institute of British Architects (1993) *Strategic Study of the Profession— Phase 2: Clients and Architects*. London: RIBA Publications.

Royal Institute of British Architects (1995) *Strategic Study of the Profession— Phases 3 and 4: The Way Forward*. London: RIBA Publications.

Royal Institute of British Architects and Architects Registration Board (1997) *Criteria for Validation, Part 2*. London: RIBA ARB.

Schön, D. (1987) *Educating the Reflective Practitioner*. San Francisco: Jossey Bass.

Shuell, T. J. (1986) 'Cognitive conceptions of learning'. *Review of Educational Research*, 56, pp. 411–36.

Stansfield Smith, C. (1999) *Review of Architectural Education*. London: RIBA.

Stefani, L. and Nicol, D. J. (1997) 'From Teacher to Facilitator of Collaborative Enquiry', in S. Armstrong, G. Thompson and S. Brown (eds), *Facing up to Radical Changes in Universities and Colleges*. London: Kogan Page.

Utley, A. (1999) 'Blackstone blesses the birth of the ILT'. *The Times Higher Education Supplement*, 9 July.

Weil, S. W. and McGill, I. (1989) *Making Sense of Experiential Learning*. Buckingham: SRHE and Open University Press.

Wilkin, Margaret (1999) *Reassessing the Design Project Review in Undergraduate Architectural Education with Particular Reference to Clients and Users*. Leicester: De Montfort University.

2 The changing context of professional practice

John Worthington

Introduction

The profession of architecture and its position in the construction and property industry has changed dramatically over the last 20 years. For architects in the UK, deregulation of the fee structure in 1981 and the rise of the knowledgeable client has eroded the architect's traditional role as neutral representative between client and contractor. Increasingly architects on larger commissions are placed in two distinct and contrasting roles: one working on the client's behalf and establishing requirements, testing options and preparing conceptual design—the 'demand' side; the other on the supply side of the industry, working as a subcontractor to the construction or project manager. Such a division at best can once again bring the construction process into the early stages of design, but at worst it can become divisive, with the client the loser. Recent inquiries into improving the construction industry's performance (Egan 1998; Latham 1994) have stressed the need for better client communication, teamwork and partnership.

The fragile position of architects is accentuated by the complexity of procurement procedures in the UK, and the increasing speed of change. There are over 80 different types of contract, and over 24 professional institutions associated with property or construction. This complexity, the most Byzantine of all European countries, is accentuated by the divisive nature of professional education.

This chapter will argue that:

- There is still a significant gap between the vision of the architect's role, as characterised in schools of architecture and the reality of practice.
- There is a need to develop a distinctive knowledge base in respect of the areas perceived as of greatest value to clients and users.
- Design thinking provides the natural skills to become the integrator across disciplines, scales and time.

- Education could provide a framework for continuous learning in partnerships with the individual, the practice, the profession and society.

Perceptions of practice

Dana Cuff (1999) succinctly summarises the dilemma of the focus of architectural education as 'numerous stereotyped distinctions: art or business orientation, star or hack architects, with design or profit motive. The basic drama puts a starving artist against a profit driven barbarian.'

David Maister[1], a leading consultant on the management of professional service firms, identifies six types of architectural practice (Figure 2.1) in two main categories: those that are practice-led businesses, and those that are business-led practices. Within this distinction, practices that reflect each of these two values are predominantly focused on delivery, service or ideas. The extreme poles in this classification are the practice-led businesses, 'signature practices' driven by innovation; and the business-led practices, concentrating on delivery.

It may be argued that the predominant culture of architectural education still accentuates the qualities of innovation and personal freedom while eschewing business disciplines. The model remains the independent architect working in a local context on a project that can be encompassed by the individual in a small firm. However the contemporary reality is that over 80 per cent of construction expenditure is with 20 per cent of the clients, who are working with large (50 plus staff) multidisciplinary, increasingly international practices.[2]

The concerns of architecture

As we shift from a machine-based to a knowledge-driven economy (Worthington 1993) the boundaries between managerial and professional roles are becoming increasingly blurred. Managers are

	Practice-led business	Business-led practice
Delivery	Production architects	Construction managers
Service	General practice	Consultancy
Ideas	Signature architects	Design consultants

Figure 2.1 Education for diversity.

becoming specialists and professionals are taking on managerial and business roles. With 'professional' clients the old relationship of passing on the problem unquestioningly to the 'trusted' professional is declining. Research at the University of Bristol (Watkins *et al.* 1992) shows a 'shift away from professionals being trusted to do their work properly because they were professionals to accountability and some kind of monitoring of their effectiveness'. The 'trust relationship' between professional and client is being eroded through external market forces. The weakening of the professional ethic is particularly poignant in the case of architecture, with its historically strong social concerns.

What makes architecture more than mere building? This question should haunt every student of the subject but it is difficult to define precisely. Louis Kahn defined architecture as 'the meaningful making of spaces in their light'. A poetic but exacting statement. Others would define architecture to include social, economic and political imperatives (Kostof 1999). Hannes Mayer, who succeeded Gropius for two tempestuous years as head of the Bauhaus at Dessau, defined architecture as 'a process of giving form and pattern to the social life of the community'.

The architectural profession has grown out of a continuous tension between the role of the 'organiser' and that of the 'artist'. As early as 1788 the architect John Soane clearly captured this balance:

> The business of the architect is to make designs and estimates to direct the works and to measure and value the different parts; he is the intermediate agent between the employer, whose honour and interest he is to study, and the mechanic whose rights he is to define.

Today the profession continues to be faced with these paradoxes, and there is uncertainty about whether its prime role is social concern for the wider interests of society and the user, or whether it is primarily concerned with the particular interests of its developer client or the success of the practice, now most probably a limited company whose economic livelihood may rest on the next job from a contractor. The architectural profession feels alienated. The professions are often no longer head of the team, being increasingly rejected by the client and user and driven by a commercial imperative.

Despite the seeming erosion of the architect's position, architecture is now probably more in the public eye than ever before. It features in popular magazines, has gained 'air time' and architects are film heroes. Architectural thinking and our education system have unique attributes to offer in a world that is predominantly stratified by speculative and management thinking.

The new professionalism

The power of management thinking (Allinson 1993) is its ability to tame 'wicked problems' by subdividing complex problems into their more manageable component parts. The failing is that whilst the parts are manageable, the coherence of the whole is lost. The strength of design education is to instil a way of thinking that leaves options open—finding form out of chaos and presenting holistic solutions. Clients and the construction industry intuitively recognise the inspiration that architects bring to a project. Without an initial design there would be nothing to manage or construct. They are often, however, frustrated with the architect's inability to work with the team and focus on the services that in their mind add greater value. Developers and clients with continuous building programmes have grown to accept that architects, in their enthusiasm to get 'their' design built, will often give away, for little or no fee, their high-value advice on framing the brief and conceptual design.

It is ironic that today the high-value services are increasingly provided outside the core of the design and construction process (Figure 2.2), at the pre-project and post-project stages. These services—master planning and estates strategies, strategic briefing, option appraisal and ongoing facilities management—are well suited to the architect's expertise and are valued highly by the client in achieving

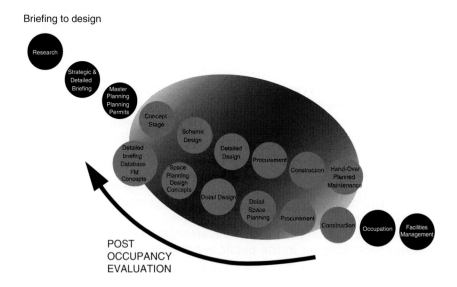

Figure 2.2 The high-value services are increasingly outside the core of the design and construction process.

business success. I have identified four areas where the profession might focus its expertise:

- *Problem seeking*: defined by William Pena (Pena *et al.* 1987) as the role in the early stages of a project of identifying, from a statement of need, the context and requirements. This step is suited to a combination of analytical and lateral thinking.
- *Concept defining*: helping users to see patterns and direction in a jumble of data and information. Many disciplines are able to collect and order data, the skill is to recognise meaning and direction from the information.
- *Solution framing*: the 'creative leap' where design draws together a myriad separate pieces of information into a coherent whole— to provide a design concept that can then be visualised through images.
- *Creating meaning*: the representation of a memorable and meaningful image.

The focal role to which the profession can once again aspire is that of 'integrator', drawing together people, process and place to create a coherent working environment (DEGW 1998). Horgen *et al.*, in *Excellence by Design* (1999), argue for an integrated design approach that brings together space, organisation, finance and technology (SOFT) to optimise the workplace (Figure 2.3).

The professions are increasingly being expected to deliver both the product and a service. The more innovative architectural practices are reconsidering their role to provide a new 'offer' that addresses both the quality of the built object and the range of services that can be provided to support it. Davis and Meyer (1998) argue that the new professional offering will be a combination of product and service over time. Taking their proposition, such an 'offer' might have the characteristics shown in Table 2.1 if applied to architecture.

The approach of recognising the project as the 'client', as distinct from the 'building design', is further reinforced when one recognises that the value of construction now increasingly resides in the building services and fit-out, rather than the construction of the building shell. A conservative analysis of the changing value of construction services (including information and communications technology) shows a shift in value for a typical office building between 1980 and 2000 for the building shell and skin from 62 per cent to 56 per cent of the total cost' whilst the fit-out and information and communications technology has shifted in value from 17 per cent to 28 per cent of the total (Table 2.2). These relative values are accentuated when one considers that the building shell has a life of at least 75 years, while on average the fit-out may be replaced every seven years and information

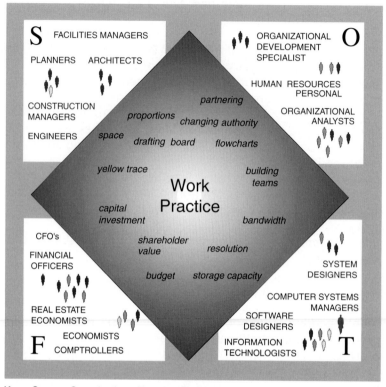

Key: ●Space ●Organisation ● Finance ●Technology

Figure 2.3 Different competences required to optimise the workplace.

Source: Horgen, Joroff, Porter and Schön (1999).

Table 2.1 Redefining the professional service

Characteristics	Product	Service	'Offer'
Time horizon	Final completion of building contract	Period of contract	Life of customer need
Client expectation	Price, delivery, convenience, image	Ongoing support	Continuous improvement and response to feedback
Cost focus	Capital costs	Contract costs	Whole life costs
Source of value	Production	Maintenance	Evolving experience. Continuous improvement
Design strategy	'One-off'	Standard and customised	Building on past experience

Table 2.2 Change in the distribution of total costs for a typical office building (per cent)

	1980	1990	2000*
Information and communication technology	2	5	8
Fit-out	15	19	20
Services	21	20	16
Building shell and skin	62	56	56

*Projected.

Source: DEGW (1992).

technology has a life cycle of two to three years. Close ongoing partnerships with client organisations that can respond to the rapid cycle of business and technological change are becoming a recognised *modus operandi* for larger architectural practices, which then are broadening their services either directly or through alliances to support the client's business.

At the core of the emerging 'offer' is the function of integrator, a role that can support client organisations in:

- Identifying needs and defining problems
- Assessing options and establishing a business case for action
- Conceiving integrated solutions to meet requirements
- Preparing designs as blueprints for action
- Procuring and delivering appropriate solutions
- Communicating solutions, managing user expectations and managing the process of change
- Establishing continuous facility management systems
- Evaluating experience in use
- Responding to feedback and undertaking continuous improvement.

Organisations such as the British Airports Authority, under the chairmanship of Sir John Egan, have established five-year partnership agreements with selected practices, which has allowed them to build multidisciplinary design, construction and facility management teams, with resulting reductions in costs and improvements in quality.

Research and learning in practice

The architectural professions worldwide are questioning their values and ways of working. Experiences in North America are not dissimilar to those in Europe: an increasing demand for more specialised, value adding services; a changing market and method of delivery; the emergence of new skills and new professional disciplines that are encroaching on architects' traditional areas of work; and new client procurement structures accountable to shareholders, with independent experts sophisticated in assessing results. The cry from the architectural profession of 'trust us and we will deliver' has to be earned, and cannot automatically be expected from past performance.

To match this changing professional context, and looking ahead to the needs of a knowledge economy, one can identify the following abilities that will be required throughout the working life of a professional. The ability to:

- Balance the traditional professional concern for the underlying social implications (society and the user) with the managerial need to use resources effectively in the interests of the business.
- Work as a team—cooperating with and respecting other skills, expectations and visions.
- Accept changing agendas, ways of delivery and roles.
- Understand the mind-set required for strategic thinking and that required tactically to achieve results. Much of architecture still mixes means and ends. Design, rather than 'giving form and pattern to social life' (Davis and Meyer 1998), does no more than provide decoration to ill-conceived problem statements.
- Learn both contextual skills (the generalist) and specialist expertise.

In a knowledge economy the individuals and professional service firms that are most likely to prosper are those that learn from past experience and are continuously reviewing and renewing their knowledge base. Tom Stewart, in *Intellectual Capital—The New Wealth of Organisations* (1997) predicts that the firms that will prosper in the emerging knowledge economy are those that:

- Establish a process of continuous feedback and learning.
- Apply knowledge that adds value to their clients' expectations over and above the recognised standard professional service.
- Develop their corporate intellectual capital by drawing from the experience and insights (knowledge) of their staff and those they work with (clients, institutions and coprofessionals).
- Establish a formalised, reliable, accessible and renewable corporate memory.

Stewart identifies the components of intellectual capital (Figure 2.4) as corporate capital (the 'company memory', composed of data information and knowledge), human capital (individual staff who manipulate tools, methods and concepts) and customer capital (clients, partners and coprofessionals). The combination stimulates innovation, insights

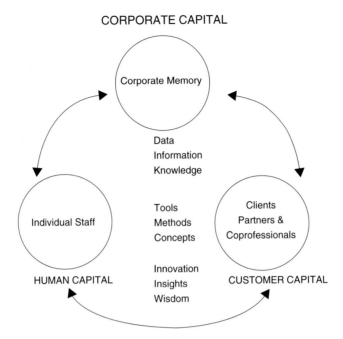

CORPORATE CAPITAL

Corporate Memory

Data
Information
Knowledge

Tools
Methods
Concepts

Clients
Partners &
Coprofessionals

Individual Staff

Innovation
Insights
Wisdom

HUMAN CAPITAL   CUSTOMER CAPITAL

Figure 2.4 The components of intellectual capital.

Source: Stewart (1997).

and wisdom. Successful professional practices are recognising these needs and establishing knowledge-management systems to capture experience, both within and outside the practice.

For instance in my own practice—DEGW—we have built up our intellectual property by investing in multiclient research projects often in association with academic or professional partners (Figure 2.5). These, subsequently published as books, have not only enhanced the positioning of the practice but also, we believe, added to the knowledge base of the profession.

Learning partnerships

Phase one of the RIBA's strategic study of the profession (RIBA 1992) set an agenda for the learning needs of individual practitioners, practices and the profession. The study proposed that in order to survive architects need to address all three levels:

• *Individuals*: the need for core sets of skills based on abstract knowledge expressed through well-practised technologies that cannot be substituted: 'The issues of motivation and training are crucial

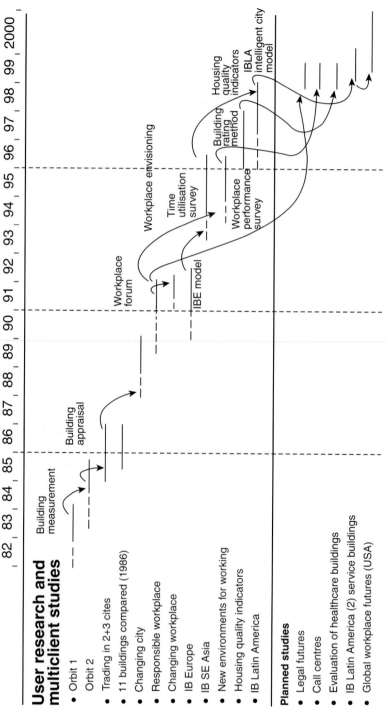

Figure 2.5 Evolution of a practice's intellectual property—DEGW.

Source: DEGW.

since architects have to be motivated to produce services which enhance the environment but they also have to accept that unless they meet clients needs, often by doing mundane tasks which seem commercial rather than professionally challenging, they will simply remain in a subordinate position' (Gutman 1988).

- *Practices*: the option of specialising or providing multidisciplinary or generalist services. Much of practice development will be focused on understanding market demand, reassessing corporate and individual aspirations, and developing skills and relevant delivery structures within the framework.
- *The profession*: recognising the balance between commercial demands and professional interests and encouraging:

    1 continuous improvement to rebuild professional status;
    2 specialist degree courses;
    3 business management expertise to result in cheaper services through better practice management;
    4 commitment to client and public objectives.

The opportunities for academic institutions to establish continuing partnerships with individuals (their alumni), local practices and the profession are considerable if they are prepared to enter a dialogue. For the individual, continuous education programmes provide a means of enhancing career prospects, developing new skills, widening understanding and networking amongst peers and coprofessionals. For practice, learning events either in the office or at an academic institution can develop team spirit and raise staff morale, improve performance by improving the corporate memory and result in more efficient use of resources. For the profession, academic research programmes and feedback courses can develop the knowledge base and protect specialist expertise.

Professional learning is a continuous process, leading individual practitioners through a hierarchy of competencies and roles (Worthington 1995). The first stage, before entering the profession, is a period of gaining general understanding where concepts, principles, an awareness of the disciplines and an appreciation of design is imparted. In the second stage competence develops in a specific discipline, design, production, maintenance or measurement. During the third, after becoming a member of the profession, further education on a full- or part-time basis may be undertaken to gain a specialism, through specific expertise. The final stage is the acquisition of finesse, where the specialist professional updates specific skills (Figure 2.6). Such a programme, if provided in modules, could be delivered as a combination of full-time, part-time and 'some-time' learning to

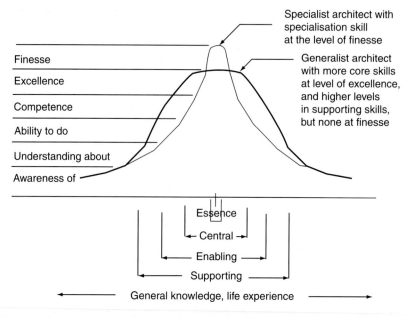

Specialist architect with
specialisation skill
at the level of finesse

Finesse

Excellence

Competence

Ability to do

Understanding about

Awareness of

Generalist architect
with more core skills
at level of excellence,
and higher levels
in supporting skills,
but none at finesse

Essence

Central

Enabling

Supporting

General knowledge, life experience

Figure 2.6 Distribution of competency and roles.

Source: Dr Rob Cowdroy. Architects' CPD: A Strategic Framework.

meet the financial and work requirements of students and practitioners.

Continuous learning in business schools has become the mainstay of the latter's income, through full-time, part-time and distance learning modules that meet busy managers' schedules. If architectural schools are to capitalise on this emerging demand they may have to reappraise their perceptions and, for example, review the first degree course as a platform for wider career opportunities. In Europe the UK is unusual in the small number of students studying at any one time compared with the number of practising registered architects. This could be due to the fact that the majority of students are expected to enter the profession. For instance in England and Wales there are approximately four architects to every student, whilst in The Netherlands the ratio is 1.8 : 1 and Spain 1 : 1 (Orbasli and Worthington 1995). On the continent an academic architectural education is recognised as an excellent grounding for a wide range of careers. The opportunity for working and learning in the final years of architectural education are well understood on the continent. In Germany a seven-year programme of study and professional experience on average takes 8.5 years, and in Spain a seven-year programme on average takes 12 years to complete. The course in the architectural faculty at Delft is organised to provide general grounding in the first two years, with specialisation in architecture, housing, technology, urbanism or real estate and project management in the final three years. An alternative with the modular system is to extend the course to gain an architectural award with an additional specialisation.

The opportunities for academia are immense if it can shake off its parochial defensive positioning and adopt the four layers of professional educational development proposed by the Stanfield Smith committee. The four layers allow the freedom of continuous learning, with study interspersed with practice, whilst integrating with the accepted degree structure of BA/BSc/MA/MSc and advanced research degrees (M.Phil and D.Phil). After the initial degree, schools—working in partnership with the profession and practices—could provide a series of integrated learning opportunities, interwoven with work experience and spread over an individual's career. Architectural practice is changing—the challenge is for practices and academia to respond.

Notes

1 David Maister was educated at the Regent Street Polytechnic as an architect and subsequently taught at the Harvard Business School. His *Managing the Professional Service Firm* (New York: Free Press, 1993) and *True Professionalism* (New York: Free Press, 1997) provide excellent insights into the changing nature of professional practices in a knowledge economy.
2 Dana Cuff (1999) points out that among US practices with over 50 staff, 53 per cent are currently working on international projects and 21 per cent are considering or actively pursuing international work.

References

Allinson, K. (1993) *The Wild Card of Design*. Oxford: Butterworth Architecture.
Cuff, D. (1999) 'The political paradoxes of practice: political economy of local and global architecture', *Architectural Research Quarterly*, 3(1).
Davis S. and Meyer, C. (1998) *Blur: The Speed of Change in the Connected Economy*, Oxford: Capstons.
DEGW (1992) The Intelligent Building in Europe, The Changing Workplace, Phaidon London.
DEGW (1998) *Design for Change—the architecture of DEGW*. Berlin: Birkhäuser UK: Watermark Publications LTD (UK).
Egan, Sir John (1998) *Rethinking Construction: The Report of the Construction Task Force*, as the Egan Report. Department of Environment, Transport and the Regions. London.
Gutman, R. (1988) *Architectural Practice: A Critical View*. Princeton, NJ: Princeton Architectural Press.

Horgen T., Joroff M., Porter W. and Schön (1999) *Excellence by Design*: Transforming Workplace and Work Practice. London: Wiley.

Kostof, S. (1999) *The Architect Chapters in the History of the Profession*. Oxford: Oxford University Press.

Latham, Sir Michael (1994) *Constructing the Team: Final Report of the Government/Industry Review of Procurement and Contractual Arrangements in the UK*. London: HMSO.

Orbasli A. and Worthington, J. (1995) *Architecture and Town Planning Education in the Netherlands: A European Comparison*. York: Institute of Advanced Architecture Studies IoAAS, University of York.

Pena, W., Parnhall, S. and Kelly K. (1987) *Problem Seeking—an architectural programming primer*: Washington, DC: A.I.A. Press.

RIBA (1992) *Strategic Study of the Profession—Phase 1: strategic overview*. London: RIBA Publications.

Stewart, T. (1997) *Intellectual Capital—The New Wealth of Organisations*. London: Nicholas Brealey.

Watkins J., Drury, L. and Predy, D. (1992) *From Education to Revolution—the pressures on professional life in the 1990's*. Bristol: University of Bristol.

Worthington, J. (1993) *Workplace Design for the Knowledge Industries in Industriebau die Vision der Lean Company*, PRAXIS report. Basel: Birkhauser.

Worthington, J. (1995) *Professional Futures: Continuous Learning through Research and Practice*. CIB W89 Conference Proceedings, Orlando, Florida.

Section 1

Communication

Developing sensitivity to the needs of users and clients

The chapters in this section are all concerned with developing students' sensitivity to users' and clients' needs in building design and their ability to understand and engage in dialogue with them.

The first three chapters concentrate on the needs of building users. Morrow (Chapter 3) is concerned with the ability of schools of architecture to prepare students to address, in their designs, the needs of those who are discriminated against in society (for example single parents or those with a disability) and she suggests ways in which design education could be realigned to make it more inclusive. One of her solutions is for students to go out into the community and spend time with those for whom they are designing. Brown and Yates (Chapter 4) start from the premise that architects, as a result of their education, perceive, experience and talk about the built environment in a way that is different from non-architects (users). They discuss a project that involved students and children (users) exploring together, through activities and discussion, different aspects of the same space in the children's school. Jarrett (Chapter 5) offers an American perspective that complements that of the two previous chapters. His concern is that urban design education is disconnected from the tangible experiences of users, from real social problems (for example unemployment, crime, sickness) and from the cities in which people live and work. He describes some community-based design projects that were developed to increase students' receptivity to the social meaning of design.

Chapter 6, by Callicot and Sheil, describes a series of exercises designed to challenge students to think about how designs are interpreted by those who are not party to the design. Like the previous two chapters, the concern is with how students learn to communicate and consider the perspective of others. However, instead of going into the community, Callicot and Sheil's students develop their skills in the design studio.

The next two chapters are focused on clients as well as users. Here the aims were to sensitise students to clients' and users' perspectives and to develop the skills required to deal with clients in practice situations (for example listening, brief-building, perspective-taking, questioning, groupworking). Both writers provided opportunities for their students to interact with real clients as well as users. Sara (Chapter 7) describes a 'live project' where students learn skills by developing a design brief (for a new roof for a cricket pavilion) in consultation with a client group (the cricket team). In this project the clients are also the users of the building. Torrington's students (Chapter 8) research and design a day nursery school. They first develop and practise their skills in groups and then refine them through meetings with a client, nursery users and an architect (with expertise in nursery design).

Chiles (Chapter 9) is also concerned with introducing students to the realities of clients in design. She describes a project in which students interact with some of the real clients of a large and complex regeneration project that was carried out in the city of Sheffield a few years earlier. The students critique the original design and present counter-proposals to a panel that incudes members of the original selection team.

The next two chapters concentrate on assessment processes in relation to the needs of clients and users and to student learning generally. Wilkin (Chapter 10) discusses the findings of a research study of the review process (the crit) that she carried out at the Leicester School of Architecture. The aims of the study were to examine the effects of the review on student learning, the effectiveness of the review in promoting discussion amongst students about the interests of clients and users, and its value in fostering the development of communication skills. Brindley, Doidge and Willmott (Chapter 11) explain how tutors at Leicester responded to the Wilkin study. The writers describe a series of alternative review formats that were introduced to make the review a more effective vehicle for learning and to promote the development in students of some of the communication skills required in professional practice.

3 Architectural assumptions and environmental discrimination

The case for more inclusive design in schools of architecture

Ruth Morrow

Context

The built environment is insensitive to the needs of a wide range of users. In particular it excludes and marginalises people with disabilities, single mothers and families on low incomes. Architects, designing in their own image, often centralise their own experiences of space and marginalise and negate the experiences of others. It currently takes legislation to ensure that buildings have physical access for people with disabilities.

These shortcomings in the built environment are part of the reason for the general public unease with modern architecture and for the growing call for user participation in architectural design.

A research project has been set up within the School of Architecture at University College, Dublin to investigate why architecture persistently falls short of fully addressing the needs of particular sets of users. The aim of the project is to find ways of incorporating 'inclusive' design throughout the curriculum of the school. Inclusive design in the project is defined as an approach to design that recognises the diversity of users, regardless of their ability, age, gender, income, sexuality, race or culture. Inclusive design challenges designers to think beyond compliance to regulations and codes, and to find inclusive solutions that incorporate the needs of diverse users without segregation or the need for separate accommodation.

This chapter draws on the findings of the DraWare research project. It identifies a series of 'barriers' to the mainstream adoption of inclusive design within schools of architecture and, for each, goes on to suggest ways of making curricula more inclusive.

Architecture apart from society: a grouping of like minds

Those studying and teaching in architecture schools typically share similar backgrounds, social class, aspirations and political affiliations, whilst teaching staff are still predominately one gender—male. As a group they will rarely have felt excluded from the built environment: and even though the experience of exclusion is not a precondition for empathy with the excluded it is a good starting point. It is contended that this homogeneity in their background and culture contributes to the failure of architects to take account of the 'otherness' that is essential to the creation of inclusive design.

Since there is no time to wait for demographic changes in schools of architecture to redress such an imbalance, strategies must be found to make inclusive design a priority. For example a wider range of people could be invited into schools of architecture—not just as consultants but as equal participants, feeding into the education of architecture students. Architecture students could be sent out to spend time with some of the people and communities for whom they may eventually design (Welsh 1998). Ways need to be devised to raise awareness in students that even in a homogeneous group such as their own there are differences in needs, desires and perceptions of space.

The architectural syllabus: complacent implicitness

An understanding of users' needs and the nature of the relationship between user and space should be an implicit part of the architecture curriculum. The study of how people perceive and interact with space is integral to the history of architecture, architectural theory, professional practice in the design studio and environmental studies. Yet even some of the most basic principles that lie behind how people perceive space, for example in relation to the senses and sensory impairment, are rarely addressed in the architectural curriculum. The Royal Institute of British Architects and Architects Registration Board document *Criteria for Validation* (RIBA ARB 1997), which acts as an outline syllabus for schools of architecture, is a good indicator of where the current emphasis lies. Within that document 'people issues' are fragmented and vague, thus diminishing their importance in the minds of those who teach architecture. Instead of being embedded in the curriculum, people issues become peripheral (Morrow 1998).

User issues are fundamental to the making of architecture. They must therefore become a more explicit part of the study of architecture. Schools of architecture should ensure that students are made aware that users of buildings have different needs and that these affect how the users perceive and use space. More importantly, students should learn to recognise that different groups are likely to have contradictory and often conflicting spatial needs, and that it is necessary to acquire the architectural skills required for reconciling such differences.

Analysis and design: an essential iterative process

Environments that exclude or discriminate are as much a product of the inadequate and inappropriate methods of analysis that led to them, as they are of poor design. However, within architectural schools it is this very relationship between design and analysis—or rather the frequent failure to acknowledge the issue—that hinders the development of an inclusive design ethos. Students typically come to understand analysis in an oppositional relationship to design. Perceiving design to be the most valued element of the course, they equate spending more time on analysis with spending less time on design. The result is a narrowness and lack of depth in analysis coupled with overreliance on traditional analytical, supposedly objective, methods of analysis. But without more depth and innovation during the analysis stage it is unlikely that more inclusive social forms will emerge.

If inclusive design is to be encouraged, students will have to develop a deeper understanding of the relationship between analysis and the design process, and of the interplay between the two. This will require tutors to adopt teaching methods that ensure an 'inclusive understanding' of the user context of design problems. One way to do this is to ask students to carry out their analysis not through the eyes and mind of an architect but through, and with respect to, the perception of others (Hester 1993).

Choice of sites: the hidden messages

When sites are used in student design projects they are invariably beautiful, 'full of character' and have strict limits. Such sites are no doubt stimulating, drawing a strong response, but they also demonstrate an element of the 'architect's indulgence'. Such choices have definite consequences.

One is that students may never develop the skills needed to deal with large, expansive sites with little character and surrounded by low-grade suburban blandness. But in reality it is sites of this kind that are, for instance, typical of those used for social housing, for day centres for people with multiple disabilities and for residential units for people with dementia.

More consideration should be given to how sites are chosen. Those responsible for teaching students need to ask themselves about the signals that are sent to students by the choices they make. Students should have the opportunity at least once during their studies to design sites that take into account the needs of marginalised groups in society.

Design programmes: typecasting

In order to allow students to spend as much time as possible on the design stage of a project, tutors usually select specific building types for study. Like the choice of sites, it is notable that many of the building types chosen more frequently reflect the needs of dominant groups in society than those of minority groups, thus reinforcing the divisions in society. In fact, as with the choice of site, the mere adoption of these building types for study helps perpetuate environments of exclusion because it encourages students to accept them as the norm.

Students should be given the opportunity to challenge the perpetuation of some of these accepted building types. For evidence of what can be achieved, see Karen Franck's account in *Ordering Space* (1994) of how a young architect reforms the design principles of a maternity ward by talking to expectant and recent mothers rather than unquestioningly accepting the brief given by the hospital authority.

Product over process: finding the balance

Evaluation of architecture—primarily by the industry itself—is presently weighted towards judging how innovative the form (the physical object) is rather than the innovation of the process (the building in use). This is evidenced by the architectural work that is published or wins awards. In turn the creators of these forms act as role models for students, with the result that students invest most of their study time in the design of form. Those students who do focus on process and develop new programmes or ways of reconceptualising space/user relationships are rarely given credit because of the current systems of assessment used by schools of architecture. In effect, what is valued in the profession—form—is reflected in architecture schools, and of course *vice versa*.

In addition, the understanding and language required to evaluate form is, of necessity, very specialised. This may be one reason why the general public, as well as minority groups, are excluded from debates about what is or is not good architecture.

Evaluation and assessment systems, in the profession and in schools of architecture respectively, must establish an appropriate balance between process and form. The most direct means of achieving this is to invite user involvement in the evaluation and assessment (formative feedback) of work.

Perception of space: representing spatial experiences

Concern with form also leads students to focus their efforts on the visual dimension. This means that students' designs often lack the full breadth of sensory stimuli and are thus, for some people in society, perceptually inaccessible.

This situation is further exacerbated by the fact that much of the discussion about students' design work is centred on the underpinning 'idea' and the organisation of space. There is comparatively little discussion about the experience of the space. But the 'idea of the space' is usually irrelevant to the user, and the organisation of space is but one part of the picture. If, as often happens, the building takes on a new programme or a new set of users, the 'experience' of the space persists.

The narrow band of representational techniques often used in architecture schools can be seen as a major source of this problem. Of necessity, some design proposals and their presentations demand wordy explanations—the root of the preoccupation with the 'idea'. Others simply deliver organisational diagrams. However the vital dimension of the experience is less easy to represent. Students need to be encouraged to explore other methods of representation—mock-ups, sensory presentations and so on—as happens when architects negotiate with users in practice. Similarly, detail design also has potential, if it goes beyond simply testing the student's technical competence and requires the student to discuss how that detail influences the feel of the space and its degree of accessibility, in the broadest sense.

Examining normal everyday life

Preoccupation with the new, the exotic, and the need to perform what Frampton (1991) calls 'acrobatic feats', are prevalent in the design studio and exist at the cost of everyday issues. Designing a transportable, multimedia environment still remains more popular amongst students than designing an accessible environment. However, as McLeod (1997) has noted, 'From the perspective of everyday life, such neo-avant-garde strategies as "folding", "disjunction", and "bigness" deny the energy, humanity and creativity embodied in the humble, prosaic details of daily existence.'

Not only are many of the qualities of everyday life currently overlooked, but observational and analytical skills, combined with the creative and intellectual rigour required to identify them, never have the opportunity to develop in students. Such skills are the key to successful professional practice, where an effective architect finds inspiration in the most mundane of places, and is able to see potential and opportunity in the obvious. Indeed this is a form of sustainability—it is sustainable thinking.

It could be argued that, as students progress through their studies, there is a need for design projects to become more modest and more everyday.

Conclusion

Change is always inevitable, even in architectural education. But for change to be constructive it must respect existing contexts and accommodate some of the traditional approaches in architectural education. This chapter has argued for a move towards an inclusive curriculum, and has tried to demonstrate how this might be achieved in small, reasonable and logical steps. It is interesting to note that all the changes advocated in this chapter are the inevitable and natural result of setting design projects that work directly with, and learn from, the end user.

If, as Frampton (1983) says, 'No new architecture can emerge without a new kind of relation between designer and user, without new kinds of programs', then, in the interests of the future of the architecture profession, schools of architecture have a pressing duty to connect with their surrounding communities.

References

Frampton, K. (1983) 'Towards a Critical Regionalism: Six Points for an Architecture of Resistance', in Hal Foster (ed.), *The Anti-Aesthetic: Essays on Postmodern Culture*. Seattle: Bay Press.

Frampton, K. (1991) 'Reflections on the Autonomy of Architecture: A Critique of Contemporary Production', in Diane Ghirardo (ed.), *Out of Site*. Seattle: Bay Press.

Franck, K. (1994) 'Types are us', in K. Franck and L. Schneekloth (eds), *Ordering Space, Types in Architecture and Design*. New York: Van Nostrand Reinhold.

Hester, R. (1993) 'Sacred Spaces and Everyday Life: A Return to Manteo, North Carolina', in David Seamon (ed.), *Dwelling, Seeing and Designing: Towards a Phenomenological Ecology*. Albany: State University of New York Press.

McLeod, M. (1997) 'Henri Lebfre's Critique of Everyday Life: An Introduction', in Steven Harris and Deborah Berke (eds), *Architecture of the Everyday*. Princeton, NJ: Princeton Architectural Press.

Morrow, R. (1998) 'People Friendly Design', *Streetwise: The Journal of Places for People*, 8(4).

RIBA ARB Joint Validation Panel (1997) '*Procedures and Criteria for the Validation of Courses Programmes and Examinations in Architecture: Part 2 Criteria for Validation*. London: RIBA.

Welsh, P. (1998) 'Teaching Universal Design through Inclusiveness', in *Proceedings of International Conference on Universal Design*. New York: Hofstra University.

4 Seeing the world through another person's eyes

Robert Brown and Denitza Moreau Yates

Introduction

> Self-regarding elite … on an artistic ego trip … don't care about the buildings and styles people really want.

> Much misunderstood … sparks of mad genius …
>
> (Fairs 1999: 2)

The first of these quotes reflects the prevailing view held by the public about architects, and the second the view that architects have of themselves. Underlying these sentiments is a fundamental difference in the way that each communicates about, perceives, interprets and values the built environment. This variance has led to a condition today where architects are producing an architecture that, however well intended, is one to which non-architects often have difficulty relating.

This chapter contends that this disparity arises from differences in experience and, most significantly, education, and that it is in education that there lies a possible way forward. This chapter will explore the role of architectural education in the creation of this disparity, and review a workshop that addressed the dialectic outlined above, run as part of the University of East London's Atelier Principle in Teaching programme. The title of this chapter, 'Seeing the world through another person's eyes', reflects in essence both the workshop's activities and the understanding it generated.

Seeing the world differently

Research in environmental psychology has examined the different ways people relate to the built environment. It has demonstrated that architects respond with an emphasis on perceptual terms and representative meaning—'concepts'. Non-architects, on the other hand, do so with an emphasis on associational terms and responsive meaning—'evaluative' (Devlin 1990; see also Hershberger 1988; Rappaport 1982).

In one study this thesis was carried further, examining how this disparity is reflected in the design (and perceived value) of contemporary architecture. It investigated whether postmodern buildings are more meaningful to non-architects than modern buildings. The findings suggest that modern buildings are designed to a 'professional' code. Architects, interpreting according to this code, responded more positively than non-architects, who interpreted these buildings using a 'popular' code. In contrast the postmodern buildings were seen as having been designed to both a professional and popular code. Being 'more easily and appropriately interpreted by those using [the] popular code', non-architects responded to these more favourably than they did to the modern buildings (Groat 1982). This suggests that the architects' design of buildings is being informed by a different value system from that which non-architects are using in their response to buildings.

There are of course a number of reasons why this disparity exists, including cultural (for example class) and historical (for example the emergence of architecture as a distinct profession). While such reasons play a part, the findings of the research suggest that the primary reasons for this condition are first-hand experience and education.

The education of the architect

In Britain today there is neither substantial nor direct primary or secondary education focused on the built environment. Thus how children relate to the built environment is, and remains in adulthood, generally informed by their own experiences. However, for the aspiring student architect entering higher education a disparity quickly emerges. Most students will undergo a distinct transformation in how they relate to the built environment: they become totally immersed in an examination of the built environment, a process continued in professional life.

By the time architecture students finish their initial formal education, they have been trained to 'think like an architect' (Weaver 1997). Traditional critiques of this training have noted its emphasis on 'formal style and proportion..., two-dimensional and externalised [design], ... [taking] place in an academy unrelated to other disciplines of human activity outside architecture' (Hellman 1987). This philosophy continues to be reinforced by those who define the agenda. For instance the recent syllabus produced for schools of architecture by the Royal Institute of Architects and Architects Registration Board noted the RIBA's view that '"architectural education" is in essence a visual subject' (Morrow 1998).

In professional practice this emphasis is reinforced by the way in which architects speak and write on architecture, and this is in turn reflected in the architectural press. It is the perceptual qualities and the 'professionalised' conceptual meanings that a building conveys that is given primary status; far less attention is given to how non-architects will inhabit it, or what they think of it. Together with the foundation laid during education, this has helped foster an elite professional code that is not necessarily reflective of non-architects' values. As architectural design is informed by the architect's training and values, architects are producing an architecture to which non-architects often find it difficult to relate—an architecture that could be interpreted as being intended primarily for the benefit, and approval, of other architects. Frank Duffy, former president of the RIBA, alluded to this when he spoke of 'the curse of architectural photography, which is all about the wonderfully composed shot, the absolute lifeless picture that takes time out of architecture—the photograph taken the day before move-in. That's what you get awards for, that's what you make a career based on' (Brand 1994).

While there is undoubtedly a growing number of architects whose work counters this and attracts a positive response from non-architects, there is still, as frequently reported in the media, a marked level of dissatisfaction amongst the public with much of the profession (and contemporary architecture). As a result the public is increasingly turning to others in the construction industry in the belief that they may be more responsive to their needs and aspirations. This poses enormous implications for the profession.

Where to now?

There are a number of ongoing initiatives to address this problem. Programmes have been initiated by the professional bodies to promote a more user-responsive approach to design in practice, as well as attempts to raise the profile of architecture with the public, and programmes that seek to introduce studies of the built environment into primary and secondary schools. However, while these initiatives are laudable and have brought improvement, we contend that it is in professional architectural education that the disparity between architect and non-architect first becomes established and that it is here that it should be squarely addressed.

It is our view that what is missing are educational programmes that explicitly investigate the disparity. These would permit architecture students to raise their awareness of how non-architects relate to the built environment. Moreover they would enable both architects and non-architects to develop their ability to communicate effectively with each other, with knowledge and understanding moving in both directions. Such programmes must, however, also allow architects simultaneously to develop their abilities in creative problem solving.

Description of the work

With this intention in mind, in July 1998 we organised a workshop to explore the nature of these issues. It involved the participation of architecture students from the University of East London and school children aged nine and ten from a nearby primary school. Its aim was to help the children to raise their level of awareness and critical engagement with the built environment, and prompt architecture students to review their own architectural values in relation to those of the children as non-architects.

The underpinning theme was design activities through which the participants might draw others into an investigation of their environment, enabling them to identify and express their interests and concerns—the exploration of other's values and interpretations as a tool for understanding and reevaluating one's own relation to the built environment.

Introduction to the workshop

Before coming into contact, each group engaged separately in a series of introductory exercises. These were intended to prepare them to work with each other and investigate issues raised by the workshop.

First, work with the children began with the introduction of basic concepts of design by focusing on something familiar to them in their everyday life: clothing. They examined why clothes are designed the way they are, based on their own observations of purposes, practicality and beauty. They were then asked to design a piece of clothing and identify the most effective way of (re)presenting it to the group.

The exercises helped familiarise them with the idea of design, and enabled subsequent cross-references with building design to be more easily established. As a final step, the children were asked to draw their ideal school, which was to be presented to the architecture students on the first day of the fully interactive session.

Meanwhile each of the architecture students had to identify a favourite building and define in three words why they liked it. Then, working in pairs, one student would show the image and words to the other, who was allowed to ask a limited number of questions with yes/no answers in order to try to determine what the other person liked about the building. This exercise highlighted the varied and personal meanings each assigned to buildings and words.

Learning to ask questions

The two groups then came together. Interaction started with a general walkabout around the primary school. When visiting the parts of the school that the children had selected, we discussed the reasons they liked or disliked these places and also what the students found interesting in terms of design. Through this the children began to discover how their feelings about these places were related to the design of them, and also how various design features complemented a room's purpose.

An example of this was the computer room, liked by the children because they had lots of fun in there. They were asked to imagine the room with a different appearance (for example smaller, darker and so on). This prompted an awareness of a connection between the design of the room and why they liked it (for example enough space, right type of light and so on). They also started spontaneously to compare it to other places where they had used computers.

The children's comments on the use of the space revealed how the same place could be perceived differently by different people, with interpretations that the architecture students might not have considered on their own. This was evident, for instance, when visiting the library, which was enjoyed by the children because they were allowed to work on the carpeted floor. The original design intention when selecting a carpetted finish (as the architecture students identified) had been to muffle sound, but in practice this soft, cosy space had turned out to be one of the most pleasurable places to sit in the school.

The children were quick to pick up the new direction of the conversation and started to comment on colours, materials, the size of windows and so on. Interestingly, the children's observations revealed aspects of the school that the students and even the children's teachers had not considered before or thought that the children would be aware of.

Looking for answers

After the walkabout the students and children engaged in a series of exercises to explore further some of the children's interests and their architectural implications.

In the first exercise the students presented images of buildings to the children. While this could be seen as a very traditional architectural exercise, here the buildings had been selected by the students on the basis that they reflected values expressed by the children in the previous exercises. For example some children had expressed a liking for small, intimate spaces scaled to their size, so one student showed an image of a space with a series of small, raised and partially enclosed platforms, to which the children reacted enthusiastically. For the children, this revealed that what they valued existed in architects' designs. For the students, it further enhanced their understanding of how the children engaged with the built environment.

The architecture students were also asked to develop and lead an investigation of an issue revealed by the children. It was to be done in small groups, and would help the children to gain an awareness of how this aspect could affect space and perceptions of it. The children were to record their experience through a drawing or other medium, as prompted by the students.

This activity proved to be one of the most revealing parts of the workshop. The exercises turned into games that made the learning fun and interesting, while obliging the students to engage with the children's views. This made the architecture students 'step out' of their own understanding and approach the built environment in someone else's terms, challenging them to rethink their own values and ways of communicating.

In one exercise a student asked the children to choose a part of their classroom that they liked, and to draw and write down what they liked about it. The student prompted them with questions to help them articulate what it was they liked. These drawings set the basis for a general discussion on the children's observations and how they had chosen to represent it.

Various observations came out of this exercise, which did not focus on tangible aspects of the room but on the interpretation of space. One child chose to study the teacher's armchair, where he enjoyed sitting. He liked the comfort it provided, in spite of it being old and worn-out. Through the discussion he also identified that he had a good view from where the chair was positioned. His observation overlapped with that of another child, who talked about the connection to the outside he gained through a window even when still inside the room.

Like these, many of the other comments and observations started to link up and the participants soon realised that changing one aspect of the room would affect the rest, and *vice versa*. While this exercise did not lend itself to definite conclusions, it raised interesting issues and gave the students an insight into how the children inhabited and interpreted the space.

At this stage the students and children were set their final exercise. The students were to make a proposal for a space in the school that would reflect the children's values. Meanwhile the children were asked to define their 'ideal' school.

Communicating ideas

For the last session together the children and the students met to present their final work. The children's design and presentations showed more control and understanding of the way they could create and affect space. At this stage the architecture students' questions focused mostly on how the children had chosen to present their ideas. The children responded positively to this, having discovered the potential of expression and intention that presentations can reveal.

The architecture students then presented their designs. Some proposals explored light, the idea of enclosure and intimate and public scale—illustrated in models, collages and drawings. Another was for a new school based on a student's investigation of scale. In one section were drawn the children he had worked with, who immediately identified themselves in the drawing and started to comment on the openness of some of the proposed spaces and the intimacy of others. Their first observations gave way to more inquisitive ones such as what the building would be made of, or how certain spaces would be inhabited, revealing their own critical views and values. Equally exciting was seeing the children break the barrier between the image on paper and visualising themselves in the imagined building.

Conclusions

It was rewarding to see the progress both groups had made by the end of the workshop. Each had gained an insight into how others experienced the built environment, and explored the potential of each other's perceptions. The children were now better able to express their views with clarity and focus, and their response to their surroundings and their ideas about it were more critical. The architecture students had developed proposals that explicitly responded to the children's architectural interests and acknowledged that consideration of the children's values had affected and contributed to their approach to the design. Thus in its more immediate terms the workshop had achieved its main aim: to establish a dialogue in which architects and non-architects could effectively share and exchange ideas.

The combination and variety of activities undertaken throughout the workshop allowed the issues to be examined from different perspectives. Moreover the nature of the exercises enabled new understanding to be gained, even within a short period of time. Such positive results provided encouragement to develop the workshop on a larger scale.

In the workshop we utilised particular teaching methodologies, selected because they would enhance the learning experience.

Moreover they were conducive to the subjective nature of the issues of perception and interpretation being addressed. These methods included:

- A process of cross-fertilisation between the two groups, where the activities of one group in one session informed the activities of the other group in the next session—a constant interweaving of activities and exchanges of information through which learning and dialogue flourished.
- Teaching as a learning tool: requiring the students as teachers to reexamine the issues critically and find effective ways of communicating their thoughts to others.
- Heuristic learning: prompting dynamic interaction among the participants, avoiding a dogmatic approach to learning, and engaging the students in a process of self-learning.
- Using students' existing knowledge and experience as a base from which to learn. That is, building on what they already knew, respecting their unique experience and thus easing the introduction of new ideas.
- Maintaining a flexible structure that was open to the unplanned activities and events that group interactions might create.

In general terms, the work supported the findings of previous research. Architects and non-architects do have a disparate relationship to the built environment, assigning it different meanings and values. Furthermore, the workshop reiterated that architects tend to reflect in their design their own interpretations, distinct from those of non-architects. Most significantly, the experience demonstrated that there is fertile ground for learning and design creativity in exploring this disparity.

References

Brand, Stewart (1994) *How Buildings Learn*. New York: Viking, pp. 52–71.

Devlin, Kimberly (1990) 'An examination of Architectural Interpretation: Architects Versus non Architects', *The Architectural Journal and Planning Research*, 7(3), pp. 235–243.

Fairs, Marcus (1999) 'Architecture Week Boring', *Building Design*, 29 January.

Groat, Linda (1982) 'Meaning in Post-Modern Architecture: An Examination using the Multiple Sorting Task', *Journal of Environmental Psychology*, 2, pp. 3–22.

Hellman, Louis (1987) 'Two way Teach In', *The Architect's Journal*, 2 December, pp. 27–9.

Hershberger, R. (1988) *A Study of Meaning and Architecture in Environmental Aesthetics* (ed. J. Nasar). Cambridge: Cambridge University Press.

Morrow, Ruth (1998) 'Degree-Centred Design', *Streetwise*, 8(4), pp. 17–18.

Rappaport, Amos (1982) *The Meaning of the Built Environment*. Beverly Hills, CA: Sage.

Weaver, Nick (1997) 'Atelier Principle in Teaching', paper delivered at the Conference on Project-Based Learning, University of Roskilde, Denmark.

5 Social practice
Design education and everyday life

Christopher Jarrett

Context

A prominent Canadian architect was recently approached by an editor of one of the American architecture journals. The editor wanted to produce a profile on the firm's work and requested a photograph of her and her partner for the piece. The following week the owner of the firm mailed off a photograph of everybody in the firm, about twelve people, including three or four summer trainees. When the editor received the photo he telephoned her and said he just needed a photo of her and her partner. The owner replied, 'if you are writing a profile on our firm's work, then you want a picture of all of us; these are the people who make it happen'. She did not send another photo, nor did she hear anything more from the editor on this matter.

About four months later she received a copy of the October issue with profiles on three firms' work, including her own. To her surprise, at the head of the article was a picture of her and her partner only. At first she could not figure out where the editor had got this from, but then realised he had exercised a 'cut and paste' command on his computer, removing her and her partner's head from the original photo she had sent. This form of editorial practice could be seen as epitomising a kind of decapitation on collaboration—the essential process of communication and exchange, cooperation and reciprocity between individuals, groups and places—on design as a mode of social practice.

Design education has increasingly become an isolated, indoor activity (Ausubel 1996), disconnected from tangible experience, real problems and the cities in which we live and work. According to educator David Orr, a great deal of what now passes for knowledge is little more than abstraction piled on top of abstraction (Orr 1992). Design education, in distancing itself ever more from the outside world, becomes abstract and utopian—literally 'nowhere'.

This chapter, in contrast to university education's tendency to segregate disciplines, or more to the point, to segregate *intellect* from its *surroundings*, explores a model of architectural design studio teaching that engages 'place'. It is divided into three sections. The first, 'Blind spots in the design studio', describes some of the problems of forgotten space/place in contemporary design education. The second—'The everyday city'—illustrates the lively, dynamic and circumstantial characteristics of the inner city. The last—'Out there doing it'—presents a studio-turned-practice project that steps over the boundaries of the design studio, inhabiting the space between architectural design education and everyday life.

Blind spots in the design studio

Design studios are too often insulated from ordinary, everyday life. Such studios, isolated from the 'street', continue to represent the normative model of studio instruction, where topics of investigation tend to promote theory without experience. The studio works as a laboratory where design methodology is contained, artificially controlled and frequently prescribed with guaranteed success.

Isolating design programmes from everyday life also excludes a world rich in colour, behaviour and circumstance, and establishes a number of blind spots in the design studio environment:

- It can lead to 'studio seclusion', autonomy and narrow-minded thinking.
- It can reinforce the production of 'objects and signatures'.
- It breeds abstraction and the propensity for the programme to be pure, hypothetical and out of date.
- It supports the premise of the 'expert', detaching the student from the very forces that induce life in our cities.

Studio seclusion

Designing in seclusion has a number of consequences. Firstly, it places students at the centre of the project and the problem at hand, pushing the concerns of the 'other'—the neighbourhood and community—to the edge. It also restricts design research/brief-building from engaging the outside world—research is confined, academic and remains narrow in scope, operating between the drawing board, the laptop, the internet and the library. Design thinking, being freed from reality and life's imperfections (Relph 1993) thus becomes abstract—designing in isolation removes oneself from the impurities of everyday life, from the clutter of transmission lines, a warped construction timber, the wind direction, the height of a curb or a conversation on the street.

The act of design can thus come to be seen as a precious, uncontaminated activity. Students retreat from the outside world, literally enclosing themselves in the project, mentally and physically. With a few sheets of plywood and a walkman, boundaries are constructed in the studio environment—tutors have been known actively to encourage students to set up their studio environment like a home, complete with family photos, bookshelves, a refrigerator and a sleeping bag.

Objects and signatures

Student work produced in isolation tends to be hygienic and injected with convoluted meaning, usually illegible or indifferent to the public or inhabitant. Operating in a vacuum, the project often takes the form of an 'object'—a distilled artefact free of use, habitation or ritual. The resultant work is pure 'signature', untarnished by the hands of another. The work is predictable, usually untouchable, an end in itself and therefore of little real consequence.

Isolated, nimble manipulations of form advance an agenda of individual authorship and overwhelm the concerns of the 'other' (Francis 1994). Promoting seduction in lieu of substance or service, such design processes, disconnected from the street, emphasise experimentation at the expense of possibility or purpose. Regardless of programme or place, person or culture, studio projects that operate in seclusion are too often formal, automatic and produced independently by a single author.

Traditional programmes

Urban advocates argue that grass-root, community-based social programmes in the everyday city can strengthen neighbourhood identity and prosperity. But in the design studios of many schools of architecture, issues such as unemployment, crime, safety, citizenship and the common good take a back seat to issues strictly interior to the formal discipline of architecture. 'Instead of [architecture] being understood as interventions into the environment that bear social, economic, and political programs, architecture oscillates uneasily between self-expression and some form of effete cultural commentary' (Ghirado 1991).

In reality, programme in the everyday city is not autonomous or pure, but an assemblage of multiple competing identities. Accordingly architecture itself is never autonomous, never pure programme (Tschumi 1994). However, stand-alone, institutional typologies such as schools, libraries and museums continue to dominate as preferred design programmes in the studio. These building types are clear and familiar, with a large collection of precedents, but such axiomatic institutions usually conflict with the changing climate of programme in everyday life. In the everyday city, 'traditional' programme types are warped, clouded, stretched, superimposed, inverted and/or fragmented by the concerns of the 'other'. In contrast, by recognising the diverse activities and events we can respond to the actual, dynamic socioeconomic forces at play on the street.

Practice as a by-product of experts

Masterplans, calculated axes, grid-iron subdivisions, boxed trees planted at ten-metre intervals, neotraditional styles and other popular parochial perspectives perpetuated in many schools of design are often detached from the very forces that induce life in our everyday cities.

Urban critic Raymond Ledrut (1986) reminds us that the city is not an object made by one group in order to be sold and used by others. Nor is it defined by a collection of neutral, isolated objects. For Ledrut, the city is an environment formed by the interaction and integration of different practices. Ledrut's definition of the city as the product of social practice strongly opposes the notion of the city as the by-product of experts. For Ledrut, 'the true issue is not to make beautiful cities or well-managed cities, it is to make a "work of life"' (Ledrut 1986).

Equally, attention in design studios cannot begin with or stop at the production of objects. While making is the definitive activity of architectural design education, the isolated projection of objects has no possibility of meaning, connection or consequence without a welcome invitation for what Elaine Scarry (1985) calls 'reciprocity'. To understand making, Scarry suggests that the object is only a fulcrum or lever. She gives the example that a woman making a coat for someone has no intrinsic interest in making the coat *per se*, but in making that person warm. Her attention to threads, materials, seams and linings are all objectifications at work to free the (physical) problem of being cold. She could, of course, do this by putting her arms around the shivering person, but instead she more successfully accomplishes her goal indirectly—by making a coat, which is just the midpoint in the total action, or the fulcrum in a lever.

Applying this example, one might argue that the architect's role in society, like the coatmaker, is working not to make the object *per se*—the building—but in cultivating a 'sense of place' and belonging—a 'work of life'. The architect could do this by assembling a group of people for the purpose of meeting, working and living, but instead more successfully accomplishes the goal by making a place to meet, work and live. Such attention to context, climate, space, movement, light, surfaces, codes, budgets, systems, materials and joints are all objectifications at work to free the larger (social) problem of isolation. In this scenario, building becomes just the midpoint in the total action of the architect's work.

The everyday city

The 'everyday city' is a lively, circumstantial, pedestrian urban landscape. Full of colour, flavour and intensity, it is dramatically fused into its surroundings. It is there and yet easily unnoticeable. There are no signature architects, no grand axes or robust civic architecture. Unlike the diffuse, barren, wide-street, automobile-oriented streetscape in a typical metropolitan area, the everyday city is dense and bustling, vibrant, full of pedestrian traffic, pavement commerce and multiple languages. It is an energetic, 'happening' place within the larger space of the city. Three specific characteristics define the everyday city and set it apart from the rest of the larger metropolis.

Appropriating the street

The everyday city is based on individual and group appropriation, ephemeral lodgings and the tactical, often illegal (but permitted) interweaving of public and private space. There are no doctrines, mandates, metanarratives or masterplans that define or regulate the everyday city. It is an aggregate of small events and places. It is an ambiguous and discontinuous urban space. It is a dynamic urban landscape of lived experience, an unfolding, incomplete context, full of unknowns and shifting grounds. It is enigmatic, circumstantial and scattered, slow, open-ended and everyday. It emerges from a world of all-too-real facts about survival, economic hardship, conflict, city ordinances, cars, rights-of-way, bureaucrats, residents' rights and street transients.

Colourful and diverse populations

The population of the everyday city is dense, colourful and culturally diverse. Young and old, the everyday city is populated with a rich mix of legal citizens, illegal immigrants, retired carpenters, active veterans, steady residents, unemployed factory workers, restless street peddlars and the homeless. The population density is higher in the everyday city than in most other parts of the city. One will also find three, sometimes four, generations living in the same everyday city. Lively conversation is readily apparent and clothing is vibrant, expressive and exotic. Several different languages can be heard in the everyday city, and is equally evident in the shop signs and billboards.

Pavement settlements

Entrepreneurial behaviour is rife in the everyday city. Everyone is trying to make a go of it. Transactions are social and impromptu, varied and fleeting. Everyday merchandise is sold in makeshift market stalls, lean-tos and grocery carts. The circumstantial, cluttered, day-to-day dynamics between curbside vendors, corner preachers, loud radios and multilingual shop signs in a typical everyday city street paints a remarkably lively urban landscape. Pavement settlements, like curbside farmers selling fresh vegetables and baseball caps, boot-leg cigarettes, perfume and music tapes from the trunk of a parked car, produce a self-made urbanism that stands perpendicular to the homogeneous views often delivered in a formal academic environ-ment. The everyday city is frankly a condition difficult to emulate by a single designer, or even by a group of designers.

Out there doing it

The gap between the limited projections exercised in design studios and the lively pavement urbanism shaped by everyday life on the street, signalled a need to reconsider the relationship between the practices of everyday life and the role of architectural design educa-tion. The challenge of engaging the everyday city from the design studio fuelled a proposal called the LA Service Station (LASS) Studio. Two years later it gave rise to a collaborative, working-from-the-ground-up effort by eleven architect-led teams called the LA Service Station Project.

The LASS Studio

The LA Service Station Studio first surfaced as a design studio proposal in March 1992 at the University of Southern California—a private, well-endowed academic environment nervously situated in Martin Luther King Boulevard and the backyards of south-central Los Angeles (LA). The proposal was motivated in part by a debate with a number of design faculty tutors who believed that studio instruction should not concern itself with social issues. To some, social problems were not architectural problems. The counter argument of those proposing the studio was that if architecture had the capacity to participate in social problems such as crime, drugs or loss of a sense of belonging or identity, then it had the capacity and power to participate in a remedy or solution as well.

The LASS project would focus on a common building type in Los Angeles—the mini-mall. Corner mini-malls run rampant in the city—they are an economically driven building type and the epitome of commercial convenience. Taken overall, in LA mini-malls 'work'. However in the inner-city neighbourhoods these malls are also replete with problems stemming from issues such as drug use, unemployment, AIDS and family strife. In an attempt to open up the strict commercial behaviour of the mini-mall, the studio would explore the possibility of introducing affordable housing and social service agencies into the unwavering formula of the mini-mall.

The design programme was to be modelled on ideas of collaboration. It likened itself to a conversation—a dialogue on the street between two or more people, full of gesture and emotion, exchange and ideas. As a literal reflection of this, from the outset a large table was permanently placed in the centre of the studio. This was to provide the collaborators—students, instructors and visitors—with a place to meet and review the work, whether between two people, a small group or the studio at large. Such a format was a deliberate attempt to depart from the normative model of studio instruction that venerated the importance of individual studio cubicles.

The design studio process unfolded in three phases. The first, two-week phase—'Experiencing, Thinking, Listening'—took place outside the physical confines of the university and began by associating groups of four students with specific neighbourhood intersections. Each group was asked to carry out a series of exercises in the area surrounding the intersection. The students would first navigate by car—driving along major streets and taking notes of things and situations. They would then return to navigate by foot—walking along neighbouring streets, sketching, notating and talking to people in the neighbourhood. The second phase—'Studying, Working, Living'—involved studying particular social programmes that seemed pertinent to the specific neighbourhood and intersection. These included a non-profit outpatient clinic, an employment agency, a women's centre, a drug rehab facility, a shelter for the homeless and a small police station. Finally, the third phase—'Designing, Making, Building'—required each group of students to design one corner site in relation to the ongoing design of the three other specific sites at a given intersection. Each site had an existing mini-mall to redesign, and a specific social service programme combined with approximately five housing units.

The LASS Project

The effort of the 22 students in the LASS Studio paved the way to a much larger collective undertaking by eleven architect-led teams and nearly 100 students—the LA Service Station Project. In contrast to the traditional view of imposing architectural solutions from above, the objective of the LASS Project was to empower 'voice over form'. Again working collaboratively, it was to be neighbourhood-based, architect-initiated and student-tested. It was to work from the ground up with little money, to form an inner-city case study that would propose lighter-weight and more localised tactics to strengthen the sense of urban life and community in the inner city.

The scope of the project was basic, raw and immediate. Not monumental—rather an 'obvious', non-striving, common-sense programme, focusing on illuminating the everyday rather than shaping the future.

Collaboration

Each team was led by a group of architectural designers in collaboration with neighbourhood groups and/or civic agencies. There was a range of cross-disciplinary exchanges, including engineers, landscape architects, metalworkers, cabinetmakers and seamers. The designers comprised a group of women and men from a variety of ethnic backgrounds and scales of architectural practice. Each team leader also taught architecture in one of six schools in the LA area. Invaluable contributions were made by more than 100 architecture students from these schools, including Cal Poly Pomona, LA Trade Tech, Parsons School of Design, Sci-Arc, UCLA and USC.

With collaboration as an overarching framework, each team was encouraged to reach out and bring the everyday actively into their design process. From the beginning, the project attempted to provide an opportunity to explore the potential contained within the collaborative relationship, whether between designer and community leader, specialist, political activist, neighbourhood advocate, student assistant, resident or 'person on the street'. As a group, the LASS teams were committed to reinforcing the design decision, which actively included and valued 'the other' over the alternative, which represented architecture as simply a formal gesture or singular object made by a single authorial hand.

Project sites

The LASS Project study areas were common places, rich in culture, shaped by local ritual and need, always with very little money. They were places that were often unnoticed, feared or forgotten by those who lived outside them. Such neighbourhoods and sites were abundant throughout Los Angeles. Undesigned by planners or architects, they tended to be marginal, ignored, lag-time places near or adjacent to freeways.

At the start, each team aligned itself with an everyday city neighbourhood and civic agency or local community group. The particular area studied would be typically selected for reasons of their familiarity to individual team members and their need for revitalisation. The project took a year and a half and was carried out in three overlapping phases.

Phase 1: listening

The first step in the process was small and light. The strategy for approaching the neighbourhood was motivated by Margaret Crawford and her call to architects 'to listen to the city (Crawford 1993). In effect, Crawford suggests the need for architects to reposition their view by focusing on the auditory rather than the visual. In other words, imposing public voice over public image. In one reading, the need to bring listening to the heart of the design process implies that, as a profession, we have ceased to listen to the voices of those for whom we are working. Further, it suggests that the very discipline that depends on the visual may in fact be overlooking the reality of the city—its inhabitants and their actual needs, desires and resources. More than just talking, which may or may not reach the 'other', architects need to rethink the importance of conversation. This may in fact be a residue of the all too often impervious nature of architectural design education.

For this project, in lieu of utilising cameras, video recorders or other mechanical distancing devices, conversation was to be the instrument of engagement and understanding.

Phase 2: enabling

The second phase of the project entailed organising collaborative working relationships. The groups built a web of connections between youth programme directors and barrio planners, curbside vending advocates and neighbourhood youth, librarians and graffiti artists, job training supervisors and day labourers. The collaborations were diverse and varied between teams. They were at times circumstantial and unpredictable, and required the teams to be able to meet wherever and whenever—ranging from early evening community meetings in church halls to late-night gatherings at a table in a neighbourhood bar.

Phase 3: constructing

The final phase of the project consisted of producing design documents and full-scale material constructions of each service station. Emphasis was placed on economy of means. The intent behind the mock-up requirement was to extend the architect's typical role of representation to one of production—moving from proposal to product. This proved a difficult and humbling venture. Most importantly, since the work was being exhibited in a municipal gallery, with access by the general public, and especially school children, the mock-ups offered everyone a direct experience of the project.

Output

Three of the eleven projects are selected here as indicative of the overall 'products' that resulted.

Vending, waiting, looking station

This focused on enhancing the street environment in the spirit of recent city ordinance that had legalised street vending. It consisted of a variety of modestly scaled pieces designed for pavements and curbsides to serve street vendors, their customers and local pedestrians. The study went beyond the requirements of the new vending ordinance by including stations for disabled vendors who were unable to manoeuvre the vending carts that the ordinance stipulated. It also proposed an opportunity for neighbourhood youth authorship in the expressive construction of other needed public street elements, such as seating, platforms, pavement surfaces and shade-tree planters.

Community access station

Recognising that funding for inner city social services had been drastically reduced, this project involved the provision of a mobile trailer to disseminate information and provide temporary space for the community to use as the need arose. It could adapt to any number of sites and uses, for example in the event of a library's shortened opening hours due to lack of funds, the station could be used adjacent to the library for book check-out and return. Alternatively it could be used in an empty lot for tutoring school children in the afternoons, in a cul-de-sac for job placement once a week, or on Saturdays for selling vegetables.

Training, borrowing, repair station

This was designed to augment the LA Housing Division's Handyworker Programme to promote daily neighbourhood 'quick-fix' building improvements. The role of the Handyworker Programme, which helped senior citizens and disabled people with modest home repairs, was expanded in the neighbourhood with the provision of a number of job stands and semipermanent, open-air workshops operated by resident workmen. Located in underutilised parking lots, these prototypical satellite 'toolboxes' were transportable and contained with roll-out equipment for light construction, training, borrowing and repair. The operator provided after-school job training for young people by working with them on illuminating local pavements, alleys and boundaries, making modest street furniture and offering advice to local residents on simple construction techniques for backyard building.

Evaluation

The LASS Project was a grand undertaking at the local level. With eleven architect-led teams and 100 students working in eleven inner city neighbourhoods, and many more community groups, the project was taxing on a number of fronts. There were times when the intention of the project was clear and manageable, and others when it seemed too broad and unfocused.

Its aim had been to find new ways of understanding the city, and the architect's role within it. Attached to a number of broad-based social issues, the project worked at a number of levels, ranging from urban design to product design. This fundamentally challenged entrenched attitudes in its participants. Moreover each team had to resist the temptation of 'form-giving' and move towards patient and sympathetic listening.

In general, the local communities were initially confused about the project. Several were sceptical and felt intimidated. They did not understand why architects were knocking on their doors. There were very few practising architects in these communities, and most residents had not had any previous encounter with an architect. Accordingly they did not know how an architect could help them with their neighbourhood issues, particularly when the problems in their communities were not architectural in nature.

A number of standard cliches about architects surfaced: architects build complex buildings; architects design large, expensive houses; design is a luxury we cannot afford. The teams spent a fair amount of time challenging these stereotypes.

Measures of success

- The scale of the individual projects was small enough to enable students to experience the entire design process.
- The students appreciated the opportunity to work directly with architects dealing with real social issues. The separation between architectural education and practice was contracted—the difference between what students do in the studio and practitioners do in the office was reduced.
- Approaching the communities with a handful of eager architecture students opened doors that would otherwise have remained closed. The students changed the group dynamic of the architect-led

teams. Initial feelings of intimidation were quickly overturned by a sense of honest intention.

- The professional community was highly supportive of the project.
- The project received local, state and national media exposure.

The final judges of success must be the communities for which the projects were intended. Although only two of the eleven projects made it to the streets, several other outreach initiatives have since taken place as a result of the LASS project. The ideas that motivated both the project and the people who participated in it continue to find their way into pedagogy and to inspire other experimental, community-based projects.

Conclusion

As Christian Norberg-Schulz (1976) reminds us, 'to dwell in a house is to inhabit the world'. Architectural education needs to place greater emphasis on direct experience of inhabiting the urban world. The LASS Studio and Project challenged a university faculty and professionals to collaborate at the local level in designing neighbourhoods that would put people's needs first. Educator Diane Ghirardo concurred at a public symposium on the LASS Project, that 'a significant point to consider in viewing this project is that it surfaced out of a university context'.

Studio instructors and schools of architecture and urban design must attend to the unexplored challenges facing our everyday cities and establish projects that address experience, collaboration and social practice as part of the ethic of architectural education.

References

Ausubel, J. (1996) 'The Liberation of the Environment', *Daedalus*, 125(3), p. 14.

Crawford, M. (1993) 'Listening to the City', *Offramp*, 1(5), pp. 101–4.

Francis, M. (1994) 'Some Different Meanings Attached to a City Park and Community Gardens', *Landscape Journal*, 6, p. 111.

Ghirado, D. (1991) 'Introduction', in D. Ghirardo (ed.), *Out of Site*. Seattle: Bay Press, p. 10.

Ledrut, R. (1986) 'Speech and the Silence of the City', in M. Gottdiener and A. Lagopoulos (eds), *The City and the Sign: An Introduction to Urban Semiotics*. New York: Columbia University Press, p. 122.

Norberg-Schulz, C. (1976) 'The Phenomenon of Place', *Architectural Association Quarterly*, 8(4), pp. 3–10.

Orr, D. (1992) Chapter 8, 'Place and Pedagogy', in *Ecological Literacy*. New York: SUNY Press, p. 125.

Relph, E. (1993) 'Modernity and the Reclamation of Place', in D. Seamon (ed.), *Dwelling, Seeing, Designing*. Albany, NY: State University of New York Press, pp. 36–7.

Scarry, E. (1985) Chapter 5, Section 2, 'The Artifact as Lever: Reciprocation exceeds projection: The Making and Unmaking of the World', in *The Body in Pain*. New York: Oxford University Press, p. 307.

Tschumi, B. (1994) Chapter 2: 'Program' p. 124, in *Architecture and Disjunction*. Cambridge, Mass: MIT Press, p. 3.

6 The degree laboratory

The work of Unit Six at the Bartlett School, University College London

Nick Callicott and Bob Sheil

Context

Past assurances about the status of a career in architecture are no longer valid—the role of the professional in society is under scrutiny. The construction world is changing—new roles, new responsibilities, new aims and expectations—and so is the role of the architect within it. What, therefore, does it mean to study architecture, let alone practice it?

Traditionally, students started their studies with the acquired belief that this was a path—not necessarily steady, but based on making the 'right stuff'—that would lead to mid-life rewards. This model underpinned many a graduate's portfolio. In the absence of a challenge to this assumption, the 'once in a lifetime' educational experience was capable of being reduced to an exercise of nothing more than mimicry and regurgitation.

This model is changing, not least due to the outlook of our students, who see how the task of practising architect is increasingly difficult, baffling and not the only arena for furthering an individual's work. What these students see in the world of the professional architect is how the range of activity involved has gone beyond the command of any one person, how a decreasing number of projects reach fruition and, with particular self-reference, how uncertain is the definition of the role of the young architect. The relevance of the traditional model of what it is to exist in practice is increasingly being challenged by an entirely revised set of beliefs.

This, in turn, should prompt educators to review and revise existing teaching methods. In our own model—the 'Degree Laboratory'—old habits have been altered to utilise the relative freedom offered by full-time education to seek out the unfamiliar, the unconventional and the methods of other disciplines. The opportunities that lie within the educational 'experience' are unique, and we believe that they should be awarded higher value than has been the case to date, with the view that templates for future practice may be discovered and unravelled over the period of a student's studies.

Learning

The motives that lay behind the creation of the Degree Laboratory teaching programme grew from our own experience. Labelling ourselves 'sixteen*(makers)', we had set up a workshop-based practice towards the end of our time as full-time students. This became a space—a 'reality'—beyond the confines of the institution in which we had become long-term inmates. It had a new set of constraints, more economic than academic, but still within a world of conventions. Some of these involved the learning of traditional crafts, not in college but from neighbours. We were part of an everyday existence—one which our work had to support.

This experience led us to accept an invitation to assist part-time in the running of a Bartlett School workshop, and in parallel to teach a degree unit of second- and third-year students. This unit—the Degree Laboratory—seeks to offer a new model of architectural investigation in a fast-changing environment. Much of its work is concerned with living and working out the transition from study to early practice, and stems from the questioning of unwritten assumptions, particularly the assumption that architects do not make buildings, but draw them.

The programme has a number of important characteristics:

- Traditional notions of authorship are challenged.
- The identity of students' proposals is no longer constructed through drawings alone—the studio is enhanced by a well-equipped workshop for craft experimentation.
- The architectural process is recognised as often more revealing, important and unique to the particular student than the product. The process springs from the fundamental properties of the project.
- Exercises are investigative, using 'real' sites and 'live' projects, with work emerging from the exploration of site, purpose and use.

Learning is doing

The acquisition of craft knowledge is a very different process from image production. Whilst image creation focuses primarily on the desire to be creative, the learning of a craft skill is underpinned by a necessity to attain a specific body of knowledge. The 'maker's' progress is measured against this set of certainties. A continual series of decisions is being made within the act of making. Work is created within a set of parameters defined by the available equipment, skills and materials, and time/budget constraints.

However the success of a workpiece, though well made, does not necessarily lie in the craft that made it. Rather a workpiece may be read as a series of decisions, some of which would be termed failures of workmanship in one environment but in the workshop/laboratory could be viewed as 'purposeful tests'. It is here that the opportunity to acknowledge aspects of a student's work developed through making can be seized, and not left until the project takes its place in the crit room.

The representation of work and the work itself are intertwined, and perhaps are even one and the same. The 'architect/maker' is in a position to challenge traditional notions of authorship for the professional. Whereas artists and craftsmen mostly withhold their work until it is complete, architects practice representation with techniques to imbue realisation, the outcome of which is made possible by others. The maker and the architect may equally possess powers of individual creativity, but to distinguish this aspect alone is not of great importance.

In the Degree Laboratory we are seeking out unfamiliar methods to provide the means of revealing and then testing our ideas—it is harder to deceive yourself in a language that is new to you. We are discovering methods that rely less on the image to communicate the nature of our work, both to ourselves and to others.

Project work: authorship and creativity

Bridging the boundaries of authorship and creativity leads to the reading of material created by others, with whom future collaboration is negotiated. With respect to drawings, clearly not all are made with the intention of materialisation, but perhaps they are intended to provoke it. In the course of a conversation they may be transformed from representations into a form of memorandum. Looking at crafted objects, some are made only to be outlived by other drawings, myths and numerous other mutations.

To be on the other side of drawings—the architect's traditional medium—makes possible a clearer understanding of the ability they have to provoke multiple readings. Working from this premise, our year's testing in the Degree Laboratory began with questions of authorship.

In 'The Author', students were asked to construct a 'drawing' to convey a spatial condition of their own choosing. The work was to be anonymous, and constrained within a given size of 300 × 300 mm × unlimited The exercise lasted five days and was without tutor intervention. Its aim was to elicit representations of individual student interests.

The work submitted included a diary of site-specific random events, a lens, a double-faced sheet embossed and lineated, a map, a post-structuralist game, a party wall award, broken glass, a lemon squeezer and an aphorism. The submission was immediately followed by the random swapping of the anonymous 'drawings'. Authors now became 'readers'. Their task in this project—'The Reader'—was to turn the drawing they had been given into a constructed 'reading', using processes available in the workshop. The project took place over four weeks. Its aim was to explore the usefulness and/or uselessness of drawings as a source of reference in making. The readers and authors—still anonymous in respect of the specific 'drawings'—were encouraged to respond to the task. However the reader was under no obligation to satisfy the author's comments. Nor was an author obliged to provide any further information. Each could elect to remain silent. It was made clear that this was not a test of skills of reproduction. The reader was to respond in any way he or she saw fit and was fully responsible for the results.

The work submitted included an ink-dripping, balanced mobile made from glass tubing and brass, prismatic spectacles, a gravity-operated ice-cutting machine, a steel/rubber/electronics desktop diplomacy game, an interactive visual and acoustic amplifier in latex and polished glass, a concrete 'TV' that switched off when approached, a cast container for forensic artefacts, a spinning footplate in a viewing refraction frame, and a moving silhouette slot-viewing box.

Projects one and two sought to clarify the investigative nature of the Degree Laboratory and develop a methodology. The next project—'Left Luggage'—tested those methods in the 'real' world. Students were to make a 'portable accessory'. For this, they had to 'record' the contents of a left luggage locker at London Waterloo international railway station for transfer and installation at a site along the meridian—a maximum of 1000 metres from London's Greenwich observatory.

This required them to select and survey a locker (there were three sizes), mindful that access was controlled by tight security arrangements. They were then to record their selected meridian site, considering one qualitative and one quantitative characteristic. Finally, they were to leave their work at Waterloo station for collection on review day.

As tutors we had selected the two sites for their perceived property of transience. It was also very important that the resultant 'made' work should be of a reasonably portable size and therefore a manageable undertaking in the confines of a six-week project.

The site was the source of most of the thematic concerns of the brief. Students were now working alone and were required to exercise individual judgement. Initially this slowed the pace. Interestingly, the majority of work was developed without the production of significant drawings. Projects one and two had killed off the established habit of letting a sketch determine the outcome of work developed in the laboratory.

The installations created included a souvenir Thames tidal barrier, an adjustable pedestrian frontier, lost and found deposit boxes, a random compass journey planner, an optical directional sign, an inflatable personal space jacket, meridian stilts and store, windial street furniture, a sectional time space projector and cast chocolate sites.

Evaluation

By their nature, the work of the first two projects became a self-assessing exercise. Projects acquired nomadic authorship and criticism alike. Students found they could not be sure that their drawings conveyed the intended message to their new owners, or whether the invitation was there to interpret freely. This proved upsetting for a few. For some the temptation to negotiate with the author was overwhelming and there were isolated rumours of behind the scenes activity. Others said the drawing did not matter that much and some struggled to make it more significant than it needed to be. Some made it easy for the reader, whereas others jealously guarded their creation as if to cling on to the authorship of both pieces of work.

The true purpose of the exercise had been to challenge conventional notions of the production of creativity, and its partner, certainty. By these criteria it was considered successful—the unit had established new methods of working, found that the search for ideas could occur in more than one place and involve more than one person, and was satisfied that the experience of process could be as revealing as the outcome.

For many students, working at the bench or the lathe was the key activity in enabling the exploration and presentation of the concepts and issues involved in project work. Although for some these constraints felt at odds with the perceived product, in its most positive form, the act of making within these restrictions required constant re-evaluation and development of the work.

This flirtation with the mechanism—or construct—contributed to an expanded vocabulary of expression, thus broadening the architectural debate within the school. The workshop was shown to enable a project to commence both as a form of site analysis and as an exploration of the specific properties of material. This investigatory method became the means by which programme and form were defined.

Overall assessment of the work can take a number of forms. The term workmanship could be used on many aspects of the work. However, workmanship of materials and making, can too quickly become a display of skill and manufacturing decisions—the assumption of usual practices to display the intent of the project. What is of greater interest is the reversal that the work experiences through its placement in the 'real' world—the world beyond the control of the author.

Here the work is open to other readings by passers-by and invited critics. The elimination of the four walls of the crit room creates an invitation to question the purpose of this way of working. The work becomes, in effect, a 'third person' to the author and is open to interpretation and appropriation by users. Students feel rewarded by assessments of this kind, away from the defining codes of the institution, and henceforth will demand a more critical and sensual relationship between subject and object in their work.

Conclusion

The concerns of education and the practice of architecture do not necessarily overlap. Indeed the gap between them could be seen as increasing and less frequently bridged. We suggest that changes in architectural education need not attempt to 'repair' such movement in order to clarify the relationship between the two. Rather the action taken needs to address the opportunities that lie in this unique territory.

The key to the Degree Laboratory's approach lies in the opportunistic position it can adopt within architectural education. This position is placed between a critical view of 'craft', exercised in the workshop, and the 'speculative' approach that occupies the studio. It bridges these practices in order to broaden the scope of any particular study.

Our work—one of many possible approaches to this challenge—has attempted a transition that has proven to be both exciting and difficult. It is, in all senses, work in progress—not just in itself but also as a basis for graduates' development in later years. It is already clear, however, that the laboratory has become a common ground where an increasing array of interests from across the school collide, and the school, in recognition of the importance it attaches to these facilities, has invested in their expansion.

7 Introducing clients and users to the studio project

A case study of a 'live' project

Rachel Sara

Introduction

According to a recent review, architects need to 'provide a quality of environment that responds to people's needs and wants' (Stansfield Smith 1998). The RIBA/ARB *Criteria for Validation* guide for the taught architecture course reinforces this point:

> Students need to be aware of why as well as how buildings are constructed. The role of the client both individually and collectively should be understood, how the users' needs are comprehended and satisfied and how the wider concerns of society are met through the planning and building regulatory systems (RIBA/ARB 1997).

If future architects are to be responsive to the needs of society then there is a need for two-way learning between architecture students and the community. The 'live project' described in this chapter was devised to address this issue.

The project was part of the CUDE (Clients and Users in Design Education) initiative, the aim being to give students the opportunity to interact with a client/user group to the benefit of both parties. It was envisaged that, in comparison with traditional studio projects without clients, the live project would offer additional learning benefits to students. As a recent diploma graduate the author felt that contact with clients and users had been lacking in her own architectural education.

The project was a practical experiment rather than a research exercise. As a result this chapter is presented as a case study rather than a research paper.

Method

The problem of finding a real project was solved by a friend of the author. This friend was a member of cricket team that needed a new roof for its pavilion. The team had little money, so it was agreed that students would design and ultimately build a new roof, in return for which the client/user group (the cricket team) would take part in consultation sessions.

The project was offered as an alternative option to students in the second year of the architecture course at Sheffield University. Eight students signed up for the project. The duration of the project was two weeks, by the end of which students, working in pairs, had produced four design solutions. Each was presented to the client/user group. (Following this, outside the two-week period, all eight students were to work together on a single scheme to incorporate the client's views from all the pair schemes.) The two-week schedule of events was as follows:

1   Group (eight students) carries out initial research into site and construction techniques.
2   Studio design tutorials for each student pair by one tutor throughout the programme.
3   Group meeting to develop questions for clients. Preparation session led by tutor with emphasis on collaborative-learning discussion groups involving role play, group work and peer evaluation.
4   Consultation with client to develop brief—run by students.
5   Student-led interim reviews. Full responsibility for running reviews given to students. Feedback from peers about the schemes and presentation skills. Tutor comment at the end of the session.
6   Presentation preparation session. Tutors provide all students with information about presentations. Emphasis on collaborative learning discussion groups. Students prepare their presentations in pairs. Practise run-through of presentation by each student pair to another with time for feedback. Each presentation recorded on video to allow students to replay and reflect on their own performance.
7   Presentation of schemes to client by students—full responsibility given to the students.

Learning objectives

The aim of the project was to develop a positive attitude towards clients/users, to encourage peer group learning, and to develop skills in communication with these groups. These objectives are outlined below.

Attitudes

• To encourage a favourable attitude towards clients that acknowledges the importance of client opinion in enriching rather than inhibiting design.

- To acknowledge the importance of a good client relationship.
- To encourage a team spirit among the students, allowing them to learn from each other through dialogue and observation.

Skills

- To develop skills in creating a brief in consultation with clients.
- To develop and practise skills in questioning and listening, and in using design proposals to develop the brief with the client.
- To develop skills in presenting to different audiences—client groups, fellow students and architect tutors.

As much responsibility as possible was handed over to the students, to emphasise the 'reality' of the project and the importance of their role in it.

Evaluation of the project

The project would be evaluated as follows:

- The students would evaluate the project according to their perception of their attainment of the skills objectives (see above), using a Likert scale, ranging from 0 (not at all) to 5 (fully), with comments.
- Tutors would evaluate the skills objectives using the same Likert scale.
- Clients would provide feedback comments on the students' final presentation.
- A designated tutor/observer would also provide feedback on the final presentation.

The following information was collected from the students prior to or after completion of the project:

- Why the students had chosen the live project option and what they expected to learn from the experience (open-ended questionnaire).
- Whether the project met their expectations and how the project could be improved (open-ended questionnaire).
- What value this project had over a more traditional studio project (observations and informal discussions with students).

There was an overwhelmingly positive response by students to the questions 'Why did you choose this option?' and 'What did you expect to learn from the experience of working with a real client'.
   The students felt they were being given a wonderful opportunity that 'had to be grabbed', and which was 'scary and exciting'. All but

one mentioned that the reality of the project made it more interesting and more of a challenge than usual projects, and that it would give them an insight into what an architect actually does, which was seen as a rare opportunity in a school of architecture.

The students were also aware of the learning potential of the project: for example, having to design while taking financial constraints into account and learning more about construction through actually building something themselves. Most of the students felt that the project would give them more realistic parameters within which to design. The majority of the group felt that the project would teach them the importance of good relationships and understanding with the client, especially when presenting design schemes. One student felt that it would provide an important lesson in how non-architects respond to their work.

Preparatory workshop before meeting with clients

A workshop was held to help students to prepare and develop questions for their consultation with the clients (see number 3 in the schedule presented above). After the consultation the students were asked how the preparation session had affected their approach to the consultation.

All confirmed that they had found the preparation session useful, and five of the eight students commented that it had given them added confidence in the consultation session with the clients. In addition, all the students believed that the consultation with the clients had been more successfully structured as a result of the preparatory session. Half of the students also felt it had given them a better idea of how to phrase questions for a non-architect.

Consultation with clients

The consultation session with the clients (see number 4 in the schedule) was held on the clients' territory—the cricket pavilion, so many of the problems expressed by the client group were easily pointed out to the students. Five clients/members of the team were present. After the session the students were asked whether there were any ways in which the client consultation was different from tutor consultation.

The responses to this question were more varied, although all the students felt that there were significant differences in presenting to clients than to tutors. Half of the students felt it was more formal and nerve-racking whilst the other half found the atmosphere far more relaxed. Three of the students noted that there was 'less architecture lingo', which was felt to be a positive thing.

Interim reviews

Halfway through the project a student-led interim review was held (see point 5 in the schedule). The students were split into two groups, with one group listening and then giving comments. At the end of the session the tutors summarised and made comments. One repeated comment was that the experience 'will be useful for Thursday'—the presentation of schemes to the clients. (The full findings of this session are described in Chapter 21 of this book, so are not discussed here.) The students' interaction with a real client/user helped them to see the value of in-school presentations.

Presentation of the design schemes to the clients

The final presentation of design schemes to the clients (see number 7 in the schedule) was held in one of the university's meeting rooms, enabling the client group to see something of the architecture students' world. The students had spent the previous afternoon in a presentation skills preparatory workshop. This had introduced the students to basic skills in presenting to mixed audiences and helped them to prepare and practise their presentations (see Appendix 1).

At the final presentation both the tutors and the client group (three representatives were present at the meeting) were asked to respond to the students' presentations. The clients reported that they were impressed with the students' willingness to respond to their needs within the design proposals. Both tutors and clients commented on the 'user friendly' nature of the presentations. None of the clients complained of jargon. These presentations drew to tutors' attention how much jargon is normally used in architectural presentations. The preparatory sessions had obviously been successful.

One of the clients commented that all the group had paid great attention to the brief, and each in their own way had found ways of addressing the problem. This implies that the project achieved its objective of encouraging a favourable attitude towards clients that acknowledged the importance of client opinion to enrich rather than inhibit design. Another major strength of the final presentation identified by the tutors was the handing over of responsibility to the students. The students themselves had been required to take the lead in initiating discussions with the client/users, and in that sense they had determined the mode of interaction and the learning that derived from the encounter. However it was noted that the presence of tutors at these meetings had created slight confusion for both clients and students. Despite prior warning about what was expected and the appointment of a student representative, both students and clients had behaved as if they expected the tutor to intervene.

After the final presentation the students and tutors evaluated the skills developed through the project. The responses were very positive—particularly regarding the resultant scheme proposals. Most notable was the comment that similar projects were needed so that the students could practise presenting to a range of people, not just tutors. The students actually wanted more client interaction.

Throughout the project the tutors had been impressed by the high level of enthusiasm shown by all the students. One student in particular previously had a very low attendance record, but during the project had been present and communicative at all but one of the group meetings. The tutors felt that the students had bonded well as a group and learnt from each other through sharing information. There had been a much less competitive atmosphere than usual—the clients had had to come first, and whichever scheme was chosen by the client, they would all be happy to work it up.

Discussion

All the students involved in this initiative appreciated the opportunity to participate in a live project and to find out what an architect does. They felt that, through the project, they had learnt the importance of the architect's relationship with clients/users and how to communicate with and present to non-architects. The project underlined the need, in the undergraduate years, to develop the necessary skills to negotiate a brief and design for a wide range of clients. It highlighted the potential for linking schools of architecture to the community—architectural courses could be enriched by taking students (and tutors) from their ivory towers and linking them to the city. The project also showed that live projects can provide mutual benefits in which both the students and the client group learn from each other.

Through the project the students learned the importance of cultivating a sense of audience for their presentations, and of adapting their mode of interaction and tone of presentation to that audience—clearly an important skill in relation to the students' future professional practice. They also became conscious of how much jargon is normally used in their in-house presentations to tutors. In addition, they felt that an awareness that a client's architectural views are not necessarily the same as a tutor's was important for learning—it encouraged in students a wider agenda for their learning beyond that supplied by tutors.

The involvement of clients made the project more interesting for the students and gave the work a sense of importance that kept their level of enthusiasm high. The 'real' aspect of the project highlighted real life issues such as the value of designing within realistic parameters.

The project emphasised the value of giving more responsibility to students, for example to lead a discussion with clients/users and to learn collaboratively. The pairings, and the interactions between the students in the development of the final design, promoted team bonding and peer group learning. Instead of being a competition, the design process was experienced as a team activity, as is the case in a professional practice. Projects of this kind give important roles to students who may not be brilliant designers but may have other strengths and abilities to contribute within a team.

Finally, it is recognised that the small number of participants in this case study mean that the results must be treated with caution. Furthermore the staff to student ratio was very high, which allowed a great deal of time and attention to be given to the students by the tutors. This might have been a significant factor in the project's success. More research is needed to establish how the benefits could be translated to other contexts and, in particular, larger groups of students.

There is also a potential problem in finding real situations suitable for studio projects if they are to become a regular part of the curricula in schools of architecture. The time-scale of real projects and how to link them into academic timetables needs to be addressed. Vertical studios (studio projects that run across all years) and in-school practices might have potential here as a means of integrating projects into the existing academic timetable. Student projects could 'dip in' to the ongoing project for short periods of time.

Finally, this project was fairly short—two weeks. More time would have allowed increased client—student dialogue during the development of both the brief and the design. And student presentations at the interim reviews could have been improved if there had been more preparation time and more practise in giving presentations. Nonetheless it is indisputable that live projects have the potential to enhance students' learning experience and boost their enthusiasm and motivation. As Carpenter (1997) has noted, 'When a project has a social relevance, it becomes more than a building; it becomes a bridge—between school and practice, faculty and student, and student and community.'

References

Carpenter, W.J. (1997) *Learning By Building. Design and Construction in Architectural Education*. New York: Van Nostrand Reinhold.

RIBA, ARB (1997) *Criteria for Validation*. London: RIBA Publications.

Stansfield Smith, Sir Colin (1998) *Stansfield Smith Strategic Review of Education*, consultation document, November. London: RIBA.

8 The development of group-working skills and role play in the first-year architecture course

Judith Torrington

Introduction

There is concern about the way in which members of the architectural profession relate to clients, building users and other construction professionals during the production of buildings—that architects are unresponsive to the needs of clients and users in building design and are not good at collaborating with other members of design and construction teams. It has been suggested that higher education is the source of these problems and that the interpersonal skills required for professional practice are not being sufficiently developed during the undergraduate years. For example, not enough is being done to develop skills such as listening, negotiating, groupworking and communicating to different audiences.

This chapter describes a project that tried to address these problems. It was carried out under the CUDE initiative by the School of Architecture at the University of Sheffield and involved first-year students. The goal was to foster the development of groupworking and communication skills through learning tasks involving real clients, users and people with expertise in disciplines related to architectural design. The project has been running for three years and during that time there have been changes and refinements. This chapter reports on the workings of the project in its third year—1999.

Background

The first-year intake to the architecture course at Sheffield is between 50 and 90 students. A further 20–25 are students studying a combined course of architecture and structural engineering, undertaking the first-year studio work over two years interspersed with engineering.

In 1996, at the beginning of the three-year period of CUDE, there was a strongly held view amongst the first-year staff at Sheffield that the course already had a focus on client and user needs and collaborative working. Several projects involved collaborative working and 'real' clients were introduced during the main design project. The programme structure was adapted for the purpose of the CUDE initiative by introducing role-play activities—the students taking the roles of client, user and expert advisor. This required students to work in groups of three, each person in the group role playing a client, a user or an expert advisor. The groups were then expected to assist each other during the design process and to comment on each others' design from the point of view of their designated role.

Although this worked reasonably well there were indications that there was considerable scope for improvement. Firstly, there was evidence that some students found it difficult to work in groups. A questionnaire was therefore issued to the next student intake to find out their perceptions of the inherent attitudes and abilities that they had in such areas. These self-assessments of strengths and weaknesses revealed that the students had greater confidence in their design/ creativity, artistic and technological ability than in communication skills, organisational ability and groupworking (Figure 8.1).

Further feedback—obtained after the main project, where groupworking and role play were introduced—reinforced this view. For example some students reported that even though they valued the group structure for social reasons, they experienced difficulties working together. Typical comments were:

> The problems predominantly arose from the inability of my group to firstly schedule meetings at convenient times and secondly to stick to them.

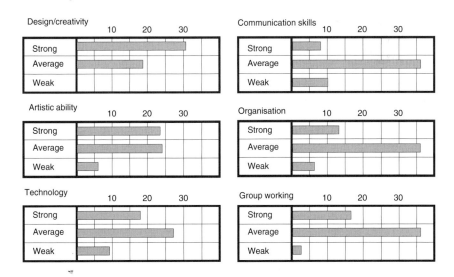

Figure 8.1 Student's initial self-assessment of strengths and weaknesses.

Unfortunately the idea of sharing and using the information was badly developed, largely due to group ill cooperation.

The swapping of information in my particular group was not all that successful. Unreliable group members meant I had to ask other people in the studio.

Depending on others was a little hard and not very successful. Perhaps larger groups would be better.

It is perhaps not surprising that these first-year architecture students lacked group-working skills. They were predominantly high achievers from an A-level culture that emphasised individual accomplishment and competition. Accordingly, while collaborative effort is common in society in general it is uncharted territory for many first-year students.

Secondly, there was also evidence that students were ill-equipped for the role-play task. It had been assumed that students coming into the architecture school from the wider community would be able to draw on their own life experiences to inform their role play, and that they would be better able to take on the 'lay' roles of client and building user rather than the architectural role. However questionnaire data contradicted this assumption. It showed that 63 per cent of students had already had work experience in architects' offices, or closely related work places, and that they were more knowledgeable about the practice of architecture than the course tutors had expected. In contrast, when it came to the other role perspectives—those of client and user—most students reported that they had difficulty assuming these roles. For example, when the design project was a day nursery it was found that very few students could remember what it felt like to be a young child and only 12 per cent had close links with children under school age. Also, when students were asked to play the role of client or user at reviews most found it very difficult, reporting that they had little insight into these roles. Given that the ability to take alternative perspectives and empathise with others is fundamental to working with clients, users and other construction professionals, it was important to address these problems. The findings, at the very least, suggested that more might be done to prepare students for the roles they were expected to play.

The project

The first-year major design project took place over six weeks and required students to research and design a small building—a children's day nursery. This chapter specifically describes and investigates the skills focus for the development of group working and role play within the overall design project in its third year of running. Since it was now clear that the students had not been well prepared in either of these areas in the past, two changes were made. Firstly, supportive workshops were inserted into the course, designed to improve group working skills before students were asked to undertake tasks involving collaboration. Secondly, strategies were adopted to give students more insight into and ownership of the roles they were being asked to play. Both approaches were intended to increase the students' collaboration with each other and their participation in reviews.

Group-working

The Students were organised into working groups of five or six at the beginning of the semester. Each group had to compile a report on the background research for the project, comprising a record of group meetings, specialist reports, site data and precedent studies. In addition, all the students were divided into three 'specialist groups'. Each was to focus on a different role perspective—client, user or expert. Each working group included one or two representatives from each of the specialist groups. The specialist groups met with a real life client (a nursery owner), a user (a mother and her child) and an expert (an architect and author of works on kindergarten architecture). This overall structure was designed to ensure that, in order best to utilise information from the client, user and expert, the students from the specialist groups had to share what they had learned with the other students in their working group.

Supporting group-working

Each group-work exercise was preceded by a workshop and followed by a debriefing session or a reflective review. The former gave the students the opportunity to consider what it meant to work in a group and to plan for group-working; the latter enabled them to review and learn from their experience in order to make improvements in subsequent group-working. The workshops were tailored to the task in hand and the level of experience of the students. By the time of the main project the students had already attended two general workshops on group-working—the first being an introduction to group-working, the second focusing on the actual skills needed for group-working.

The reasons for using collaborative learning were also made explicit to the students to ensure that they were motivated to work in groups. Practising architects joined the early workshops to talk about group working and its relevance to professional practice, and an educational rationale for collaborative learning approaches was also provided—it was emphasised to the students that group learning can in many situations be more powerful than individual learning.

Supporting role play

In order to learn more about the roles they were being asked to adopt, each of the three specialist groups met their role model—a client, user or expert. At these meetings the role model gave an introductory informal talk, which was followed by a question and answer session. Afterwards the students fed back the knowledge they had gained from the role models to their working groups, through discussions about design issues within their working groups, both informally and in group tutorials. In addition they made a written contribution to a research report on the project from their role perspective.

A listening and questioning workshop preceded the meetings of the specialist groups. The aim of the workshop was to clarify the purpose of the specialist meetings and to get the students to think about how to elicit information from a client, user or expert. Inputs into the workshops included an architect talking about the relevance of questioning and listening for professional life, and discussions about questioning and listening skills. The students worked in sub-groups to devise questions to ask at the meeting with the specialist. The questions were then discussed, refined and typed up at the end of the workshop. A chair and a spokesperson were appointed by the group for the forthcoming meeting with the client, user or expert. Lastly, the students met with their working group after the specialist meetings to review the success of their questioning strategy and to share their learning experiences.

Design reviews

Specialist groups also played a part in the design project reviews. Formal reviews were held at the interim and final stages of the project. In previous years the introduction of role perspectives in the reviews had been problematic. Students had felt uncomfortable about criticising each other's work and therefore tended to make unperceptive remarks such as 'This scheme seems to work really well from the user's point of view'. This problem disappeared after the introduction of the specialist groups. Instead of individual students being asked to take the perspective of client, user or expert in the reviews, the specialist groups formed a panel and were asked to contribute to the discussion about the design schemes.

The design project review began with each of the working groups of five pinning up their work together. The audience for each design consisted of a staff panel and three specialist group panels. Each individual gave a short introduction to his or her design scheme. The specialist groups were then given a short time to discuss the schemes, after which they were asked to make two comments—one favourable, highlighting a strength of the design, and one constructive suggestion for improvement. After a discussion of the comments the staff panel made their own commentary and summarised the review. In addition each student appointed an observer to record the proceedings on a feedback sheet, to which the individual student added his or her own comments and self-assessed mark. The process is summarised below.

Review timetable (audience in four panels—staff, users, clients and experts)

1   Working groups pin up work.
2   Observer appointed for each student to record comments on feedback sheet.
3   Short introduction to schemes by each student in turn.
4   Specialist groups discuss schemes and formulate two observations, one favourable and one constructively critical.
5   Discussion of specialist group observations.
6   Staff comment and sum up.
7   Students record their own comments and self-assessment on feedback sheet.

Evaluation of the project

The project was evaluated in three ways. Firstly, each workshop was evaluated as it took place—typically students were asked to record their expectations of the workshop at the start of the session, and at the end to record one significant thing they had learned. Secondly, the written research reports produced by the working groups were assessed and marked at the end of the project. Finally, at the end of the year all the students completed an evaluation questionnaire designed to elicit information about how they felt they had progressed in collaborative working, and how they rated the various inputs into the course. The questionnaire also asked open-ended questions about what they felt had been the most and the least valuable aspect of the explicit skills focus within the design project.

Group-working

Both staff and students felt that group-working had improved as a result of the specific targeted skills input. According to the teaching staff, students who experienced this in the first year were better at group-working in subsequent years than had been the case in the past. For the students, an evaluation questionnaire showed that 40 per cent felt they had been good or very good at group-work when they began the course, but by the end of the year this figure had increased to 79 per cent.

In addition, a strong correlation emerged between achievement and successful teams. In general, but not always, the best group project work (achieving the highest marks) had been produced by teams that, by their own judgement, had worked well together.

After the support workshops were introduced teaching staff noticed improved participation in reviews and in the ability of students to take different role perspectives. Moreover the difficulty students experienced with taking different roles was highlighted during the workshop on listening and questioning skills, held just before the meetings with client, user and expert. At this workshop it was apparent that the students found it hard to compile a list of questions for the forthcoming meeting 'because they did not know what they needed to know'. This is the classic dilemma of the inexperienced designer. However the workshop forced students to think through and discuss the potential questions at greater depth and to focus more effectively on the role perspective. The result was that the students managed to produce more penetrating questions and were able to go on to the meetings with the client, user or expert with a clearer structure for their questioning and a clearer idea of the kinds of answer that would help them to tailor their designs to the needs of those parties.

However, while it was clear to the staff that students in previous years, having not been given preparatory workshops, had got less value from their meetings with clients, users or experts, the students themselves did not value the support workshops as highly. Only 39 per cent of the students rated them 'good' or 'very good' (43 per cent 'average' and 18 per cent 'below average' or 'poor'). Those who rated them 'poor' felt that each workshop should have been more differentiated in style and content to avoid repetition, and that the objectives should have been made much clearer. Improvements in these workshops are planned for subsequent years.

Role play

Meeting 'real' people was highly valued by the students. Sixty-nine per cent reported that the specialist meetings with clients, users or architects were a valuable experience, and only 3 per cent saw this as not valuable to their learning. The staff reported that student participation in reviews had increased enormously since the introduction of this project, and that the level of debate had improved. The students also reported that they found the reviews useful, with one third finding them a good or very good learning experience. More student involvement in the reviews resulted in less pressure on the staff. By coming in after the students had made their contributions and debated some of the issues the teaching staff were able to give more thoughtful feedback. Attendance at reviews also increased after the specialist panels were brought into play. Moreover, instead of leaving after their own reviews were over, the students were more likely to stay and join in the discussion of other students' design schemes. In summary, the reviews became less stressful, less confrontational between staff and students, and more enjoyable, with a deeper level of analysis and discussion.

Conclusion

The initial reaction of the teaching staff to the concern to make students more sensitive to clients and users had been to provide students with more information about the needs of clients and users. However, over time it became clear that to develop skills in dealing with clients and users changes had to be made in the way students interacted with each other, with tutors and with real clients and users.

This project was successful in sensitising students to the needs of clients and users in the design process, and in introducing students to group-working skills—both of which are essential in professional practice.

There had been some staff concern before the project began that, by concentrating on the client/user perspective, design issues would necessarily be neglected. In the event, student feedback showed that, far from being a problem, events such as the specialist meetings were frequently seen as the starting points for design ideas. Comments from students included:

> I saw this method of gaining information extremely helpful in generating my scheme for the nursery.

> I found the meeting with [the client] very informative and it went a long way to shaping my design.

> A comment that [the user] made was a major contribution to my nursery design. That was her dislike of pokey corridors.

Paradoxically, the students who appreciated the CUDE initiatives were often those with the least need of being taught them—students with preexisting strengths and empathy with the subject. However this does not mean that these students would necessarily be considered the high achievers on a design course. In architectural education it is the natural designers who are best rewarded from the outset by the traditional system. They may see no need to nurture their communication skills. In turn, their dazzling tectonic performance in the early years of a course can induce such a lack of confidence among their fellow students that the latter may retreat into other areas where they know they can perform well.

It is clearly as advantageous for natural designers to take the client and user issues seriously as it is for other students to be able to nurture their natural strengths in communication and brief-building. Together they will be more effective practitioners. The challenge for the tutor is to foster this climate.

9 The 'real' client and the 'unreal' project

A diploma case study

Prue Chiles

Context

The curriculum of the postgraduate diploma course at Sheffield University is designed to develop the problem-solving processes introduced in the undergraduate years. A central underlying aim is to foster in students a way of thinking about the world and architecture's place within it, in both an intellectual and a practical sense. This involves the development of more complex skills and expansion of the knowledge base gained from previous experience. The overall aims include:

- Enabling a more fluent and sophisticated ability to design.
- Encouraging students to develop their own particular academic interests.
- Fostering a more in-depth understanding of the role of the architect.

Diploma students have just returned from a year in practice, thus each brings to the course the knowledge she or he gained during the undergraduate years in architecture plus a year of practical experience.

This chapter describes a project, partially funded through the HEFCE CUDE initiative, that was carried out in the first semester of the diploma course at the University of Sheffield 1996/97 session. It discusses how we tried to reconnect architecture students with the profession and the building industry, and encourage better communication between the architect and the outside world. We chose to do this by situating the project in Sheffield, basing it on a real public project that was under way at the time and bringing the client body into the architectural studio.

The studio project was based on Sheffield's 'Heart of the City' project (HoC). This £100 million urban regeneration scheme involved the redevelopment of the civic centre and included a 'signature building'—a new art gallery (the Millennium Gallery, sponsored by the

Victoria and Albert Museum)—and an attached winter garden. It had been initiated by Sheffield City Council in 1995, when a firm of architects had been commissioned to look at the unpopular 1970s town hall extension and adjacent vacant ground, and to propose ideas for its regeneration. In the following two years the project went through various material changes in pursuit of a fundable scheme. During this process the original architects were replaced, the developers were selected and the project became a reality.

In the 1996/97 academic year staff from the school of architecture decided, in the light of the CUDE initiative, to reinvent this project with a carefully structured and intensive input of taught material to promote a greater understanding of the client's requirements and the procurement of such a complex project.

The studio project

The studio project took place over nine weeks. It was divided into two parts and, as with the real HoC project, was based on the remaking of the heart of Sheffield. Forty-two students participated, with three studio staff and additional visiting critics and tutors.

The first (four week) part required the students to work in self-selected groups to make an 'academic critique' of the original urban regeneration project. This critique would then form the basis of a counter proposal that the students would present to a mock Millennium Commission Selection Panel. This panel contained some members of the selection panel from the real project.

It was, however, made explicit in the briefing to the students that their proposal could stand back from the reality of the original development process and assume a utopian or idealistic standpoint. In the event this proved difficult for many of the students, who responded to the reality of the situation.

The second (five week) part of the project required the students to take off their masterplanning hats and assume the role of architect of the 'signature' building in the masterplan—the Millennium Gallery. They continued to explore the themes of Sheffield's *genus loci*, but now the vehicle was the gallery. In addition to questions of place and regionalism they were asked to consider the 'nature' of the museum and gallery—arguably the most prolific and culturally significant building type of the late twentieth century. This again was an attempt to mirror reality. In 1996 a short-list of architectural practices had been invited to make a presentation to a selection panel and describe how their firm would approach the commission to design the Millennium Gallery.

The briefing sessions for this part of the project described the conception of the gallery idea and the generation of the brief, and then followed the complex procurement process from initial concept to studio project. Students were to follow the brief given to the winning architects and individually produce a detailed design for the gallery or winter garden, including a detailed exploration of space, structure and environmental control. Although the students were now working individually, their proposals were to respect their group's urban design proposal adopted in the first stage of the project.

Three members of the diploma tutor team had themselves been members of practices on the shortlist for the real project and so had direct experience of the process. The winning architects were also involved in the student briefing process. The city architect, who was the enabler of the HoC project, acted as the main 'client' contact for the students. He was briefed by the tutors regarding the project's learning goals and took the role of an informed client, also participating as one of the critics of the final student designs.

As for the tutors, their direct professional involvement in the HoC project gave them a degree of ownership over the project and meant they could better mediate between the client body, the individual students and the learning goals they were trying to facilitate through the project.

Throughout, the tutoring staff made a conscious effort to encourage clear explanations from the students of the design process and to discourage the private language and priorities that only architects understand. Students were assessed through presentations to the 'millennium panel', which included non-architects. They were also assessed through written reports. Their first written report on teamwork took the form of a diary and an account. The second asked for a journalistic account of the two-day seminar. Each was designed to encourage ongoing reflection.

Knowledge and skills input

Central to the students' overall briefing for the project was a two-day intensive course, where the complex procurement process—from idea to reality—was described by a series of speakers drawn from academia, practice and the city. The subjects covered ranged from specific briefings from members of the client body to more general architectural management issues, to sociological lectures on understanding Sheffield city centre. Nearly all the speakers were personally involved in the HoC project and used this as a case study to discuss the principles of management, procurement and legislative issues.

An understanding of the wider parameters of the HoC project in terms of the socioeconomic and cultural reasons for a building's purpose and meaning was provided by lectures. An economist gave a broad view of the political and economic changes in Sheffield over the previous 20 years, while a sociologist and author of a recent study explained what gave Sheffield its particular identity, and identified the local 'structure of feeling' of the city (Taylor *et al.* 1996).

The project was centrally concerned with skills relevant to the relationship between the client and the architect, including:

- Listening skills: skills relating to the development and negotiation of a brief with a client/user.
- Presentation and communication skills, both visual and verbal.
- Teamworking and the role of the individual within a team.

These were specifically addressed either through workshops or through briefings from 'real' clients and subsequent discussion with those clients.

The intention behind the presentation workshops was always to link the skills that the students were learning or reviewing to actual tasks, so there was no separation of skills from the application of those skills.

Just prior to the project the students had worked in teams on a short project with structural engineering students. For this they had been taught some specific skills in teamworking dynamics, and had subsequently reflected on the experience and their attitude towards teamworking in written accounts. They therefore came to the project with some teamworking experience. The students had also been given guidance about how to present, as a team, to a panel through two workshops on presentation techniques, and as part of these workshops, had participated in exercises with a voice coach.

Evaluation

The external 'expert' input into this project was evaluated through a student questionnaire.

The students reported that the workshop input on teamworking and presentation techniques immediately prior to the project had been highly valued. A common reflection was that 'doing a project where we had to consciously think of how we performed as a group taught me a lot about teamwork'. Others commented that being taught to understand their role in a team—that is, to see their natural personal strengths and weaknesses as identified in a Belbin analysis—greatly helped team dynamics. This was borne out in the final presentations for the four-week group urban proposal where nearly all the students presented their work in supportive functioning teams. The opportunity that had been created for students to reflect on group processes was, in hindsight, seen to be one of the primary enabling experiences of the subsequent studio project.

Similarly, the workshops where the students had practised their presentations and been given advice and feedback from a voice coach were valued by the students. Again, as evidenced by the final presentations, students had gained confidence and clarity through this coaching. Overall, the opportunity to look at basic skills, practise them with professionals and then relate the skill to an actual assessed task was greatly appreciated by the students.

The main criticism was the intensity of the two-day course. Even the most conscientious students said they had struggled to absorb everything. Some of the input was seen as unsuccessful in its attempt to reveal of the 'real life' processes in building procurement, since this was too far removed from the students' own experience. However, many students commented that they appreciated the different viewpoints that each speaker had brought. For example the project manager's 'worldly' view was memorable to many. The most popular and memorable lectures were those concerning the political and economic context.

There was also concern that there had not been enough time for discussion and critical debate—most students would have preferred a longer briefing period. Yet this revealed a contradiction in the students' responses. Although most felt that more time on this would have been useful, they also felt that larger amounts of taught input would have compromised the time needed to develop their designs.

The students also reported that it was difficult to connect the intensive two-day seminar course with the studio work. Might the 'real' client input have been more effective if the students had been producing a written case study on the HoC project rather than trying to draw out messages for their own work?

The structure of the overall project had been designed to achieve a broader inclusiveness of the 'real' issues and their integration into the design proposals. However it became clear from the feedback that it had in fact inundated the process with too many constraints. This had weakened the project at the very point where the students' imagination and intellectual rigour should have taken over—many students found it difficult to break out of the constraints and offered no critique or interesting new angle through their design. Neither did many make any serious critique of the role of the gallery/museum generally or to Sheffield specifically.

However, for the few students who had grappled with the critique and were also strong enough to reevaluate the constraints of the real project brief, the result was, as hoped, a better ability to open a broader debate. Furthermore the project then became 'owned' by them and was to sustain them intellectually for the rest of their diploma years. For example one student, keeping closely to the real accommodation brief for the gallery, totally reassessed the idea of what a gallery in Sheffield should contain. He became interested in the notion of craft, which in turn opened an enormous and rich area of investigation. This resulted in a dissertation and a final diploma project that contributed something entirely new to the whole debate on craft and Sheffield's traditional role in this field.

For another student, his group's urban proposal enabled a completely fresh look at the whole conception of the HoC project. Although not able fully to express this in his gallery project, the seeds had been sown for a radical new urban proposal that was to grow into two years of postgraduate investigation for this student.

Overall the success of the project lay in its power to aid students' understanding of the complexity and reality of how a public building gets built, its inevitable compromises, and the role of the client body and the architect in the whole process. The tutors were reminded that different students excell at different skills, for example verbal communication or taking the lead in teamwork, and that these should be encouraged, rather than expecting all students to be 'excellent designers'. Clearly, an architect needs a wide range of skills to work with a client. This project encouraged the development in students of a range of abilities, particularly empowering those who saw their role in the more managerial areas of the architectural profession.

Implications for the future

It was clear from student feedback and tutor realisation that the project had been overloaded, and that a nine-week programme was too short for an endeavour of this complexity.

From the tutors' perspective the project had been very time-consuming to set up. Structuring the project was a logistical challenge—getting the clients and the other professionals in the 'right place at the right time', time spent briefing and agreeing inputs. It was also expensive and only affordable with the 'external' funding provided through the CUDE initiative. Even so, the project still had to rely on the goodwill of the clients, who gave much of their time.

Paradoxically, to be cost-effective—with the high level of organisation and expense required—there should have been a larger number of students, yet working with a still smaller group of students might have achieved more discussion, a closer relationship with the client body and a generally more successful experience.

The project had tried to incorporate a direct, authentic relationship with the client. However in many senses the project had not been authentic. Another project, carried out the following year, to design and build an opera set in Sheffield Cathedral for an individual client achieved a more authentic experience because the relationship between the client and the students genuinely focused on a 'real-time' project. The students were actually contributing to, and controlling, the project as it was happening rather than working on an already completed project. Hence the need for the communications skills necessary to develop a good relationship with the client was immediately perceived as highly relevant by the students. The briefing process became a set of direct instructions that had to be interpreted by the students. This contrasted with the Heart of the City project, where there had merely been a sharing of past information. On the other hand, because it was so real, and ongoing, there was little time for reflection, which had been one of the most successful aspects of the Heart of the City project.

Exposing students both to a real client body, with their different expectations and aspirations, and to a complex procurement process has great potential as a learning experience for students. However the Heart of the City project would have undoubtedly been more successful if it had had a sharper focus. When planning a similar project in the future it will be necessary to pay particular attention to the size of the client body and the scale of the project. If the actual project is too large then the learning focus will have to be narrowed to a specific building or specific aspect of the project. Alternatively, different groups of students might focus on different parts of the project and interact with smaller numbers of clients so that the experience is not overwhelming. At a later stage in the project these groups could be brought together to draw out the larger perspective. All this will require tutors to clarify which of the many aspects of the client–architect relationship and brief-building process should be the focus for student learning.

Reference and Bibliography

Bines, H. and Watson, D. (1992) *Developing Professional Education*. The Society for Research into Higher Education and OUP. Milton Keynes: Open University Press.

Brady, D. (1996) 'The Education of an Architect: Continuity and Change', *Journal of Architectural Education*, 50(1).

Eraut, M. (1994) *Developing Professional Knowledge and Competence*. London: Falmer.

Ruedi, K. (1996) 'Beyond the Building Site', *Building Design*, June.

Taylor, I. (1994) *Developing Learning in Professional Education: Partnerships for Practice*. The Society Research into Higher Education and OUP. Milton Keynes: Open University Press.

Taylor, I., Evans, K. and Fraser, P. (1996) *A Tale of Two Cities—a study in Manchester and Sheffield* London: Routledge.

10 Reviewing the review
An account of a research investigation of the 'crit'

Margaret Wilkin

Introduction

The 'crit' or project review is a form of teaching to which schools of architecture have subscribed for decades, and this historical continuity would seem to suggest that in the past it has been a successful mode of transmitting the knowledge and skills of the architect to the next generation of the profession. But as Vowles indicates in Chapter 26, continuity of a social institution may reflect more than functional effectiveness. It can also reflect broader social processes such as the exercise of power and influence. Thus, for example, the review is an established mode of teaching, whereby students learn from tutors' comments on their own and their peers' work. But it may also be a means of ensuring the recruitment to architecture of students of a certain personality type or artistic inclination, thereby preserving design traditions.

   However suppositions such as these, which refer to the value of the review either as a teaching method or as a forum for perpetuating particular design perspectives, need to be verified. We know little about either of these aspects of the review. Considering how dominant a feature of architectural education the project review has been and continues to be, remarkably little has been written about it, and even less has it been the object of serious investigative research. This chapter is an account of an early attempt to analyse the review process from the perspective of the learning opportunities it provides for students. Analysis of the data also provides some hint of the way in which students learn to become architects—rather than just practise architecture—as they participate in reviews over the three years of their undergraduate course.

Reviewing the review

In 1996 funding was granted to the schools of architecture at the universities of Sheffield and De Montfort to consider how their courses might focus more fully on accommodating the needs of those ultimately to benefit from the architect's expertise—the clients who fund buildings and the users who work and live in them. This could be seen as evidence of the more pragmatic approach to higher education adopted by governments in recent years, but it also reflects an emergent concern within the construction industry and within the profession itself regarding the 'human dimension' of the industry.

This was a broad brief, and required a review of all current practice in this light, in order that a basis for further development might be established. The project review was chosen as a central subject of research on the ground that it is such an important and comprehensive element of the student's training. It incorporates the content of lecture courses and tutorials, and the student's use and interpretation of this material. It provides an opportunity for design initiatives, and it acts as a vehicle for assessment.

The enquiry was limited to inviting tutors from the various disciplines represented in De Montfort's then School of the Built Environment, and their students, across all three years of the undergraduate course, to give their personal views on the project review. No direct observations of the reviews were undertaken at this stage. A total of 22 members of staff and 41 students participated. Questionnaires of various types were sent to staff and to students, and the staff also had the opportunity to express their views in discussion groups. Module guides or project briefs were also analysed for their emphasis on clients and users.

A full account of the process—its methodology, findings, analysis and recommendations—was subsequently published.[1] This chapter provides a summary of the key points. When the participants' responses were analysed they seemed to cluster into four issues, two of which were concerned with conditions for learning and two of which referred to the concerns expressed above about the consideration given to the concerns of clients and users in the project review.

Emerging issues

Is the project review a learning opportunity or an assessment point?

Of course assessment of one's work provides an opportunity to learn. The distinction between the two activities is an analytical one, drawn for convenience, since different rules of interaction between tutor and student apply in these two situations. In the case of an assessment, students can rightly expect that their individual efforts will be judged on common criteria. But personal progress in learning may be measured on the basis of the individual's development in any dimension.

There is no need to compare one student's progress with that of another, and therefore there need be no common criteria. It is, however, essential that students should know which of these intentions governs the particular review process, because unless they do, they will be unable to direct their efforts.

Analysis of the tutors' comments suggested that while most tutors think that the review is an opportunity for learning, a few regard it as an assessment point. Moreover, while—in the interests of equity—some tutors prefer to evaluate students' work according to set criteria, others aim to focus on diverse issues in their review comments in order to broaden the basis of student learning. In effect, tutors may not be maintaining the important distinction between the two activities. Just how confusing this can be for the student was implied in the comments of one of the tutor participants:

> I think the answer is probably both [learning opportunity and assessment point]. It depends on how a particular presentation is being used in that particular project or at a particular stage in the project, and so it might be more biased towards learning ... or it might be more biased towards assessment.

If the focus of tutors' responses is unpredictable in this way, students will be uncertain of the basis on which their project work is to be appraised. The tutors' actions and presentation of the material to be learned—whether process or fact—will tend to be random and disjointed, rather than coherent and systematic. Twenty five per cent of the student respondents claimed that tutors were inconsistent in their responses, and their dilemma was summarised by the student who, when asked for suggestions for improvements in the review wrote: 'Make sure all the lecturers are on the same wavelength and want the same thing.'

Nevertheless the analysis of the data suggests that the great majority of staff believe that a considerable amount of learning does take place in reviews, and the students' comments support this assumption. According to their responses the project review provides an important context for learning from tutors in the first instance, but also from other students. But of greater interest is how, across the years, students vary in the way they utilise the review as a context for learning. For example first-year students attribute to their tutors an almost parental interest in their work, and they look to their tutors for support in helping them to access the discourse of architecture. By the third year, however, students view their tutors primarily as a source of expertise, of technical advice and guidance. Similarly, first-year students refer to the review as a chance to pick up ideas and to compare themselves with their peers in order to confirm their position as a member of the group—attitudes that reflect their concerns and insecurity as novitiates. In contrast third-year students refer to the review as a chance to test out their own ideas and to assess, either individually or as a group, the ideas of their fellows. As might be expected, by this time personal anxiety is much less in evidence.

In summary, the data collected on this issue suggests that students, across the years and in their respective ways, do recognise the review as an important forum for learning. But it also suggests that the lack of a shared perspective by staff on the purpose of the review, and the subsequent randomness of their selection of issues for discussion, may impede students' coherent understanding of the material. Therefore the project review, as traditionally conducted, is not as fully effective a learning context as it might be.

The organisation of the project review

If the coherent and systematic presentation of learning issues aids understanding—and it is reasonable to assume that this is the case—a further condition for learning to take place is that the material to be learned should be readily accessible. This may seem an obvious assumption, but the large student groups that schools of architecture host today, present a problem in this respect. Nearly half of the staff respondents agreed that students were constrained from participating by their 'distance from the action'. As one tutor put it: 'The thing I remember most as a student was that [the project review] was largely a waste of time. You can't see the drawings that are being criticised, and if you can't see the drawing, you can't understand what is being said.' If this was the case when groups were smaller, then how much more is it so today?

In addition, learning is promoted by a positive state of mind. The above situation is demotivating for students for further reasons. Large groups mean extended reviews: 'What do I dislike about reviews? Waiting around all day for my turn.' This, in turn, can lead to students feeling that they have had insufficient tutorial time or tutor interest: 'If a student spends six weeks of their life on a project, the least staff can do is to spend time to listen and understand the scheme.' In their questionnaire responses, both staff and students indicated that they would prefer smaller groups in order to maximise the opportunity for proactive involvement.

Finally, the cultural traditions of how the review is run impose their own constraints on learning. Both tutors and students agreed that all-day reviews are unproductive. Concentration is difficult to sustain and tutors become less effective as teachers as fatigue sets in. Furthermore, voluntary intermittent attendance must interrupt the flow of ideas and the concentration of the group.

The students made a large number of comments that were critical of the organisation of the review—they would have preferred a more disciplined event. The tutors too were critical of some organisational aspects of the traditional review process. Large groups and lengthy reviews in particular were considered to inhibit learning. By its nature intermittent attendance is disruptive, and therefore must be similarly regarded.

To what extent does the review focus on clients and users?

The previous two sections considered the efficacy of the review as an educational event. This is an important and fundamental consideration since, if the review as it is conducted is already an event that supports student learning, then it could be redirected without too much difficulty to focus more fully on a specific issue—in our case, clients and users—if need be. If, on the other hand, its potential as a forum for learning has been reduced for whatever reasons, such matters will have to be addressed in the first instance.

In the majority of the 18 project briefs analysed, client and user issues were identified, and about 50 per cent of the students agreed that these groups do feature adequately in the briefs, thus giving shape and direction to the design project. But third-year students in particular commented that they would like to see even greater emphasis on client and user interests, perhaps because they were nearing the end of the course and would soon have to work within the parameters of actual clients' and users' wishes. The staff were also almost unanimous that clients and users should contribute to design projects, particularly in drawing up the brief. However they were less willing to invite them to share assessment responsibilities. They pointed out that there were certain constraints on the greater involvement in the course of outside consultants of any kind—in particular a lack of funding and insufficient time to set up their visits.

If clients and users are readily identifiable in project briefs, and if staff and students are united in their wish to see their involvement in the processes of designing and monitoring design projects, then how do these two groups fare in the project review itself? Are they a regular focus of tutor questioning for example? First- and third-year students perceived the review as a sound forum for promoting and learning about client and user issues, though second-year students tended to be more sceptical. This issue is, however, inseparable from the first of the issues discussed above—that tutors, in their desire to develop individual students' ideas as well as to ensure that their evaluations are rigorous, may question students about their work in what appears to the student to be a random rather than a systematic and predictable manner. Students expect to be asked questions about their designs that directly reflect the project brief. The tutors agreed that the criteria given in the brief were an important influence on the form of questioning, but in their responses they also indicated that, as might be expected, their first consideration was the strengths and weaknesses of the student's design. The tutors also suggested that members of staff had their own preferences and priorities, and would tend to bias their questioning to accommodate these personal interests. It therefore seems unlikely that, in the traditional form of the review, the requirements of clients and users are a predictable and prominent feature, largely because the review itself is an ongoing, relatively unstructured exchange, which is interpreted by tutors as the means of advancing the individual student's learning, and therefore is not predetermined in its details.

In summary, the data suggests that both tutors and students support the involvement of clients and users in architectural education, though students to a greater degree than tutors. Although clients and users feature in module briefs, it seems unlikely that their interests and preferences are a regular focus of project reviews.

Student participation in the project review

The development of students' communication skills is perceived by both tutors and the HEFCE (the funding body of this research project) to be an important aspect of their professional preparation. Once working in a practice, they will be expected to discuss preferences and possibilities with clients and users, and to negotiate with them on projects. To what extent does the review prepare students for this important professional requirement?

The data suggests that for a range of reasons, and despite tutors' encouragement, student participation in reviews is limited. Some of the reasons for this are personal (for example some students are made extremely anxious by the review situation), some are organisational (see above), and others are cultural. Architecture is a discipline in which individual recognition is the reward, and some of the students admitted to enjoying the public display and defending their designs. Whether an unspoken agreement exists within review groups that discourages the practice of commenting on another student's work is unknown, but it is a possibility. Nevertheless the tutors agreed that students learn through discussion, and they supported the mandatory training of students in interaction skills.

In summary, the importance of students acquiring and demonstrating communication skills during their course was a strong theme in the tutors' responses. There was little evidence, however, that students actually participate, either fully or regularly, in the discussion of general topics or of other students' work in the project review.

Conclusion

The research investigation reported in this chapter, coupled with prior concerns about the effectiveness of the review as a teaching method, have prompted the staff at the De Montfort University School of Architecture to revise and redesign the project review as a more structured event with more explicit learning outcomes. Such an undertaking is a challenging task, all the more so since, as Vowles indicates in Chapter 26, the review is such a well-established and institutionalised procedure in architectural education that it is difficult either to view it objectively or to disregard its status and question its conventions. Moreover, relatively little has been written about the pedagogy of architectural education over the years, and even less about the evaluation of it, so knowledge of, rather than hearsay about, developments over time in the review process is scant and so can contribute little to its reassessment.

If concern about the intrinsic inconsistencies of the review process is now stimulating its reassessment, developments in the wider political and economic context of architectural education are having a similar effect. Student groups are now far more cosmopolitan. Higher education in the UK has been opened up to students from across Europe and beyond, and from a diversity of educational and social backgrounds. Budgetary constraints have led to fewer tutors being in charge of larger student groups. Furthermore the trend towards greater public accountability in all areas of education demands tighter management of courses and increased explicitness about the student experience. All of these external influences impact to a greater or lesser degree on both the content and the pedagogy of higher education courses, for they oblige institutions to reassess their current practices.

For those involved in teaching the next generation of architects, this enhanced managerialism may be unwelcome. The demand for more closely regulated courses, explicit criteria and a predictable student experience could be interpreted as opposing the spontaneity and creativity of architecture as a discipline. But accountability and openness, and freedom of personal expression are not incompatible. Courses and assessment procedures can be designed in such a way as to incorporate areas of freedom. For example reviews can be planned that devote some time to considering particular and predetermined aspects of a student's work, but which also designate time for either tutor or student to comment on any aspect of the submission. The task confronting schools of architecture today is how to remain true to the principles of their discipline while at the same time accommodating necessary changes in the nature of professional preparation.

Note

1 The full report of this research project—M. Wilkin 'Reassessing the Design Project Review in Undergraduate Architectural Education with Particular Reference to Clients and Users' (1999) can be obtained from the Secretary, the School of Architecture, De Montfort University, Leicester.

11 Introducing alternative formats for the design project review

A case study

Tim Brindley, Charles Doidge and Ross Willmott

Introduction

The project review or 'crit' has been the cornerstone of architectural education for generations. In it the student explains and defends his or her design ideas in an open forum—a situation that is considered to mimic, and therefore is an important preparation for, professional practice. Despite an underlying concern in most schools of architecture about the format of the review, its effectiveness and even its morality, it has retained its position as the predominant teaching method in undergraduate courses in architecture.

In 1998 the Leicester School of Architecture (LSA) commissioned Margaret Wilkin, an educational researcher, to undertake an independent assessment of the review process in the LSA. Her report (Wilkin 1999) suggested that there were weaknesses in the 'typical' review process, but it also pointed to opportunities to develop the review as a positive learning experience to promote attitudes and skills in the students that could improve relationships between design professionals and clients and users in the construction industry in their later working lives. The report concluded that the formative stages of this process should begin during the students' undergraduate years. This chapter looks at the response of the LSA to Wilkin's report.

The report's recommendations

Two broad conclusions were identified in the report and adopted *inter alia* by the LSA:

- The review needed to be more clearly structured; learning outcomes should be explicit and students should receive consistent feedback; and the status of the review—assessment or learning opportunity?—should be clarified.
- The review should more closely reflect the range of skills needed by architects in professional practice, with particular reference to

communication with clients and users; it should develop and build these skills cumulatively during the undergraduate course.

Structuring and clarifying the review's purpose

The LSA's initial response to the first of these conclusions was to consider modifications to the conventional review, but a number of alternative review formats were also suggested. Some of these were derived from occasional experiments in the past, others were new ideas for introducing explicit skill training into the review. These alternative formats (Table 11.1) were matched against design project

Table 11.1 Alternative formats for design project reviews

Format	Method	Professional 'parallel'
Traditional	Conventional review format for an academic audience; well-organised, clear objectives; normally two staff, 20 minutes per student	In-house presentation to fellow architects in the office
Selective	Staff review submissions without students present; staff present summary of main issues to whole student group, based on selected examples	Competition submission to an informed client; selected architects invited for further discussions
Talk	Illustrated verbal presentation, using slides or OHP, in medium-size group of about 20 students	Illustrated verbal presentation, various contexts, including to clients and users
Client	Presentation to real or role-playing client, based on models, 3D graphics; small group of about six students	Feedback from client in brief-building phase
Meeting	Short individual presentations in a small group; group establishes common agenda for discussion and decisions; student-led	Design team meeting, to analyse issues and develop options
Brochure	Individual or small groupwork in brochure format, using text and images; round-table discussion	Project summary used, for example, in practice marketing
Exhibition	Self-explanatory display, in poster or panel format; private review by staff, short discussion with author(s) for clarification	Public exhibition of proposals, for example to potential users
Computer	Computer-based presentation, text and graphics, with a small, medium or large group	Summary presentation to clients, sponsors, public authorities etc. using IT

objectives and a programme of trials was set up with the first- and second-year design tutors.[1] The trials stimulated a wide-ranging debate on teaching and learning methods, and on objectives and intended learning outcomes throughout the LSA.

Each trial format included a number of changes to the review process, to the content or substance of the review, and to the medium or media of communication. Each also required a consideration of educational objectives and intended outcomes, including the following:

- What were students expected to learn from the process (learning outcomes)?
- How could the learning objectives be made explicit to all involved?
- What, if any, additional teaching inputs and learning opportunities would be required to support the new format?
- How could effective feedback to staff and students on the process outcomes be ensured?

Implementation

The programme of trials commenced during the second semester of the 1998/99 session. Not all staff were comfortable with these innovations and some resistance to change was experienced. Some doubt was expressed about introducing major changes for students in the third year, and graduate diploma students were omitted since the diploma staff were reluctant to be involved in the trials. In addition, discussion revealed that some of the proposed formats did not match well with some design project's stated objectives and planned review stages—these cases were omitted from the trials.

The first and second years were chosen for the trials, their respective year coordinators being enthusiastic supporters of the initiatives. The implemented trial formats are presented in Tables 11.2 and 11.3.

Critique

Each of the trial reviews was observed by at least one member of the project team and an external advisor was present for some of the reviews. At the end of the session the project staff held a workshop to discuss the outcome of the trials and to share experiences and conclusions. Feedback from students was received informally during the review process, and formal feedback will be available at a later stage. The trial formats are considered in turn below.

Table 11.2 Alternative review formats selected for first-year students

Format	Project	Method	Special teaching inputs
Exhibition	Design for a simple structure in a landscape: initial design	Pin up student drawings; selective review by staff	Workshop on drawing and communication skills
Computer	As above: design development using CAD	Computer-based presentations by individual students, based on 3D Autocad drawings	Specialist tutorials in appropriate software (2D and 3D drawing, £D rendering, DTP page layout)
Talk	Design of a terraced house: research studies	Small groups present results of initial research studies using OHP	

Table 11.3 Alternative review formats selected for second-year students

Format	Project	Method	Special teaching inputs
Exhibition	Design of a temporary structure	Pin up student drawings; conventional review	
Talk	Design a medium sized building in a dense urban context: initial investigations	Small groups prepare illustrated talk based on site studies	Workshop on summarising key findings and planning a presentation
Meeting	As above: conceptual ideas	Individual student presentations to small group, using drawings, models and OHP	Written guidance on the review process and objectives
Selective	As above: sketch scheme proposals	Individual student presentations to small group; selected schemes form basis of feedback to whole student group	Written guidance on the review process and objectives
Exhibition	As above: final review	Self-explanatory display reviewed by staff, followed by questions to individual students	Written guidance on the review process and objectives

Exhibition

In both years the first trial format to be introduced was the exhibition. This is a well-established format for a project review, and had been planned before the trials began. The planning and observation of early reviews were not as consistent as desirable because of time pressures. Later stages of the trial process were better planned and more systematic—the final exhibition for the second-year urban project being prepared well in advance and students being fully briefed on the format. This was generally successful, with staff spending half a day reviewing the exhibited work privately, and then holding short sessions with the individual students. A tendency was observed, however, for the individual sessions to revert to the conventional project review format. It was clear that, over time, both students and staff had developed certain patterns of interaction in the project review. Even with a clear and explicit intention to do so, it proved difficult to shake off or modify such well-established habits. The lesson learned was that if any alternative practice was to be effective, it needed to be put in place from year one.

Talk

The talk format was also implemented in both years, using the overhead projector as the presentation medium. In first year, initial research findings were presented by small groups of students. All members of the group were expected to speak, but with a time limit of two minutes for each student. The students responded well to presenting as a group, with good graphical coordination and group self-management, but presented large quantities of factual information that left little time for interpretation or commentary. As had been the objective of this trial situation, comments by the staff focused on the presentation process rather than content. This exercise highlighted the difficulty of treating content, commentary and communication techniques as discrete elements for review.

The second-year students, in groups of eight, presented an analysis and interpretation of their initial site studies, together with a study of the urban design context of the site. The presentation had been immediately preceded by a workshop on the skills of summarising and techniques of analysis. The intention was to encourage students to reflect on the essentially descriptive exercises they had undertaken on the site and in the studio, and to interpret the meaning and relevance of the material in the context of the project. Most groups responded to this challenge, producing effective summaries of key findings and conclusions. However some found it difficult to go beyond the limitations of the original descriptive task. The student groups were allowed to determine the format of their presentations. Some elected a group spokesperson, others chose to speak as individuals. The exercise exposed those groups that lacked coherence and common purpose, as well as a few students who resented being asked to do more on something they thought they had completed.

Meeting

The second-year students presented their conceptual ideas in the meeting format at the second interim review stage. The intention here was to promote effective cross-learning and encourage students to take more responsibility for each other's progress. Each student, as part of a group of six to ten, firstly made a three-minute presentation of their work to date, and then stated the areas of feedback they would like to see covered with regard to their work. The issues were then prioritised according to the number of students requesting each item, together with other issues added by the tutor, and an agenda was compiled on a flip chart. The selected items were then discussed across all projects and all students were encouraged to participate, although not all of them did so.

This trial highlighted the need to look in depth at how students, particularly those from non-UK cultures, can be encouraged to contribute their views in discussion when the very basis of such an approach can be unfamiliar and uncomfortable due to cultural differences and language difficulties.

Selective

The selective review format was employed in the second-year project at the sketch scheme stage. This is an established project review format in the LSA and, in practice, tends to mean a conventional review followed by selective reference to particular students' work in a summing-up session. The reviews were conducted in three parallel sessions, each run by a design tutor working alongside a visiting practitioner. The objectives and format of the review had been clearly documented and circulated in advance, and the tutors provided with a pro forma listing the issues to be considered. However, in spite of this thorough and careful preparation, the presence of the visiting practitioners tended to shift the review back to the conventional style, with some loss of focus and structure.

A crucial lesson coming from this was the vital need fully to brief visiting practitioners in the process and objectives of the review—to agree roles and responsibilities so that the expectations of students and critics alike were reflected in the reality of the event.

Computer

In this trial the first-year students presented a project directly from a computer, using a data projector. The project was designed to introduce them to a range of computer programmes—Autocad as a basis for 2D and 3D drawing; 3D Studio for rendering; and PageMaker for the presentation itself—in three consecutive weekly lab sessions. This was highly ambitious for a first-year project, but most students adapted readily to computer-based presentation and demonstrated a remarkable degree of skill. The standards of graphical presentation were high, with effective page layout and composition. In the process the students had become aware of the demands of computer presentation—difficulties encountered included students failing to finish their PageMaker presentations and technical problems during the review itself. For the staff, the trial showed the need for them to be adequately briefed and trained in the software and hardware. It was clear that there was still considerable work to be done in future years to maximise the potential of computer presentation.

Conclusions

These trials of alternative design project reviews initiated a process of gradual change in the Leicester LSA of Architecture. The staff recognise the inertia within the conventional format of the project review, and generally accept the criticisms in and findings of Wilkin's study. There is a raised awareness of client and user issues through the pervasive presence of the CUDE project in the LSA, and, more generally, a heightened awareness of the importance of explicit educational objectives and outcomes. The common purpose of all the trial review formats had been to bring normally implicit learning intentions to the surface, where they could be scrutinised and debated, made clearer to students and developed. The trials showed that explicit skilling objectives can be built into the project review, and that students' communication skills can be noticeably improved. There is a clear need to develop a programme of reviews over the period of the undergraduate course that builds on early established good practice. This could mean greater concentration on the skills of communication, summarising, groupwork and analysis in the first year. The specific workshops in these areas to date have been welcomed by students.

At the LSA we have demonstrated to ourselves that project reviews can indeed be improved, and can become a more positive learning experience for students and staff. The trials confirmed that smaller groups are a more effective forum for student learning—an issue identified in Wilkin's report. They also showed the need for further clarification of whether the objective of a review is assessment or learning opportunity. Whilst not incompatible, these two objectives have differing implications. For instance interim reviews that, in the absence of clarification, may appear to students to be assessable, will lead to the students focusing on that as an end result (the mark or grade awarded) rather than on the learning that takes place.

There are, of course, some costs to be offset against the trials' benefits. In particular the time pressures, large student numbers and the need for high-quality personalised teaching through the review need to be reconciled. Some of the review formats described above have required tutor time to be redirected. Effective project reviews necessitate additional planning and organisation, with a clear specification of the process, objectives and outcomes. The staff involved in the reviews, including visiting practitioners and critics, have to be fully briefed in advance. This all involves leadership and consensus building in a context of some disagreement, where not all tutors will agree that the traditional way of running a project review needs to be altered. Finally, there has to be effective feedback on the review process from staff and students, contributing to continuous development.

Note

1   The members of staff involved in the developments described in this paper were Tony Archibold, Mike Ashley, Sahap Cakin, Charles Doidge, George Henderson, John Lee, Mel Richardson and Richard Short. The external advisors were Angela Fisher, Simon Pilling and Margaret Wilkin.

Reference

Wilkin, M. (1999) 'Reassessing the design project review in undergraduate architectural education with particular reference to clients and users'. Obtainable from The Secretary, the School of Architecture, De Montfort University, Leicester.

Section 2

Collaboration

Developing teamworking skills for
professional practice

The chapters in Section 2 focus on developing teamworking skills in students. Design in practice is a participative activity: architects need skills not only to work with other architects in practice but also to work with other built-environment professionals to provide clients with a cost-effective and integrated service. All but one chapter in this section (Chapter 21) describe and discuss ways in which schools might equip students with the teamworking skills necessary for professional practice.

Rüedi (Chapter 12) describes a community project in which students of architecture and planning worked together on a strategic plan and detailed designs for commercial development, housing and transport in a poor neighborhood in Chicago. Through the project the students became aware of the skills in each discipline in relation to design and of their interrelationship in design. Howes (Chapter 13) describes a series of experimental design projects in which students from different built-environment disciplines worked together as multidisciplinary teams using information technology. One of the aims of these projects was to identify how breakdowns in communication across the disciplines occur during the design process. Fisher (Chapter 14) describes a series of workshops that were designed to improve interpersonal skills in students as a preparation for professional practice. She explains and gives examples of how to organise and sequence skills development and how to encourage students to reflect on and review the effectiveness of these skills in use. This chapter provides valuable advice for those in schools who wish to provide students with structured support for the development of both communication and interprofessional skills.

The next two chapters move beyond local changes in design studio practice and describe whole courses (centred on design projects) that were specifically created to teach students learn how to work in teams with people from other construction disciplines. Manley and Claydon (Chapter 15) describe the development of a joint degree course in Architecture and Planning at the University of the West of England.

This course not only gives weight to teamworking and project design, but is also organised to enable students to become more independent as they progress. Howieson (Chapter 16) describes a degree-level course entitled 'Building Design Engineering', developed at the University of Strathclyde in 1988. Students from architecture and engineering (structural and environmental) follow a common programme for two years in a studio-based environment before entering their vocational stream. The course emphasises design ability, interprofessional respect and communication, and cross-disciplinary knowledge. Many issues are discussed that might be of interest to others considering similar developments.

The last chapter in this section, by Wood (Chapter 17), is based on interviews with senior academics from a range of built-environment disciplines about their attitudes towards interdisciplinary working and learning. He discusses the differences in opinions that emerged in respect of the course structures and teaching methods appropriate to the development of interprofessional skills; and he explores the perceived barriers in schools of architecture to the development of these skills.

12 Habits and habitats

Interdisciplinary collaboration in a community architecture studio

Katerina Rüedi

Introduction

Most architectural educators see community architecture as unglamorous. It is often associated with a 'do-gooding' attitude, conservative design solutions and student paralysis in the face of seemingly overwhelming political issues. In the UK it hardly figures in design-conscious architecture schools in 'cool Britannia'. However in the USA the devolution of the social contract from the (no longer) 'welfare' state to secondary state institutions, such as universities, foundations and non-profit agencies, has meant that 'architectural advocacy' (as community architecture is termed here) is moving back into the architectural curriculum across the nation.

Community design centres, many of them in universities and serving local populations, used to be fairly common in the 1960s, numbering close to 200. Now, after two or three fallow decades, they are beginning to make a mark once again. At the Rural Studio, led by Sam Mockbee in Auburn, Alabama, a professor and students work their way through from scheme design to the actual construction of individual buildings. At the University of Illinois at Chicago (UIC), the College of Architecture and the Arts and the College of Urban Planning and Public Affairs jointly support the City Design Centre (CDC). This is a multidisciplinary research, education and service programme to promote the study and practice of architecture in the public interest and provide architecture and planning advocacy. In a university with a strong commitment to urban outreach, and operating in a city with a powerful minority vote and some of the worst housing in the USA, the growth of the CDC reflects the political agenda and real needs within and outside its academic home. For a number of years the CDC has been running a community architecture design studio called CityLab, funded by the US Department of Housing and Urban Development.

The CityLab studio

On taking up the directorship of the School of Architecture, University of Illinois, in January 1997 I felt it important to find ways of teaching design that would involve a shared visual language between architects, clients and professionals in related disciplines. There was a need to deny the falsely dichotomous stereotypes of 'high' and 'low', architecture and building, good taste and kitsch, aesthetics and politics. The CityLab design studio served an under-represented client group, worked to a realistic brief and a tight time frame, and was interdisciplinary—architecture and planning students being taught jointly by architecture and planning professors. The opportunities for examining and crossing the boundaries of class, race, professions, disciplines and aesthetics were all there.

The CityLab project in autumn 1998 (the semester of my participation) was to be the production of a strategic plan and detailed architectural designs for the district of Pilsen—the biggest Latino neighbourhood in Chicago. The client, a coalition of two Latino community organisations, needed proposals to strengthen the identity of their lively but poor neighbourhood and thus provide a focus for fundraising and political consciousness raising. In the client's view, Pilsen should become a 'community of choice'—a place where second-generation Latinos would choose to stay, rather than moving out to industrial suburbs for work, or to middle-class suburbs for better housing and education.

There were many political issues associated with this agenda that affected the work of the studio:

- Just to the north of Pilsen, the university was developing plans for a new campus, including market-rate housing. This led to a real fear of gentrification in Pilsen.
- Pilsen had long been a focus of many planning and sociological studies. There was some weariness about yet another survey/unrealised proposal.
- The neighbourhood had different constituencies—new (and sometimes illegal) rural immigrants were moving in, while assimilated second-generation Latinos were moving out.
- Despite being poor, Pilsen was powerful—the Latino vote forms the biggest minority bloc in the city and Pilsen is its heart.

Good relations between the studio and the client were going to be vital. To achieve results it was felt that, broadly, the studio had to cross two specific types of boundary: boundaries generated by 'habits', which divided the architect from the planner and one student from another; and those generated by habitats, which divided the largely white American middle-class urban intellectuals in the studio from the largely rural Latino blue-collar and service industry workers who were the broader client body.

Habits: the role of the stereotype

The studio had twenty students—twelve from architecture and eight from planning. The teaching team consisted of four full-time professors (two each from architecture and planning), a community coordinator and a regular Latino architectural guest critic. It took some time for this large group to agree to the teaching programme.

The first questions we asked ourselves concerned working methods:

- What teaching methods would bridge the gap between planners and architects?
- How should we teach planners visual narrative, composition and spatial awareness, using techniques that architects and planners could handle with equal confidence? Similarly, how should we teach architects the analysis of activity in time, data research and gathering and report writing?
- When should the students work separately and when together?

We agreed that planners and architects both routinely use combinations of image and text to communicate. Architects use these to develop compositional and spatial awareness, planners to develop temporal and narrative awareness. We therefore looked for image/text combinations that both groups could understand and use. In dealing with narrative, composition and time we singled out the newspaper 'weather map' and the 'cookery book' as image/text models that would be familiar to both groups of students and the client. We reckoned that if the images and narrative in the final report to the client could provide architectural 'pictures and recipes' for their neighbourhood, then client, architect and planner should be able to understand and use it. The 'weather map' would be used to explain to both sets of students the graphic representation of change over time.

Studio work in this framework successfully broke the ice. Students worked together, tutoring each other but producing individual work. In week one we asked each of them to use a collaged narrative sequence to represent the Pilsen neighbourhood. Perceptive and well-presented work came from both groups. In week two we asked for a spatial/narrative representation of the neighbourhood. This too proved successful. Week three consisted of building the site model. Here the architecture students did most of the work, the planning students being unused to Exacto knives (the US equivalent of scalpels) and scale rules. Week four shifted to traditional planning issues—the history of the neighbourhood, economic development, traffic flow, income levels, patterns of property ownership and so on. The architects and planners did equally well here too, although the planners were much better at finding and accessing sources of information. Generally, the architecture students then used the information with greater visual impact for quicker understanding, whereas the planning students were more expansive in the information presented.

However by this time the planning students were getting very nervous. Privately they were asking their professors when they were going to start the 'real' planning work. Why did they have to wait so long? The architecture students, used to aesthetic exploration, were less concerned—they were not yet working against stereotype, although they too wanted to get on with 'their' design work.

HABITATS: 'high Latino'

Design did not begin until week five, when work began on an interim proposal that was to be presented to the client in week nine of the sixteen-week semester. For this work the studio was split into two groups of ten students, with planners and architects in each group. It quickly became clear that it was hard for such large groups to establish visual and textual consistency within the short time frame. In response, one of the architecture professors improvised by allocating the work of a Latino architect as a model for each group: that of Louis Barragan and Ricardo Legorreta, respectively. This 'off-the-cuff' decision helped with the interim presentation, and it was only afterwards that we found out from the students just how stressful this period had been, working so quickly without knowing each other's strengths.

Nevertheless, at the interim review the work was remarkably clear and coherent. The Barragan group made a strong presentation that became known as 'the football stadium project'. The group proposed a new football stadium as an economic magnet for the neighbourhood, and had found a Chicago football team with the funds required to acquire the land. However, to our dismay the football stadium turned out to be a real problem for the clients. It became clear that, sited on largely derelict land zoned for industrial use, a stadium threatened to alienate the largely blue-collar constituency of both community groups because, amongst other things, it would symbolise the actual and progressive loss of blue-collar jobs in the area. The students, who were very excited about the proposal, were begged by the client representatives to remove the stadium from the presentation in order to avoid embarrassment with their constituency.

In fact 'high Latino'—to us implicit in the concept of 'a community of choice', as represented by university investment in the neighbourhood, intuitively embodied in Barragan and Legorreta and now reinforced by the students' ideas—was generating great unease.

The real needs of our clients were far less glamorous: to make small-scale commercial activity more economically viable through the provision of more on-street parking, indoor car parks, better streetscape and shop signs, and visual markers identifying the community. The planning students were indeed aware of the centrality of parking in US urban development, but for the architects this was a very unromantic lesson. Moreover, since both groups of students were 100 per cent behind the football stadium, and generally less excited about parking, there was a significant loss of morale after the interim review.

Political sensitivity

A further political hot potato emerged a little later. Just north of the project's boundary was the south end of a new campus area, to be called South Campus, which was being designed as our work was proceeding. The university, in an effort to make its limited public funds go as far as possible, had enlisted the help of the city and a private developer as partner to make its plans financially feasible. Funded by major tax-incentive legislation and a large area of market-rate housing, the proposal involved the demolition of existing buildings along Maxwell Street, where a much loved market had been in operation for decades.

In many ways this was a smaller-scale re-enactment of the first university development in the 1960s, which had involved the displacement of a significant section of Chicago's Italian community and had not been forgotten by the media. The Pilsen community's fear of gentrification, resistance to the redevelopment of Maxwell Street and the long memory of the university's first engagement with its neighbourhood led to the university having an understandable sense of caution in sharing information about the South Campus project. Therefore not only were our clients therefore uneasy about our proposals, but so also was the university.

After the interim review the architecture students moved on to the design of visual markers that the client called 'gateways'. A small group of architecture students decided that prominent buildings would make the best markers. One selected a tall warehouse building owned by the university just beyond the northern edge of our project area to work on as a gateway. His search for existing plans led to a call from the university querying the precise boundary of our study and a concern that information about university property might fall into the wrong hands. As the student had strayed beyond the contractual edge of the project and into a politically unresolved debate, he had to look for another site.

As a result, student morale went down still further. Professors also differed on the issue. Those in planning were more pragmatic than the architects—the former trying to expose and deny the autonomy of the academy, the latter trying to maintain it as academic freedom. Whichever position we took up, we—the professors—had egg on our face for not spotting this problem within our own institution in advance.

The Final proposals

The students worked extremely hard in the last four weeks to produce an exhibition for the final review, to be held in a Pilsen meeting space: an old church. The final presentation to the community included all the elements that the client had asked for in their initial brief—a strategic report outlining the main issues of commercial development, housing and transport. The timeline included the historical development and future prognoses for the area. The individual projects included a central plaza with a market, cafe and health centre, several smaller plazas and the conversion of several existing buildings—one becoming a Latino Heritage Centre, two others artists' studios and another consisting of work units. The projects also included improved parking designs, street sculptures as gateway markers, and a new park on disused railway land acting as the northern gateway. The last project in particular had real formal, symbolic and social merit.

Despite a few rogues on both sides, communication between the architecture and planning students in the final phase was impressive. The planners, impressively articulate as public speakers, introduced the 'strategy' and report, after which the architects described their individual projects. The clients claimed to be impressed by the professionalism of the presentation (the stadium was gone). However, as not many of their grass-roots members attended and saw the work, it is hard to say whether they were simply being kind. We, the professors, were pleased with the breadth of the work. However, as in previous CityLab studios, and with a few notable exceptions, the design quality was average, largely due to the time constraints. I was therefore personally disappointed, as were a number of students who knew they could do a lot better.

What lessons did we learn?

Reviewing the overall project, the first lesson we learnt was that in a teaching structure already involving two clients and a number of visiting critics, there had been too many academic staff. Despite a relatively clear outline brief from the client, it had not always been easy for all the professors to understand or follow the agreed format. We clearly had a case of 'too may cooks'—some being 'ad-hocists' and others 'organisers', some 'heroes' and others 'compromisers'. This dichotomy had led to changes in the timetable and policy, which had frustrated the students. The irony of opening up boundaries in an academic setting was that it needed tight leadership.

Secondly, too much emphasis had been put on visual exploration at the beginning of the studio. The content and sequence of the exercises had privileged the architects, and had delayed the gathering of important information, which in turn had delayed the start of the design phase. The planners had not had enough information to give to the architects and *vice versa*. In fact the first two weeks of the semester could have contained the work of the first four, with each student learning the skills of the other discipline at the same time as developing existing ones. The device of the 'cookery book' and 'weather map' had not really worked. The collages and the mutual tutoring, however, had been a real success. (A year later, I am told, some of the planning students, having graduated, were using collage as part of their professional work.)

The structure and difficulties of collaboration had not been adequately and clearly explained to the students. While we had provided a structure for producing work, we had left them to organise themselves within it—a process that had proved remarkably stressful for them. Although collaboration had not been a pleasure for them, they had done a good job and my respect for their ability had grown over time. We, the professors, should have at least warned them that collaboration is never easy, and that it is difficult to design a coherent structure for it in advance without knowing the personalities and skills of the students. The positive lesson, however, was that a genuine respect had developed amongst the students for each other's discipline—the architects had been impressed by the focused way in which the planning students had gathered knowledge, while the planners had been impressed by the architects' dedication to their work (in particular the studio culture and the all-nighters).

Not enough time had been allowed for the creation of a feedback loop for integrating architectural and planning knowledge. The students had needed strong aesthetic, technical, intellectual and professional skills to handle the complexity and irregularity of information. These take time to acquire. If the design studio is for the traditional 'twenty-something' student it needs a lot of time for design, with well-timed feedback from the client, students and the teaching team. If, however, the studio is for mature professionals who have background knowledge of the issues, then a looser structure may work.

Finally, and most importantly, a close and open relationship with the client is central to the success of the project. This is obvious, but hard to achieve. Client relationships grow over time, and depend on individual personality as well as collective commitment. In the case of the Pilsen studio, the two community leaders already had a well-established relationship with the City Design Center, yet their lack of real involvement in the specific studio eventually became a problem. With hindsight, this should not have been a surprise. As the studio provided free design services, the clients had not been under pressure to get maximum productivity out of the meetings. Equally, since they had had no great say in the content of the studio's work their sense of involvement had lessened. A less powerful and busy community client might, ironically, have been more successful in this scenario.

One additional issue came up after the final presentation, and has apparently come up repeatedly in other CityLab studios. Concern had grown in the community, especially among the property owners whose sites the students had proposed to redevelop. As a result we were asked to change the final report, and in particular not to give the names or descriptions of the particular properties involved. In hindsight it is understandable that this type of nervousness should occur when the larger body of the community has not participated in the design process and hence has not been given a chance to 'own' the redevelopment schemes. The democratic process cannot fully come to fruition in the partially 'artificial' setting of an academic design project, which lacks the financial incentive for full commitment and participation by all parties.

Conclusion

Was the client well-served by the work of the students? Were the students well-served by the studio experience? What did the teaching team get out of the collaboration? The answers are difficult to evaluate. We did not organise a formal feedback process from the client, so can only go by the appreciation expressed in the final review. However we did issue a long anonymous questionnaire to the students. The feedback was pretty damning. Disorganisation among the professors was the main criticism—the 'too many cooks' factor—but inadequate preparation, too many exercises in the beginning and insufficient client commitment were also cited.

Speaking personally, I was humbled by the experience. I learned an enormous amount about group dynamics, negotiation and leadership. I also came to appreciate the extent of preparation necessary to run a community architecture studio, and sadly acknowledged that, as the director of the school, I did not have that kind of time. Nevertheless, and most importantly, I was very glad to have worked with my planning colleagues, whom I found highly intellectually stimulating, creative and sensitive to group dynamics. The trust that developed between us is still there.

Postscript

There was a final and very positive outcome. At the end of that year the school was fortunate to obtain, jointly with Washington University, a two-year grant from the Graham Foundation to develop a curriculum in advocacy architecture, the first of its kind in a US school to join planners and architects across two universities in a joint educational community design programme. At the time of writing (1999) the pilot studio is running and will be followed by a collaborative theory course, culminating in a symposium in 2000 on issues of advocacy architecture and urbanism.

Notes

The work of the 1998 studio is presented on the web at http://www. uic.edu/aa/cdc/citylab98/homepage.html. I would like to thank Dr Roberta Feldman for her comments on some of the content of this chapter, but emphasise that the views expressed are entirely my own.

13 Is working together working?

Jaki Howes

Background

Teamworking and collaboration have been buzz-words in the construction industry for several years. But where is the evidence of their application in education?

Leeds Metropolitan University (LMU) is one of the few academic institutions in the UK where the full range of design and construction disciplines is taught. Peculiarly, the Schools of Art, Architecture and Design (AAD) and the School of the Built Environment are both in the Faculty of Health and Environment. In addition, the disciplines of architecture, landscape architecture, interior design, construction and project management, building surveying, quantity surveying, civil and structural engineering, and urban planning all occupy the same building.

The built environment courses have a common modular framework, and students from all the disciplines are taught together. However, despite a great deal of commonality in the taught material, the AAD courses have neither a common framework nor common teaching with the built environment courses. This may stem from a disastrous foray into common teaching in the 1980s, from which there still remains some covert animosity between staff who were there at the time. Simply stated, architects are thought of as elitist and 'arty-farty', and builders, at best, as non-academic. This attitude is reinforced by the fact that the AAD courses have higher entry standards and are oversubscribed.

Context

One of the themes of the conference on Education in Computer Aided Architectural Design in Europe, held in Vienna in September 1997, was collaborative teamwork. However it was clear from the papers that the intended collaboration was between schools of architecture, and that the teams referred to were generally composed of architects—no other professional disciplines and no building industry. Later that year the Construction Industry Computer Association (CICA) annual convention took place in Cambridge. That event, by contrast, was dominated by information technology (IT) managers, engineers and contractors, with only a small handful of architects and an even smaller number of academics. The topics included object-oriented modelling, international data standards, a common building model, single intranets for all project partners, industry standards and new ways of working. The underlying message that came across was that academia was thought to be well behind, and unaware of, what was happening at the cutting edge of the industry.

Finally, at the Construction Industry Council (CIC) Heads of Courses conference in January 1998, keynote speakers had made clear that, in their opinion, adversarial professional attitudes, 'inculcated by single discipline staff in higher education', were a major cause of non-collaboration in the building industry.

The TIME IT project

The TIME IT project (Team-working in Multidisciplinary Environments using Information Technology) was set up to look at this range of issues. It was to be an experiment in multidisciplinary working that would attempt to mimic what was happening in industry, and would be based on the use of IT. Research funding and industrial support was to be sought for the programme—where final-year students from architecture, quantity surveying, civil engineering and construction/ project management would work in teams of four, on real projects that were being carried out in industry. Students would not be told how to work, would not be 'taught' anything, rather they would be encouraged to work as much as possible using IT, and would be closely monitored.

Potential industry collaborators were approached and, surprisingly quickly, five internationally known firms became committed to the proposal—two commercial architectural practices, a contractor, a firm of quantity surveyors and project managers, and a bank. (The two architectural collaborators already worked exclusively with CAD, the quantity surveyors, project managers and contractors did not.) There was also an offer of university accommodation for a dedicated laboratory; and hardware and software, to the specification used by both the architectural collaborators, had been promised by external suppliers. A member of staff from quantity surveying, who had attended the Cambridge Interdisciplinary Design in the Built Environment Master of Studies course (IDBE), became a natural ally on the project, and it proved not difficult to find like-minded staff in civil engineering and construction management. The collaborators and the staff then held monthly meetings to devise suitable projects and prepare material.

Since the project could be seen both as a 'research' project—where students were being used as 'guinea pigs'—and as a 'teaching' project, the aims were wide-ranging. Additionally, we were not sure what would be measurable, how the variables could be controlled or how the project could be monitored until it was running. At the outset, the aims of the project were to:

- Examine the efficacy of teamworking as experiential learning.
- Identify where the non-use or inappropriate use of available IT tools forms a barrier to effective teamworking.
- Identify the potential of IT to contribute to close integration between briefing, design and construction.
- Identify the opportunities for and barriers to IT-supported inter-disciplinary working.
- Develop and test ways of exploiting IT to improve communication and collaboration between clients, design team members from different background disciplines, and contractors.
- Monitor the quality of the product.

Testing professional attitudes

Firstly, seeking to test the assertion from the CIC regarding adverserial attitudes, TIME IT selected ten students from each of the five years in architecture, and each of the three years in quantity surveying and construction management to take part in an attitude survey. Each was asked to rate, on a scale of one to five, how closely they felt various descriptions fitted themselves and the other two disciplines. The adjectives used were practical, logical, realistic, methodical, personable, creative, intelligent, imaginative, forthright, rude, uncaring and woolly.

We were surprised to find that students, most noticeably quantity surveyors, seemed to arrive in their first year with fixed opinions but that the strength of these opinions tended to diminish as students gained more experience. The areas of consensus were that architects were the most creative, intelligent and imaginative; construction managers were the most practical and realistic; and quantity surveyors were the most logical and methodical. Architects and construction managers were mildly personable; quantity surveyors were not—except to other quantity surveyors. Forthrightness was rated more or less the same for all three disciplines (just over 3 on the 1–5 scale). Rudeness, uncaringness and woolliness were rated low by all groups of students about all professions.

This suggests that the problem of adversarial attitude is not engendered in further or higher education, nor in initial industrial experience (the more senior students having already spent time in practice), but that students do enter courses with preconceived ideas of their own and other's professional identity.

Logistics

By October 1998 a dedicated IT suite had been set up to the same specification as that used by both architectural practices. The server was to be administered by the IT managers of the practices, and supported a network of four workstations—one per student group. Initially the only software supplied was AutoCad R14, 3D Studio Viz and AEC. However we had secured additional external funding for further software to be provided when students found they needed it. We have since added Office 97, CA SuperProject 4.0 and Photoshop. Despite all exhortations not to use paper, the students found that a plotter and a colour printer were essential to internal communications between groups. To some extent it might also have been because, for security reasons, the students did not have physical access to the server, nor access to e-mail or any external network services via the server. The IT suite was to be unsupervised.

Four teams of four students from the final years of each discipline were asked to work together on the project for one day a week. Anticipating difficulties with assessment and perceived fairness, it was decided that the students, apart from the civil engineers, should not be assessed on the quality of the outcome—the 'product'—but on their ability to monitor and assess the process. The evaluation of the process would become the dissertation subject for the construction managers and quantity surveyors, the interdisciplinary option for the project managers, the special study for second-year graduate diploma architects and the option for the first-year graduate diploma architects.

The projects

The first project, devised by the contractor, was based on a recently completed housing scheme. The students were provided with a site plan in electronic form and 'woolly' architect's plans of the house types required. They were to work on the project for one day a week over five weeks, and produce brochures that would contain layouts and perspectives of the scheme, costing analysis, full design and construction schedules, including calculations for the roads and drainage. The proposals were to be evaluated and compared against the 'real' solution in terms of quality of design and value for money.

The second project was to design a pedestrian bridge over an urban motorway as a landmark for the bank. Again, this would last five working days, during which time the teams had to produce a PowerPoint presentation with full visualisation, calculations, costs and construction schedules.

The third, three-day, project was for the commercial development of a brownfield site in Leeds, again with a final PowerPoint presentation.

The fourth, seven-day, project, which took place in the second semester, was to convert an eighteenth-century building from a restaurant to a health club with swimming pool. For this project the teams were changed and a completely new set of architecture students—drawn from the first year of the graduate diploma—came in. The built environment students could, however, choose to stay on if they wished. In the event, three out of four of the quantity surveyors and civil engineers stayed. Only one construction manager remained. Three new project managers joined. No student was allowed to remain in the same group as anyone with whom they had worked before, and the students were encouraged to work outside their professional roles.

The final project was to design a flat-packed dwelling that could be manufactured in Leeds and used in a wide range of climates for relief housing. The work was to be a set of non-verbal assembly instructions, which were to be deposited on the server for assessment by the architectural collaborators, and an electronic report on logistics and cost.

Evaluation and feedback

At the end of each working day the students were asked to fill in a questionnaire that monitored their attitude towards professional roles and the relative contribution of team members: who had done what, and how they had used IT. There were also feedback meetings with the collaborators and staff.

Teamwork and attitudes

In the first project, in three out of the four teams the construction managers had taken the lead. The architecture students felt hampered by this, one commenting that 'if this is what it's going to be like in practice I don't want to be an architect'. The construction managers felt they 'knew' about housing because they had done it in practice. The students had become highly competitive within each team and produced far more 'work' than had been expected.

In the second project (the bridge), the intensity of the competition increased further and discord set in. The architects 'ganged up' with the civil engineers, united in their opinion that quantity surveyors were unimaginative, boring and superfluous—'if it's not in Spons they don't want to know'. The construction managers kept their heads down—they knew less about bridges than housing. Despite threats of homicide and retribution during the project, all the teams managed to present a picture of harmony, confidence and competence to the collaborators and staff at the final presentation—'It is amazing how the presence of external people sharpens presentation skills.'

For the third project (the commerical redevelopment), the quantity surveyors were instructed to take the lead. They found this difficult and waited for ideas from the architects. For their part the architects had difficulty proposing 'realistic' ideas. The final presentations were considered to be 'slick and professional' and commercially realistic. But the quality of the architecture was mediocre, and for the first time in the overall programme the graduate diploma course leader expressed concern that the work of the architecture students was not of an appropriate standard for the course.

The change of teams in the second semester was beneficial. The self-selected new students knew what to expect. Also, Higher National Diploma (HND) building services engineering students from Leeds College of Building had become involved in the project. These were 'mature' part-time students. Two were allocated to each team to act as consultants. However the LMU students felt that their contribution had been minimal since the engineers were not prepared to make suggestions, only to make corrections. At the interim presentation the staff and collaborators were impressed by the professionalism of the delivery—the PowerPoint presentations and two of the animations were considered excellent. However, by the final presentation the students were struggling to overcome technical difficulties caused by the huge files that architectural 'walk throughs' generate.

For the final project the timescale was so short that students had to undertake tasks that were usually carried out by other disciplines. Professional roles dissolved. It was a frenzy of activity and one computer for each team was not enough. The computer became the drawing board, note book and meeting room. As designed, there was no 'verbal' presentation to the collaborators—the files being left on the server for 'remote' evaluation by the architectural collaborators. Feedback confirmed that both students and collaborators had missed the excitement and 'buzz' of face-to-face working. In the end the work produced proved to be overcomplicated, lacked the hoped for 'invention' and had to be printed out to be understood—thus defeating a primary object of the exercise.

Presentation/communication

Over the course of programme the improvement in self-confidence, understanding and verbal presentation skills, particularly among the built environment students, was remarkable, as was the improvement in the inventive use of IT.

Leadership

The range of projects had been devised such that if the students maintained their professional roles there would be an opportunity for each discipline to become a leader, but in practice this did not happen. Student feedback suggested a belief that leadership is 'more to do with personality than profession'. In general the architects felt that, given time, they could do everything, though they would need to 'brush up their structures'. The project managers and the civil engineers thought they could do everything, but might need an imaginative idea from an architect. The quantity surveyors clearly considered themselves as financial advisors and business people. Teamworking and leadership is being reexamined.

Assessment

Apart from those from civil engineering, the students were not assessed on the outcomes but on their ability to monitor and assess the process, which became the subject for their dissertation. This work is still in progress so it is not yet possible to evaluate the success of this approach.

Quality

All the external collaborators were impressed by the quality of the work produced. (Although neither of the representatives from the architectural practices were architects—one was an IT manager and the other a quality manager—both had considerable experience of commercially successful design.) The architecture tutors, however, were not impressed. They felt that, at best, the buildings produced had been 'polite but boring'.

On the other hand, the 'service' to the imaginary client had been comprehensive—certainly in excess of a typical architectural diploma scheme, for instance there was a PowerPoint presentation (including a 3D animated model of the proposed building), a design and construction schedule, a full set of structural calculations, and predictions of costs both in development and use.

This cannot be dismissed as an issue of quantity versus quality, but goes to the heart of the thorny question 'what is a good quality building design and who are the arbiters?'

Resourcing

The overall programme was expensive in terms of time. Five members of full-time staff—an architect, a construction manager, a project manager, a quantity surveyor and a structural engineer—committed at least three hours a week. In addition, each of the five industrial collaborators ran a project, spent a day in initial preparation and final review, and attended regular planning meetings. That is a lot of time input for 25 students.

For this first experiment all the students had volunteered. The groups included 'high achievers' from the built environment courses, whereas the architects were not considered to be high-fliers in design, but 'realistic and competent'. Student feedback suggests that the experience should be extended to all students. However not all students may be so motivated and able, and would require more guidance and tuition than might be available. It is also questionable whether we would be able to assemble enough external collaborators to cope with significantly larger numbers of students—still less complete years. Alternative possibilities are being investigated.

The project's future

The overall experiment will continue until at least 2001, without further external funding. In response to the graduate diploma architecture staff's concern that the level of architectural design was not of graduate diploma quality, the future intake will be year-three degree architects—the work forming their 'additional curriculum' module. It will be interesting to see how they react, because unlike the graduate school students they have not had a year out in the 'real world'. Built environment students will undertake the work as their interdisciplinary module.

All places for the 1999/2000 session of the project were taken up three months in advance, but it was not oversubscribed. This implies, but certainly does not prove, that less than 10 per cent of students in all the disciplines are prepared to step outside their perceived roles.

The nature of the individual projects has been altered. There will now be two four-working-day projects in each semester: the housing and the relief housing in the first semester, and the bridge and the refit in the second semester, limited to sixteen students at a time.

Measures of success

As this chapter has described work in progress, there are no conclusions and a number of questions remain to be answered:

As a process:

- Is it a successful educational exercise? (We believe yes, but it is certainly resource-intensive.)
- Is it role-playing or gaming? (We would suggest it is neither—it is a competition.)
- Is it feasible to extend the exercise to all students? (Very difficult.)
- Is it a model for successful practice?
- Is the way in which students chose to use IT significant for practice?

Is the product:

- Better than would be expected from students working in a traditional way?
- Comparable with work in practice?

Overall:

- Who would be advantaged by the adoption of this method of working?
- Who are the arbiters of the quality of the product?

Of these, we believe that the most important and strategic question is 'What is meant by quality in design?' and that this must be rigorously addressed before we can, with any confidence, make fundamental changes to architectural education.

14 Developing skills with people
A vital part of architectural education

Angela Fisher

Introduction

What skills with people does society want its architects to possess and how can students be helped to develop these skills during their time at university? During the three years of the CUDE project at the Sheffield University School of Architecture, the focus has been on two interconnected areas in the particular context of architecture:

- Skills as communicators.
- Skills as team workers.

Architects' skills as communicators, particularly as verbal communicators, must be founded in attitudes that respect other people's points of view and actively seek their ideas. Architects must be able to listen effectively, recognising and utilising the different ways in which it is possible to listen and the importance of checking they have understood what is said, instead of simply assuming they do. They must know how to develop dialogue around representations of design proposals, acknowledging that non-architects may have difficulty reading these. They must have the collaborative skills needed to negotiate options. They need effective and flexible verbal presentation skills, matching what they say and the language they use to the needs and interests of different audiences. Finally, they must be skilled in contemporary communications technology and be aware of the impact of different media on different audiences.

Architects as teamworkers must start from a willingness to work collaboratively with other people, to be equally comfortable as team member or team leader. They need to know something of how teams work and how to contribute in ways that help the team to function most effectively. This includes an awareness that, in addition to our functional role in a team (client, engineer and so on) we have individual preferences as teamworkers—for example some of us prefer to keep the team to task, whilst others like to introduce new ideas and directions. It also includes being aware of, and able to use appropriately, a range of teamwork methods.

Why do these skills matter?

Skills with people are an absolute necessity in professional practice. The practice of architecture is founded on establishing and maintaining good working relationships. Even in the earliest stages of a simple job, the architect has to develop an atmosphere of trust with the client, find ways of eliciting what the client wants and can afford, develop a set of proposals to assist this process of clarification and so on. The use of appropriate language and the ability to engage in one-to-one dialogue are essential skills here. Within the office, young architects have to be competent to work as a member of the office team, capable of taking instructions and checking they have understood what is needed and by when. When one considers the potential complications of the multiprofessional team, the complexity of contractual relationships and the tendency for the unforeseen to happen in construction, it is clear how important it is for practising architects to be both excellent communicators and adept at working with many different people. Yet a series of government and professional studies indicate, amongst other criticisms, that architects are perceived as arrogant, uninterested in the values and requirements of their clients and users and poor at teamworking.

In discussions of architectural education the question is often asked 'To what extent is it the school's responsibility to prepare students for the realities of practice? Isn't that the responsibility of practice itself?' CUDE's belief is that there is a strong relationship between the skills needed to promote effective learning in university and the skills needed in professional life. Current research on learning in higher education demonstrates the importance of the social environment of learning and motivational factors for effective learning. When appropriate group tasks are set as part of the course, students have access to a greatly increased range of ideas. Discussion and shared reflection on what the team is doing leads to extended learning for both the team and the individual. Shared work can increase engagement with the task, which in turn increases individual motivation.

The CUDE project contends that if the schools of architecture introduce and develop these skills as an intrinsic part of the course, then students entering practice are already equipped to learn how to apply them in the professional situation.

Developing skills with people during an architectural education

Many schools already go a long way towards setting up situations in which the need for these skills can be recognised and the skills themselves practised. Most students experience a live project and have access to real clients and users at some stage in their time at university. Team projects form part of each year of the course. Students work with tutors in the studio, with each other in the informal context of the studio and more formally in shared tutorials. They have to present their work to peers and outsiders at regular intervals during the course. Clearly, architectural education provides many opportunities to develop skills in working with people.

However CUDE's evidence is that merely putting students in situations like these, creating the experience and hoping they will learn something from it, is not an effective way to develop skills. It is important to do more, particularly by making the skills explicit. We have identified six conditions that we think need to be met if students are to be helped effectively to learn skills with people. In putting these together we have drawn on current learning theory and the practice of other disciplines. (It is significant that other areas of professional education emphasise these skills: medical students, for instance, can now fail their course if their patient communication skills are assessed as inadequate.)

- Students need to see the skills as relevant, both in their current situation and in the eventual work context. Helping them to see this relevance when they may have little direct experience will require careful explanation on the part of the tutor.
- The skills should be broken down into small sections, introduced sequentially and practised in a workshop environment.
- Skills should be applied in the project situation soon after they have been introduced and initially practised. This is important if students are to retain the skills and adopt them as standard practice.
- Students should regularly review together the effectiveness of the skills learned and be encouraged to develop a personal portfolio of skills. Both are aids to reflection, a necessity for effective long-term learning.
- Students will be helped to develop skills if they see them modelled by tutors.
- The institution should value these skills and acknowledge them in its own working practices.

A further justification for the explicit introduction of these skills into the course comes from a consideration of the previous educational experience of new entrants, who may have had little previous oppor-tunity to develop these skills. Typically in the UK, these students are the high-achieving products of a competitive system, accustomed to individual working and dependent on teachers for their direction and feedback. This suggests that focused work needs to be done in the early stages of the course to develop collaborative and productive ways of working with each other.

Cude's approach

The project started by looking at what tutors were already doing in the two partner schools—Sheffield and De Montfort—to promote awareness in this area. There was clearly an awareness of clients and users, and of the related communication and team skills as important issues. Tutors were experimenting with a range of approaches:

- Getting students to role-play clients and users within a project in order to help them to look at design from other perspectives.
- Bringing in real clients.
- Using student groups to research and expand a written brief.
- Getting students to act as clients for each other.

Both tutors and students reported that although the intentions were right, the achievement of them was sometimes difficult. The CUDE grant allowed us to seek advice and conduct some learning experiments, bearing in mind two constraints emphasised by the design tutors:

- Nothing was to be lost from the course to make way for the development of these skills.
- Any interventions must support the students' design work and contribute to the design projects.

CUDE responded to these requirements in two ways. An educational developer worked with the design tutors to devise ways in which their existing aspirations could be helped to work better, for example through improved briefing and preparation for team tasks. Other members of the CUDE team supported this by devising and testing a series of short workshop inputs that could be run at appropriate stages in a design project to prepare students for the next phase of work.

Cude workshops

A suite of workshops, which could be tailored to fit specific project situations, was devised on teamwork (see Appendix 1) and communication. The workshops have a number of common characteristics:

- They focus on explicit skills, for example devising appropriate questions to put to the users of a particular building.
- There is an emphasis on students' activity rather than tutor inputs. The tutor's role is that of enabler, facilitating the students' activities and getting them to review what they have done.
- The workshops take place during design projects with the aim of moving forward the work on the project, and are timed so that students are able to apply skills quickly as part of their project work—for example a workshop on preparing a presentation of a scheme will be run three or four days before the presentation is to be given.
- Students are asked for brief written feedback after each workshop, in part to reinforce what they have learned and in part to improve the workshop when it is rerun.

Teamwork

CUDE's teamwork workshops have the following aims. Through them, students:

- Develop respect for different contributions and points of view.
- Recognise that as individuals we all have different team role preferences and experiment with how to use these to the benefit of the team.
- Plan how they will work together (instead of just starting), devise team contracts, including guidelines for team behaviour, and agree to work to these for the duration of the team project.
- Try out methods of working together to achieve team tasks: for example, how to generate ideas as a team, how to select ideas to develop, how to resolve possible conflicts, (recognising that there is more than one style of meeting).
- Reflect on the effectiveness of their teamwork through discussion, team journals and project records.

Communication

Communication workshops have also been developed, based on the skills needed at different stages of the communication process—ranging from informal one-to-one interactions through to formal presentations to large mixed audiences. The workshops are designed to help students to:

- Recognise that effective communication involves transmitting and receiving. Both sides of the interaction have to be managed.
- Be aware of the importance of listening, recognising that it is possible to listen in many different ways. Practice active ways of improving listening.
- Devise and ask effective questions, especially in the briefing situation.
- Select the essential information to communicate in a given situation.
- Start by considering the audience in preparing for a presentation and realise the need to use language appropriate to that audience.
- Develop ways of managing presentations that include drawn as well as spoken material.
- Give and receive constructive feedback.

Workshops as part of a design project—an example

This example shows how workshops on teamworking and presentation, devised in collaboration with the design tutors, were utilised in an eight-week design project in the second semester of a first-year architecture course.

An overall CUDE aim for the year was to develop students' teamworking skills. The major project—to design a nursery for preschool children—included the aim of bringing students together with a client, a user and a nursery 'expert' to experience what is involved in developing a brief, and to recognise and practice some of the communication skills involved. The students were required to work in teams to research the brief, with each student taking on a particular role perspective and ensuring this was considered by their colleagues in working up their designs. The students were assessed on the team element of the work through a research document that included a record of what they felt they had learned about teamworking. The students later developed their designs individually and were individually assessed on these.

CUDE ran three workshops during the semester. None lasted longer than two hours.

Preparation for teamwork: planning and group processes

This workshop was run at the beginning of the project and brought the students together in their project teams for the first time. The workshop began with a discussion of what the students had identified as their individual team role preferences from a Belbin-based questionnaire issued before the workshop. The students were then introduced to a method of generating and selecting ideas as a team, and were invited to use these on a task related to the project. The task was to agree what they would collectively research in the brief development stage and make a plan of how to carry out the work and record their findings.

Asking questions and communicating research findings

This workshop, which was run three days before the students met the client representatives, focused on how to ask questions in preparation for meeting the client, user and 'expert' representatives in the brief development stage of the project. The students worked in small groups to devise and practise questions to put to the client representatives. Each student met only one of the client representatives and was required to adopt that role perspective when working with colleagues. The workshop helped the students to plan how to communicate effectively to their colleagues what they had learned from the client meeting.

Presentation preparation and delivery skills

This workshop was run a week before the students presented their work and was in two parts. The first helped the students to identify what they would say during the five-minute presentation of their individual design scheme, and required them to produce a simple story board connecting what they would say with what they would show. The students did this preparation in pairs, listening and paraphrasing each other's summaries. The second part, run by a voice coach, helped the students with breathing and posture, using the opening statements devised in the earlier workshop as a vehicle for practise.

Evaluation

The students have been almost unanimously positive in their responses to the workshops. They clearly value the skills that CUDE is trying to teach and recognise their importance in the world they are preparing themselves to enter. However this attitude is not always shared by the tutors, who sometimes occupy a different (academic) world in which teamworking and communication skills may not have the same importance and emphasis. This has implications for the role model that students perceive within the academic environment, and the further concern that, with increased student numbers and diminishing resources, helping students to develop skills such as these requires the sort of teaching skills that design tutors may not always possess.

Next steps

Collaboration with the design tutors has been an important element of the work and the design tutors have usually corun the workshops with the CUDE team. The workshops have also been run at other UK schools of architecture and it is planned that the design tutors will take over the running of these sessions in later years. In the 1999/2000 session the CUDE team is disseminating the work in five other schools of architecture as a follow-on to the initial three-year project.

The workshops have been written up in the form of tutor guides, examples of which can be found in the appendix to this book. The guides include a script and running order for each workshop, outlining in tabular form what the tutor does, what the students do, time allocations and comments on relevant aspects of teaching and learning. Where relevant, the guides include material for overhead projector slides and notes to issue to students. The intention is that design tutors interested in helping students to develop these skills can run a workshop experimentally, with minimum preparation time, refining or adapting the outlines to fit their own circumstances.

15 Achieving richness and diversity

Combining architecture and planning at UWE, Bristol

Sandra Manley and Jim Claydon

Introduction

It is significant that, in introducing the latest review of architectural education, Stansfield Smith (1998) places greater emphasis on the anxieties facing the architectural profession than the potential opportunities. Construction industry practices are under pressure to change following the recommendations of the Latham and Egan Reports (Latham 1994; DETR 1998). So is higher education, with government strategies to ensure quality through the audit, through the implementation of the Dearing recommendations (NCIHE 1997) and through the Research Assessment Exercise (RAE). Pressure for change is also building from practitioners, and there is mounting public concern about the lack of quality in the built environment.

Such a climate presents an opportunity for educators to examine the nature of the changes that might be required, and to provoke discussion on the issues that should be addressed in responding to professional and public opinion. This chapter seeks to contribute to the debate by describing the experience of developing a new combined course in architecture and planning at the University of the West of England in Bristol (UWE).

Background

During the 1980s there was little government commitment to the importance of design quality as part of the remit of planning. The provisions of Circular 22/80, which exhorted planners to allow the market to determine the quality of design, had far reaching effects. Even when its advice was eclipsed by new guidance (DOE 1992, 1997) its provisions still lingered in the minds of many local authority planners.

This did little to promote the importance of design education for planners or give any incentive to local authorities to employ architects as members of staff. Few local authorities were able to maintain specialist design teams to advise on architectural matters after the reorganisation of local government in 1974, 1985 and 1996. This contributed to a further reduction in the number of architects working in planning teams and, perhaps accordingly, the number of people with a dual qualification in both architecture and planning also declined.

The two professions have moved even further apart. Typically, planning courses now devote relatively little time to design issues and the style of teaching has moved away from studio-based project work.

The combination of lack of design education, lack of design skills and even the lack of the right vocabulary to express design ideas has led to a crisis of confidence among planners in respect of articulating the legitimate demand for higher quality design. The dearth of local authority architects has exacerbated the problem.

The breakdown of communication between the two professions has fuelled longstanding antagonisms (Punter and Carmona 1997). Many architects claim that neither planners nor local councillors are equipped to make design decisions. The absence of quality in many of the built environments that have been granted planning permission could be seen as supporting this belief.

The problem has become ever more acute as greater recognition has been given to the urban design agenda. In recognising the need to fill the gap between architecture and planning, Tibbalds (1988) and many other commentators have also recognised the need for educational developments to address this need.

Origins of the combined course

Our starting point in determining the scope of a combined course in planning and architecture was recognition of the urgent need to address the acute shortage of design skills in the planning profession. However, as the development process proceeded it became increasingly apparent that there was also a need, expressed mainly by practitioners, for changes to be made to the education of architects. Three key issues emerged.

Firstly, it was necessary to consider the development of architectural specialisms. There is a tendency to believe that a qualified architect has the capability not only to design buildings, but also to offer expertise in all manner of specialisms under the heading 'design'. This belief in the powers of the generalist is not well founded, given the complex nature of today's development industry and the diverse environment in which development takes place. Indeed it could be counterproductive—there is ample evidence of other specialists taking over roles, to the extent that the architect is no longer considered a leading player in the development process.

Secondly, there is a belief that architectural education should ensure that architects are equipped to work as effective members of multi-disciplinary teams. Educators often presume that the development of such essential interpersonal skills will somehow be absorbed by the embryonic architect during the educational process. It is assumed that the student will learn how to cooperate with colleagues, respect their varied expertise and become good team players, without any special emphasis being placed on the development of these skills. Evidence suggests otherwise.

Finally, there is a need to meet society's increasing demand that the agenda for design quality should be widened to embrace the social and environmental consequences of design. Design should be responsive to the needs of the whole population—client, user and community. This implies the necessity of placing greater emphasis on the pursuit of sustainable development and an awareness of the environmental impacts of design decisions. Design is a 'core problem solving activity that not only determines the quality of the built environment—the buildings, public spaces, landscape and infrastructure, but also delivers many of the instruments for the implementation of an urban renaissance' (Urban Task Force 1999). Successful urban renaissance, as part of an energy reduction strategy, is only likely to succeed if high-quality environments can lure people back to the city in the face of competition from the perceived safety and serenity of suburban environments. Architects need to be equipped to rise to the challenge that this represents—to develop a commitment to their role in this urban renaissance and the confidence to engage in debates about how it can be undertaken in a way that will avoid the repetition of past mistakes.

Consultation

The process of consultation for the development of the new course, involving discussions with the local and national architectural and planning communities, the respective professional bodies (the RIBA and RTPI) and the university/faculty, was regarded as a crucial part of the course design.

The initial idea to develop the combined course was greeted enthusiastically by the RIBA, although it was stressed from the beginning that the course should be different in character from existing courses. Within the university, for a number of reasons the existing organisation of the Faculty of the Built Environment provided a sound base for the development of an innovative new course. Firstly, because it already comprised a series of schools that embraced most of the built environment professions, including construction economics, management and engineering, housing and urban studies, land and property management, geography and environmental management as well as planning.

Secondly, the faculty's stated mission was to achieve an ethos and ways of working that were interdisciplinary, interprofessional and integrated.

Thirdly, the merger three years earlier between the three former departments of construction, surveying and planning to form an integrated faculty meant that the barriers between the professional and discipline groups within the faculty had already been partly surmounted. (Although the staff and students had found this a painful process, and there had been initial resistance, the benefits for both teaching and research were already becoming apparent and had generated a new energy and enthusiasm.)

Finally, interprofessional work in new areas of interest had drawn attention to a missing area of expertise in the faculty: architecture. Extensive local consultation revealed that architectural practitioners still felt a keen sense of loss from the closure of the original architecture course at Bristol University in the early 1980s. Their enthusiasm for the idea helped to establish the commitment of the faculty and the university to the proposed new course.

Interestingly, there were no major differences between the two professions about the aims and philosophy of the course. Both seemed to view the proposal as a tangible recognition of the necessity for architects and planners to develop mutual areas of interest rather than promoting the differences between the two professions. The consultation with architectural practices revealed a primary need for a wide range of 'soft' skills to be embedded in the curriculum. They strongly supported the emerging approach to such skills development in the faculty—ranging from an initial concentration on ensuring that all students reached adequate levels of numeracy and literacy, through to the development of the more sophisticated skills associated with interdisciplinary and group working.

That students should gain an understanding of the agenda for urban design as a central part of the course was considered paramount by consultees in both the planning and architectural communities. It was also thought crucial that students should learn how national policies for a more sustainable form of development could be implemented locally. Architectural practitioners underlined the importance of gaining experience of housing design—the intellectual rigour of designing good housing and everyday buildings should not be undervalued by the course teams in the development of appropriate design projects. Planning practitioners and academics stressed that students must develop an awareness of the effects of design solutions on people and their everyday lives, and felt that building users' needs should be given the highest possible priority.

Promotion

The success of the new course would, to a large extent, depend on the ability to show the outside world exactly why the course had been designed. To attract students, it would be necessary to promote clearly the basic ideas upon which the course was founded and ensure that these ideas permeated the course. This meant emphasising the reasons for the establishment of a new way of educating people to work as architect-planners. Three key words were used to facilitate this communication:

- *People*: students would be constantly reminded of the importance of ensuring that designs meet the needs of all users of the built environment, and not only those of the client.
- *Context*: emphasis would be placed on gaining an understanding of the physical, social, economic and environmental context of development before proceeding to the detailed design stage—their physical context.
- *Sustainability*: opportunities would be provided for staff to explore with students the ways in which individual designers at the local level might put into practice the principles of sustainable development being advanced at the global level. The faculty's strong commitment to sustainable development and the research being undertaken there (Barton *et al*. 1995) underpinned the inclusion of this theme.

It was hoped that these key words would convey to students, and new staff, the principle that every design scheme would be considered against a set of criteria that embraced the three key words, providing an identity for the course that reflected its essential character.

Course structure

Translating the ideas of the consultees and the core educational requirements of both institutes into a feasible course structure whilst meeting the specifications of the university's modular programme was a challenging task. The eventual course structure (Figure 15.1) emerged from a combination of the course team's own vision and the outcome of the consultation process.

The structure has already been amended in response to feedback from an advisory panel of academics, practitioners, external examiners, staff and students. The fine-tuning is likely to continue as the course develops and responds to changing situations. However the early decision that, in order to meet the requirements of both institutes and the university, it would be necessary for students to study for

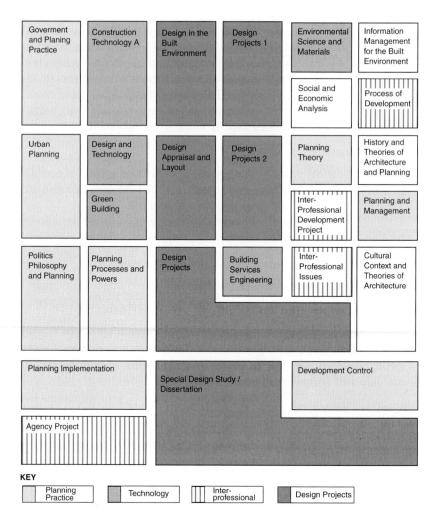

Figure 15.1 Award structure diagram BA(Hons) Architecture and Planning.

four years rather than three to achieve a BA (Hons) in Architecture and Planning, is unlikely to change.

Design, the architect's vital intellectual and conceptual contribution to the process, remains at the core of the course structure. Design projects take up a greater proportion of the overall study time as the student's design capability matures. In the early years the student is strongly directed and given relatively small amounts of independent study time. However, as the student's capabilities and understanding mature, greater independence is facilitated by the course structure. The economies achieved through the joint teaching of large groups of students in the early years facilitate one-to-one tutorial sessions for final-year students. By the final project module, which includes a research element as well as a more traditional final-year design project, the students are able to pursue their own interests and work with considerable independence.

Skills development permeates the course from the early diagnostic tests (designed to identify students who lack crucial skills) through to the final year of the course. Students keep their own records of their development and are expected to discuss their progress and personal strengths and weaknesses with their personal tutors.

The specific intention to develop particular skills in certain modules is reinforced by fostering the development of knowledge and experience through the course. For example the module entitled Cultural Context in the third year of the course helps students to make explicit links between architecture and the arts and the cultural context in which it develops. This allows issues to be raised about the nature of contemporary culture and gives students the opportunity to explore unfamiliar cultures.

Throughout the course, the importance of working cooperatively with others is given great weight. The course, by its very nature of combining two disciplines, is predicated on a belief in interdisciplinary and interprofessional cooperation. This builds on an existing faculty ethos that, since 1994, has been positively promoted through a series of project initiatives (Manley and Guise 1993). All undergraduates take part in a series of interprofessional modules in which they work in interprofessional groups on specific projects from their first year of study right through to graduation. The decision to foster this approach from an early stage of the student's career was based on a belief that prejudices and stereotypical views of the other professional groups exist even before enrolment on the course. Working in teams helps to break down barriers.

The interprofessional modules also nurture many of the essential skills that have been identified as common to all the built environment professions. It can be a difficult experience for both students and staff alike, but evidence suggests that students benefit greatly from these activities and develop new skills, as well as gain an appreciation of the legitimacy of the aspirations of other professionals. Even the conflicts that develop can be used as an educational tool since students are faced with the need to justify their own position with their team members.

What have we learnt?

The lessons learnt from the introduction of the combined course have informed the development of other initiatives in the faculty and established a model for the development of joint awards. The key lessons learnt include the following.

Consultation

Any new initiative tends to be treated with suspicion, and interdisciplinary cooperation is an obvious area in which people may be resistant to change. For us, the extensive consultation process was crucial to developing common views on how the course should be developed, and in piloting the first cohort of students through the system.

The collaboration of a diverse group of practitioners and academics proved invaluable in breaking down barriers and constructively addressing problems that arose as the course developed.

Inter professional working

In our case, the idea of interprofessional working had already been addressed by the UWE before the commencement of the combined course, and the faculty had embraced the interprofessional ethos as part of its mission statement. The transition to interprofessional working was aided by the tangible benefits that had become apparent over time—not only direct benefits to the student group and growing evidence of competence amongst graduates, but also the opportunities that had opened up for academic staff in terms of collaborative research and consultancy.

However it is likely that promoting genuine collaboration would prove difficult for many academic institutions where the traditional divisions between the various professions remain very obvious.

Interpersonal skills development

The academic nurturing of skills such as teamworking is likely to be a matter for debate amongst staff. Our experience clearly shows that some staff regard this to be outside the remit of their subject specialism, and that such skills should be prerequisites for entry to higher education. To a degree this problem can be overcome by employing specialist staff for some aspects of skills development. Also, identifying the skills that staff were already teaching proved informative as part of the initial introduction of an emphasis on skills throughout the faculty. It helped to reinforce the importance of skills acquisition as part of the learning process, and also made staff more aware of what they were trying to achieve in their own teaching.

Conclusion

Progress to date on the BA (Hons) Architecture and Planning course has been encouraging. Over 140 students have been recruited during its four years of operation, and there is evidence to suggest that many students chose to study the combined course because they were attracted to its philosophy and the opportunities it presented for variety of future job opportunities. The RIBA and ARB have granted candidate status to the course and in 2000 will visit the university to consider whether it can be accepted as equivalent in status to Part 1. In the same year the RTPI will visit to determine whether the course provides a programme of study that can be accredited by the institute as a full academic qualification for membership of the institute.

This is an on-going consultative process and will not end with the graduation of the first cohort of students. The intention is to maintain links with an expert committee of practitioners and academics from both professions. The development of graduates' careers will also be closely monitored and feedback obtained from them and their employers to ensure that the course is meeting its aims.

Overall, the course seems to have added richness and diversity to the faculty, the university and the city. The consultative process established the school as a 'presence' in the design community at large as more students and staff become involved in that community. In the university and faculty a 'design culture' is emerging. In the wider arena, it has introduced the idea that there is a role for architect-planners to help create higher-quality designed environments that will help to raise the quality of urban life.

References

Barton, H., Guise, R. and Davies, G. (1995) *Sustainable Settlements*. London: University of the West of England, Bristol, and the Local Government Management Board.

Department of the Environment (DOE) (1980) *Development Control and Practice, Circular 22/80*. London: HMSO.

Department of the Environment (DOE) (1992) *General Policy and Principles, Planning Policy Guidance 1*. London: HMSO.

Department of the Environment (DOE) (1997) *General Policy and Principles, Planning Policy Guidance 1*. London: HMSO.

Department of the Environment, Transport and the Regions (DETR) (1998) 'Rethinking Construction: The Report of the Construction Task Force' (the Egan Report). London: DETR.

Latham, Sir Michael (1994) *Constructing the Team: Final Report of the Government/Industry Review of Procurement and Contractual Arrangements in the UK Construction Industry*. London: HMSO.

Manley, S. and Guise, R. (1993) *Urban Design Quarterly*, Issue 47, July 1993 pp. 20–21.

National Committee of Inquiry into Higher Education (NCIHE) (1997) *'Higher Education in the Learning Society'*, (the Dearing Report). London: HMSO.

Punter, J. and Carmona, M. (1997) *The Design Dimension of Planning*. London: E. and F.N. Spon.

Royal Institute of British Architects (1992) *Report of the Steering Group on Architectural Education* (the Burton Report). London: RIBA.

Stansfield Smith, Sir Colin (1998) 'Stansfield Smith Review of Architectural Education', consultation working document. London: RIBA.

Tibbalds, F. (1988) 'Mind the gap!' a personal view of the value of urban design in the late twentieth century', *The Planner*, 74(3), pp. 11–15.

Urban Task Force (1999) *Towards an Urban Renaissance*. London: E. and F. N. Spon and DETR.

16 Integrated architectural design
Issues and models

Stirling Howieson

Introduction

The construction industry, which has traditionally been based on craft skills, is changing to one based on the synthesis of information and technology. Recent improvements in the speed and cost of construction has proven the value of an integrated team-based approach. The market will now drive such fundamental changes and those involved in education will be forced to adapt and change the way that architects and engineers are educated.

Architects are typically seen to be trained as individualistic prima donnas, systematically subjected to the capricious and pseudo-intellectual vagaries of fashion—often referred to as 'style'. Engineers, on the other hand, are rarely exposed to concept design and generally operate using deductive or inductive logic. Much of what engineers call design tends to be a combination of analysis and appraisal rather than exploration and synthesis. Few schools of architecture and engineering currently provide genuine opportunities for multidisciplinary, integrated architectural design.

In 1985 a report by the National Economic Development Office called for a greater number of graduates to be trained as construction professionals. This coincided with a recommendation by the University Grants Commission that 'given the importance of the construction industry to the national economy ... universities might try to direct some resources into the field of building engineering' (UGC circular). The dynamic was further reinforced by the Chartered Institute of Building Services Engineers (CIBSE), which concurrently suggested that the building industry would need at least twice as many graduates. For the University of Strathclyde, having one of the few schools of architecture in the UK to be located within a faculty of engineering (encompassing civil, structural, environmental, mechanical and electrical engineering) and having already modularised all its courses, the opportunity to produce a multidisciplinary, integrated course with the design studio at its core was seen as a relatively simple administrative task. In 1988 it initiated an undergraduate course entitled Building Design Engineering (BDE), which would aim to educate architects, engineers and other construction professionals in a joint studio-based environment. This chapter reviews this multidisciplinary educational model and discusses the critical issues surrounding integrated architectural design in an institutional context.

A multidisciplinary integrated course

The BDE course was conceived with the following aims:

- To provide a basic background in the necessary sciences.
- To introduce the design process.
- To introduce all facets of building design (architectural, structural, services, construction/manufacture).
- To provide experience in design tasks involving concept creation and detail design.

As the course was to be submitted for provisional recognition to the Royal Institute of British Architects (RIBA) and the Architects Registration Council (ARCUK), the Institution of Structural Engineers (ISE), the Institution of Civil Engineers (ICE) and the Chartered Institute of Building Services Engineers (CIBSE), the syllabus and curriculum had to address a range of fundamental professional requirements. It was decided that a structure that would allow students two foundation years—during which they would be exposed to several facets of the various professions before choosing a particular vocational stream—would give students greater choice and, more importantly, allow staff to assess the individual student's suitability for a particular discipline. Initially four streams were offered: architecture, structural, environmental and general. But although students would now be joining the dedicated cohorts located in the respective departments, integrated design studio projects would continue.

Although the curriculum (see Appendix 16.1) and syllabi have been subject to several revisions, the initial ethos remains substantially unaltered. A recent RIBA/ARB (formerly ARCUK) validation visit prompted the course to revise and restate its aims and objectives, as follows:

- To produce graduate architects, engineers and construction professionals with a high degree of design ability.
- To foster interprofessional respect and communication through common roots, shared curriculum and project work, culminating in the inculcation of a 'design team' approach.
- To produce graduate architects who are numerate and can grasp the fundamental principles of structural mechanics and environmental physics, and engineers who understand the design process

and can thus provide strategic input at the preconcept and concept development stage.

- To provide students with transferable communication skills—
graphic, written and oral.
- To provide students with the necessary skills and design methodologies to allow them to evaluate options and exercise judgement.
- To allow students the opportunity to explore the context in which
they will operate as professionals.

Issues

The debate, both internal and external, about such an educational
approach continues. The course, despite the quality of its output,
has its critics and could still be seen as relatively fragile given its context, both academic and fiscal. The following issues have been identified for closer examination to allow those who may be interested in
developing (or possibly adapting) a course along similar lines.

Choice and career flexibility

One of the main marketing angles that students say attracted them to
the course, was the opportunity to spend two years indulging in a
'Chinese meal' of credits before choosing a vocational route.
Students are more informed and aware of what each profession
involves, and more importantly their aptitudes and motivation can
be assessed. In light of the financial debt burden that they are now
accruing over a four-to-five-year course, it is possible for students to
choose a specialist area where employment opportunities are greater.
For this reason alone environmental engineering has, within the past
three years, become the dominant stream. Graduates from this seg-
ment of the cohort are typically offered more positions with significantly higher salaries. Although this may simply reflect a market
shortage, few environmental engineers from traditional courses can
present to a prospective employer such a comprehensive portfolio of
design work—demonstrating both analytical and creative skills.

Teamworking in a competitive academic environment

With few exceptions, students have traditionally become used to an
educational regime that is both individualistic and competitive. In such
a climate, although some assessment regimes may be based on crite-
rion referencing, particularly in the area of architectural design, norm
referencing the various design outcomes is inevitably the method
adopted by most schools of architecture. If this is made explicit
students will recognise that their performance is simply being benchmarked against their peers, and thus, if their aim is to be the top

student, it is in their interests to ensure that any information and strategies they have developed individually are not shared with the rest of the cohort. There is thus a significant psychological barrier to teamworking that has to be addressed from the outset.

Research evidence (Entwhistle *et al.* 1992; Higgins *et al.* 1989) shows that group/teamwork can produce a significant improvement in the quality of student work. Assessing the relative contribution of each individual is, however, notoriously difficult (Gibbs 1990). Therefore, for teaching such as the BDE course, whose entire ethos is to stimulate integrated design in multidisciplinary teams, much effort has to be put into team building. This is done using a variety of techniques, the most successful of which has been the use of games and quizzes in the early years to demonstrate that the whole can be much greater than the sum of the parts. Once a degree of trust is established in this way, a variety of possibilities can present themselves—from simply allowing students to share the total sum of the research effort generated for a given project, through to awarding group marks for their final design thesis project. As this summative assessment contributes a significant proportion of their honours degree classification, by the fourth year students need to have been won over to the benefits of such cooperation. Where doubt or suspicion remain, a student can opt out of the group marking regime and be treated as an individual. However those who have chosen such a route have, in general, faired poorly when benchmarked against their peer groups.

Stereotyping

One of the main obstacles to implementing such a course is finding individuals who are able and willing to teach in such a complex multidisciplinary environment as the design studio. The original idea was to staff all studios with equal proportions of architects and engineers. However it soon became clear that this would not be possible, based on the staff resources available within the faculty.

Engineering academics, who were familiar with traditional 'chalk and talk' didactic lectures, became uncomfortable when complex and open-ended design problems were the main vehicle in the unfamiliar territory of one-to-one studio consultations/tutorials. The architects appeared to have a higher degree of self-confidence in this educational environment and invariably assumed control, with the result that the engineers, who had been trained to solve a specific part of the puzzle rather than orchestrate the process, became marginalised. Therefore practitioners who were familiar with the broader picture were brought in on a part-time basis to bolster the studio operation. However most still brought with them traditional views on the fundamental principles and features of design.

Overall the staff, like the students on the course, have had to learn how to build integrated teams and act not as architects or engineers, but as quasi 'renaissance men' (and women).

Professional attitudes

There is, of course, an opposite view of design that is commonly held, if not openly and coherently articulated. Individuals normally domiciled in divisions of history and theory can claim that architecture is essentially an art—a cultural activity, in the main divorced from the rather grubby business of technology and construction. A past president of the RIBA, joining a visiting board to the Strathclyde school, was appalled at the aims of the BDE course. He expressed the opinion that the course was polluting young creative minds with nuts and bolts and plumbing—'it simply, should not, and cannot be done!'

The descent into unqualified subjectivism is not uncommon in schools of architecture and can be viewed as an essential defence mechanism. At a recent conference entitled Design Education, organised by the Royal Incorporation of Architects in Scotland, Professor Bryan Lawson commented upon the reticence on the part of architects to attempt any objective assessment of product and process, saying that the motivation of many architects when they discuss their work appeared to be 'to impress rather than to explain' (Lawson 1999). This can also be linked to the continuing discussion on the title of the course. The more commercial title 'Architectural Engineering' has been floated—the implication being that adopting the term 'architecture', as opposed to mere 'building', would give the course a more intellectual aura. As Lawson maintains, 'To be an engineer in Germany is to be a highly respected member of society. In England you are assumed to wear a boiler suit and carry spanners' (ibid.)

Curriculum issues

There has always been a somewhat artificial schism between art and technology—between the concerns of the more specialist researcher and the design studio master, who may be more concerned with ideology, typology, style and fashion. In a chaotic world, where students can be presented with a range of 'isms', usually combined with a mind-numbing anthology of star names and dates, the history of building and design needs to be revisited and represented. For the BDE course, since 1999 a new compulsory credit has been included in the second-year curriculum. Entitled the 'Philosophy of Design', the syllabus deliberately ignores the formalist obsession with 'the great and the good', and looks instead at the historical process of design, emphasising the role that scientific and technical innovation have played in generating new building prototypes and paradigms.

Finding a balance

Since the course requires students to fulfil the basic requirements of three separate professional institutes, each protective of their 'tablets of wisdom', the curriculum is under pressure from three sides. The engineering departments complain that students are overburdened with design and presentation. Conversely the architecture tutors remark on the lack of presentation skills and contextual studies. We contend, however, that the students—albeit developing skills and competencies at an initially slower rate—can go on to use this broad generalist approach more strategically at a later stage and surpass the traditional scenario.

Assessing across departments

If assessing groupwork within one department presents many complex problems, assessing students across departments and disciplines could be a recipe for disaster. Although the credit-based system purports to reward equal effort across the curriculum, in practice the syllabi and nature of some subjects do not lend themselves to direct comparison. We are, however, required to classify student degrees and have developed protocols that give greater weighting to the design theses and the dissertation against the more didactically taught credits. Although the university has a standard marking regime, how each department interprets such broad categories can vary. The Honours Board has to take this into account and adjust the marks around a class average if it appears that one division is marking more generously than the next. The course also encourages the external examiners to meet and interview all the honours year and moderate any marks/classifications as they see fit.

Internecine ownership and resourcing

Having a school of architecture situated within a faculty of engineering was undoubtedly a key factor in enabling such a new approach. However, the course, being the responsibility of three departments in concert, still required to be 'ring-fenced' for its first five years—given special status to cover additional staff and running costs. When combined with the vagaries of the full-time equivalent (FTE) internal economy, where FTE-rich departments are impeded from filling vacancies due to the direct cross-subsidy of debtor departments, there are considerable possibilities for resourcing disputes. Furthermore, until the course is domiciled in one department, the contributors can see it as direct competition with their more traditional menu. Our goal in order to minimise this is to achieve a critical student mass—30 students in both the first and the second year and 25 in both the third and fourth years.

Course evaluation

Although in one sense it is the graduates themselves who are the product, any final analysis of the course must attempt to evaluate those graduates' impact on the construction industry as a whole. It would be inappropriate, however, to equate the relative success of any particular graduate, or the current course employment statistics, with the quality of education that is offered. Although one could assume that professional success would, at least in part, depend on the type and quality of the academic experience, a study by Goldschmid (1991), based on interviews with over 800 architects and engineers who graduated between 1946 and 1987 from the Swiss Federal Institute in Lausanne, found no correlation between a student's grade point average and subsequent career success. (For this study the criteria of success were degree of responsibility, income, decision-making power and number of subordinates.) Indeed if anything there appeared to be a negative correlation—those with the lowest grade point average were in fact more likely to own the firm!

The research also revealed that these engineers and architects spent almost 50 per cent of their time in some form of communication—writing, meetings, phone discussions and so on—which they claimed their academic training had, on the whole, ignored. In conclusion, Goldschmid called for the engineering curriculum to include teaching methods that would encourage dialogue, participation, reflection, discussion and presentation. These were all key components of the BDE ethos.

In terms of more objective markers, the Department of Architecture and Building Science has received a rating of 'excellent' under the total quality assurance (TQA) audit procedures and a research assessment exercise (RAE) rating of 5 and 4 for research activity. The course has also been through a second round of validation and accreditation visits, where all professional institutes have granted further exemptions from their respective professional exams—RIBA, I.Stuct Eng., I. Civil Eng. and CIBSE.

Theory versus practice

The process of validation, however, has raised some fundamental issues and concerns that seem to indicate a gulf between theory and practice in multidisciplinary education.

Over the last 10 years there has continued to be a call from many areas for the development of such multidisciplinary, integrated courses. For instance the Design Council (1991) considers that all chartered engineers should be able to appreciate 'the aesthetic aspects of design which relate to shape, colour, visual detail, graphics, styling, proportion, materials, surface treatment, packaging, tactile properties and the user's perception of functional elegance, which may conflict with an engineer's desire for maximum functional efficiency' .... The RIBA, in its strategic study of the profession (RIBA 1992), and the government-funded Latham Report on the construction industry as a whole (Latham 1994) both called for more courses to 'promote multi-disciplinary undergraduate and postgraduate degrees and greater commonality in professional education with particular emphasis on design, technology and basic skills'. More recently the Egan Report (1998) called for more 'multiskilling', and claimed that 'The experience of other industries is that heavily compartmentalised, specialist opera-tions detract from overall efficiency.'

However in our experience of validation, each professional body argued hard for the curriculum to have more of their own chosen 'basics and fundamentals' inserted into the course. In other words the appointed representatives of each professional institute have tended to fall back on their own view of the world, defending the familiar and traditional. The irony is clear.

Why is this so? Is it that practitioners, subject to commercial market forces, are perhaps more likely to innovate, adapt and diversify? In academia, conversely, being rarely exposed to such forces, there appear to be fewer 'drivers' to force significant changes to 'ivory tower' methods and attitudes. The major concern of departmental heads remains that of annually recruiting the requisite target student numbers and ensuring that staff publish articles—often in increasingly obscure and incestuous journals—to maintain RAE bounties. Even the criticisms and concerns expressed by external examiners may, in real-ity, carry little weight since there is no fiscal penalty for ignoring their recommendations.

Summary

To quote from one of the external examiners of the 1998 course:

> It must be stressed that the BDE undergraduate course is unique, nationally, and it responds to a perceived need for professionally-based interdisciplinary learning within a university context. If stu-dent needs are perceived as a broad education to equip the three strands for careers in the building professions and industry, then the course succeeds admirably. The keynote is the interdisciplinary nature of student learning—often aspired towards but seldom realised.

The course has faced many problems, both internal and external, as it has progressed through its infancy—and may face further problems in its adolescence. It still appears to sit awkwardly in its surroundings—both fiscally and ideologically—and has few peers with which to share experiences and successes. However we believe that the project, in breaking new ground, has the potential to produce a new breed of professional, more suited to a construction industry that will have to restructure in order to survive. Enough evidence has now been accrued to confirm that such an experiment in multidisciplinary, integrated design is worthy of replication elsewhere.

Appendix 16.1   Curriculum

First year (12 credits minimum)

Compulsory classes

Building Design Project 1A	72 hrs, design studio
Building Design Project 1B	72 hrs, design studio
Building Design Project 1C	48 hrs, design studio
Design and Information Technology	24 hrs lectures, 12 hrs tutorials
Building Technology and Environment 1A	24 hrs lectures, 12 hrs tutorials
Building Technology and Environment 1B	24 hrs lectures, 12 hrs tutorials
Civil Engineering Mechs I	24 hrs lectures, 12 hrs tutorials
Civil Engineering Design	12 hrs lectures, 24 hrs tutorials
Energy and the Environment	12 hrs lectures, 24 hrs tutorials
Engineering Mathematics I	24 hrs lectures, 12 hrs tutorials
Engineering Mathematics II	24 hrs lectures, 12 hrs tutorials
Elective classes	Normally two additional credits are chosen

Second year (12 credits minimum)

Compulsory classes

Building Design Project 2A	72 hrs, design studio
Building Design Project 2B	72 hrs, design studio
Building Design Project 2C	48 hrs, design studio
Building Technology and Environment 2A	24 hrs lectures, 12 hrs tutorials
Building Technology and Environment 2B	24 hrs lectures, 12 hrs tutorials
Structural Engineering 1A	24 hrs lectures, 12 hrs tutorials
Structural Engineering 1B	24 hrs lectures, 12 hrs tutorials
Electrical Technology for BDE	24 hrs lectures, 12 hrs tutorials
Environmental Engineering Science I	24 hrs lectures, 12 hrs tutorials
Energy Systems I	24 hrs lectures, 12 hrs tutorials
Engineering Mathematics III	24 hrs lectures, 12 hrs tutorials
Elective Classes	From an approved list

Third year (12 credits minimum)

Compulsory project classes

Building Design Project 3A	72 hrs, design studio
Building Design Project 3B	72 hrs, design studio

Building Design Project 3C	72 hrs, design studio
Compulsory, optional and elective classes	Depend on professional route, nine credits

Fourth year (12 credits minimum)

Compulsory project/dissertation classes	
Building Design Projects 4A	72 hrs, design studio
Building Design Projects 4B	72 hrs, design studio
Dissertation (2 credits)	Unscheduled
Compulsory, optional and elective classes	Depend on professional route, eight credits

References

Design Council (1991) engineering working party report. *Attaining Competence in Engineering Design*, London: Design Council.

Egan, Sir John (1998) *Rethinking Construction*. London: HMSO.

Entwhistle N., Thompson S. and Tait M. (1992) *Guidelines for Promoting Effective Learning in Higher Education*. Edinburgh: Centre for Research on Learning and Instruction, University of Edinburgh, pp. 41–50.

Gibbs, G. (1990) *Assessing Teamwork Skills*, Teaching and Learning Bulletin 5. Sunderland Business Education Publishers, p. 6. Sunderland.

Goldschmid M. L. (1991) 'The Training and Professional Success of Engineers: an Empirical Study', *International Journal of Applied Engineering Education*, 7(6), pp. 440–3.

Higgins J. S., Maitland J., Perkins S., Richardson S., Warren-Piper D. (1989) 'Identifying and Solving Problems in Engineering Design', *Studies in Higher Education*, 14, pp. 169–81. London: Taylor and Francis.

Latham, M. (1994) *Constructing the Team—Final report of the Government/Industry Joint Review of Procurement and Contractual Arrangements in the UK Construction Industry*. London: HMSO.

Lawson, B. (1999) 'Design Education: the issues', Paper presented at the RIAS and CSA Conference on Design Education, September 1999, The Lighthouse, Glasgow.

National Economic Development Office (1985) *A Strategy for Construction Research and Development*. London: HMSO.

RIBA (1992) *The Strategic Study of the Profession*. London: RIBA publications.

17 Interdisciplinary working in built environment education

Gerard Wood

Introduction

A number of reports in the late 1980s highlighted the relatively divisive nature of the construction industry in the UK compared with Japan, the USA and other European countries (Collier *et al.* 1991). A recurring conclusion was the need for greater collaboration amongst professionals, and attempts to encourage an interdisciplinary approach have since been gathering momentum through further reports (Andrews and Derbyshire 1993; Burton 1992; Latham 1994) and conferences (University of Cambridge 1991; UCE 1995).

The essence of such reports and conferences appears to be consistent. Many of their recommendations are compatible in terms of the desirability of greater cooperation and collaboration amongst key built environment disciplines, and all recognise that higher education plays an important role. For example Collier *et al.* (1991) identified the following objective for future developments: 'to encourage the view that students of related disciplines benefit from working and learning together and that collaborative working is a positive and important component in an education programme'. Andrews and Derbyshire (1993) also concluded that 'there is considerable scope for greater commonality in the education, training and continuing professional development of the construction professions'. However, changes in programmes of study require careful consideration if they are to be effective.

Context

This chapter explores attitudes towards introducing interdisciplinary working within built environment education by presenting the opinions and experiences of a number of senior academics from a multidisciplinary faculty at Leeds Metropolitan University (LMU).

With over 20 000 students and more than 800 professional staff, LMU is one of the largest and most popular of the new universities.

The Faculty of Health and Environment has a long tradition of providing vocational education, offering courses leading to professional examinations since the 1940s. Two of the schools in the faculty have a range of accredited undergraduate and postgraduate courses associated with the design, planning, development and construction of the built environment.

As a basis for the study, exploratory interviews, considered to be an appropriate means of obtaining honest opinions and experiences (Oppenheim 1992), were undertaken with senior faculty academics—the two heads of school and the course leaders of BA(Hons) Architecture, PG Dip Architecture, BA(Hons) Landscape Architecture, BSc(Hons) Building Surveying, BSc(Hons) Civil Engineering, BSc(Hons) Construction Management and BSc(Hons) Quantity Surveying. (The absence of a key discipline within the traditional overall team—building services engineering—is due to there being no such course at LMU.)

Each interviewee made an opening statement on the interdisciplinary nature of the design process—the involvement of many professions, the need to understand the different roles and, more importantly, the common objective. Most described the nature of professional practice as crucially being about 'working with others' and how it is important for the education process adequately to prepare students by offering exemplars of best practice. Indeed it was felt that a prerequisite for a successful project is the ability to establish good working relationships—professionals must be able to enter into a full discussion, understanding the constraints, pressures and requirements of others. The result is improved client satisfaction and a more positive experience for all disciplines.

Almost all set their comments in a scenario of a rapidly changing world of business and the built environment, where there is seen to be an ever increasing blurring of the boundaries between the professions:

> The interdisciplinary nature of design—people who do not usually see themselves as designers are nevertheless very heavily involved in design at some level.

> The process and traditional roles are changing. For example, contractors are not just involved in constructing, but designing, financing, managing the whole process through mechanisms such as the Private Finance Initiative.

> We must acknowledge the reality of overlapping design practice and seek opportunities to reflect this change in the education process.

From this basis, three specific themes emerged:

• Course structures and modifications thereto.
• Teaching and learning in interdisciplinary studies—commonality or project-based activity.
• Barriers to further developments.

Course structures

The most radical opinion was that the existing professions are 'useless', and that current practice is anachronistic—quantity surveyors being obsolete, elitist architects being obsolete and so on. Consequently a new breed of people was seen to be required, which would only emerge from a completely different approach to the nature of built environment design. This respondent compared performance in the built environment to other industries that have embraced technology and change: 'Man can design buildings to go over, under and across the surface of the oceans, even orbit the earth, yet we still live in draughty, leaky, funny little dwellings that gobble energy and flush away too much water.'

Another view was that the increasingly rapid change in society meant that the future would not require lines of professional demarcation. Rather it would demand people who are more flexible and adaptable, and education must therefore prepare students for this future: 'Traditional models of teaching professions in compartments is wrong, has always been wrong, but has now been proved to be ineffectual and wrong.'

The third radical view was that education should begin by considering the basic functions and operations involved in design, rather than deriving the functions from existing professional disciplines. The traditional notion of, for example, soft pencilled architects on the one hand and technical experts on the other, was considered unacceptable, since each of their influences on the finished product is profound, as is the way they relate to each other. There was therefore a need to look at the whole education process: 'If we do not change at the beginning then we have lost the battle because the eyes of the specialist may be opened at postgraduate level, but they will retain a specialist focus that affects overall vision.'

The consensus evident in these views is that the compartmentalisation of professional education at undergraduate level is undesirable since it militates against collaboration and broader understanding. The notable difference is that the third view does not necessarily consider professional disciplines to be redundant, but regards the appropriate sequencing of specific knowledge acquisition as fundamental.

The solution, according to this group, was some form of common undergraduate programme, after which students would develop specialisms: 'The notion of maybe two years of generalist education with later levels of specialism would be a challenge, but could in fact be quite liberating.' Suggestions ranged from sixteen-year-old pupils taking a two-year course in the built environment, to a more moderate two-year undergraduate foundation course. Although there is some synergy in these views there were differences regarding the nature of this foundation, as will become apparent later.

Pragmatists

The approach of the majority of respondents was more pragmatic. They saw a need for, and benefits to be derived from, education in specialisms at the undergraduate level. The challenge was to devise appropriate means of developing this expertise alongside equals from other professions within existing programmes. Some expressed the view that professions had developed historically for good reasons and that the problem is the consequence of the protectionism that professions and their institutions bring. Nevertheless it was considered important not to move away from the justifiable demands and needs of individual disciplines.

There was some agreement that common programmes are actually problematic, in that students first go to university with a fairly clear, if naive, notion of the career they wish to pursue—identified by the Construction Industry Board (1996) as 'professional intent'. If they lose that identity from day one, then the likelihood is that they will either react against it or find it difficult to focus their minds. One member of staff cited anecdotal evidence of a common approach having been tried unsuccessfully elsewhere.

The pragmatists considered the crucial issue to be working together within multidisciplinary teams, and felt that students must be given the opportunity to do so in order to simulate professional practice. The question was where and how this should be introduced. Some saw the need to introduce the idea at level one (first year), but generally it was thought to be more beneficial at later levels when students could actually understand the nature of the problems they were facing. It was felt that at the beginning of the course they are not even aware that such problems exist. There was further agreement amongst this group that there is a need for this type of work at postgraduate level, because the lack of collaboration that currently exists in practice must not be disregarded and allowed to run its natural course for the next 30 years.

In summary, there appeared to be an interesting divergence in the approaches described. The radicals could be seen as reflecting the historical meaning of degree structures in British universities—a bachelor's degree traditionally meant that the recipient had obtained a general education, a master's degree was a licence to practise (Phillips and Pugh 1987). The pragmatists' view, however, could be seen as maintaining the postwar tendency of emphasising specialist vocational learning earlier in the education process.

This may be a peculiarly British phenomenon. Haenlein *et al.*'s (1989) study found that the US, French and German construction industries embrace only two professional groups—engineers and architects. Consequently engineers in France and both engineers and architects in Germany have a much broader-based university education, which enables them to carry out a wide variety of tasks after industrial training. It also points out that in the USA it is generally held that the first degree is a general education, with professional training provided by a higher degree.

Teaching and learning

A crucial aspect of the debate on interdisciplinary education is the place and value of common studies—'commonality'. Those in favour of a foundation programme obviously saw benefits. However they did not necessarily agree on the nature of the work students should undertake within such a programme. The first view was that foundation studies should be essentially academic: 'Courses should comprise more word and thought mongering than rote learning. Students should be encouraged to experiment, not taught how to do things in the conventional way.' It was felt that such studies should go back to fundamentals and question everything about what we need for human habitats and workplaces.

The second view was based on the notion that foundation studies should comprise problem-based scenarios: projects with a range of problems and solutions, where 'professional' individuals operate on an equal level rather than replicating conventional roles: 'In reality a quantity surveyor has as much to say about architecture as an architect, and an architect has as much to say about cost and value as a quantity surveyor. We must encourage this debate.'

Whether this is entirely true is open to question. But it is perhaps valid to propose that we should challenge the tradition of educating students to operate solely within their own discipline's knowledge domain, because in that way they will only ever be able to approach problem solving in terms of that knowledge. This militates against finding properly coordinated design and construction solutions.

There was broad agreement amongst all the respondents on the common transferable skills necessary for all professionals—communication, interpersonal skills, teamworking, research and analytical skills, and so on. However these were seen more as common 'outcomes' that could be achieved through a variety of educational experiences, than as common 'studies'. The majority of interviewees commented further on the concept of commonality, and although they agreed it has a place for reasons of practicality and efficiency of delivery in core built environment subjects such as construction technology, contract law and so on, nobody concluded that it was truly connected with interdisciplinary working.

Elective studies were also identified by some as a potential area for encouraging dialogue between the professions, although again success will be related to the subject matter and the learning vehicle. For example a civil engineer and an architect taking a module in French does not make it an interdisciplinary activity.

Integrated project work

Almost all the interviewees saw the value of project-based activities where students from different disciplines are grouped together and role play some aspects of practice. Integrated project activity of this kind was seen as a proactive method of fostering collaboration. It could act as formative learning, enable students to experience working together and encourage them to appreciate the abilities and roles of others, as well as putting their own specialism into some form of context. Role swapping was also considered to have some benefit because it exposes students to the pressures and problems faced by others, thereby helping them to understand and value their contribution to the design process. Nevertheless it does impose severe limits on the complexity of the scenario and learning outcomes, and thereby has limited use.

Despite this broad agreement, some staff were disturbed at the remarkable ability of students to role play their disciplines stereotypically, and therefore exhibit worrying degrees of prejudice within weeks of entering a multidisciplinary faculty. In the light of this experience, they felt that the nature of project work must be considered in more detail. What is it trying to achieve? It can often follow and reinforce conventional roles, and therefore simply becomes learning by default. For instance if the product of a group project proves a success (for whatever reason) then students will feel they have learned something. If, on the other hand, the product is a failure (again for whatever reason) then students will feel they have learned nothing. Equally, requiring students to work in a multidisciplinary team, even repeatedly, does not automatically ensure that individuals will collaborate or solutions will be coordinated. In fact learning to work effectively in teams was not necessarily considered to be a cross-disciplinary exercise: 'It could be about a group of architects trying to cross a river with an old shoe and a bucket.'

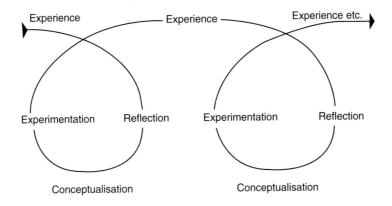

Figure 17.1 The Kolb learning cycle as a developmental spiral.
Source: Waterhouse and Crook (1995).

Further examination of this view revealed reflective observation as a critical activity that must form part of any project work. Students should be encouraged to address the process issues that arise out of multidisciplinary work, confronting the problems and opportunities more explicitly, rather than being left with a vague notion of what went right or wrong. This could then be used to feed their approach to the same type of work next time to create a cycle of learning (Figure 17.1): a learning style promoted by Kolb (1984).

Consequently, at advanced levels students could be expected to challenge norms and conventional approaches and explore alternative ways of achieving more effective and coordinated responses to multi-faceted design and construction problems. This was seen as crucial in nourishing ideas for a changing future, and of particular importance at postgraduate level.

In summary, it was apparent that project work was widely considered to play a major part in fostering truly interdisciplinary working. This is perhaps unsurprising. However, more critical was the emergence of an important distinction between 'teamworking and its associated skills', and the 'collaboration of distinct expertise in such a way as to achieve comprehensive and coordinated solutions'.

The most interesting aspect of this distinction was not between the outcomes themselves but the learning environment in which it was felt they could occur. Whereas teamworking could be fostered in either a monodisciplinary or multidisciplinary environment, collaboration could only occur in a multidisciplinary environment.

This analysis helps to clarify both what we are trying to achieve and how we may be able to achieve it.

Barriers to further developments

The respondents identified three key barriers to the further development of interdisciplinary studies:

- Staff relationships.
- Resource pressures and faculty structures.
- The influence of external accrediting bodies.

Staff relationships were cited extensively as a crucial factor. The interviewees commented that some staff seemed to feel threatened if others encroached on their territory, and therefore resisted any involvement. Whereas informal discussions with other disciplines could often be relaxed and open, when they became specific there was an immediate strain on both sides. As one course leader explained: 'I can have an interesting discussion with individuals [academics] in Architecture about design, but I know that they will never allow me to speak to their students about design.'

Indeed staff attitudes towards their own professions could cause difficulties. This was identified particularly in relation to architects, whom some considered to be elitist. This comment came from three respondents, one of whom was a particularly surprising source and added that: 'We have an incredible tendency to want to create students in our own image.'

There was also seen to be a problem with achieving a consensus amongst all academic staff. Inevitably some people regarded other issues as more important, and consequently were reluctant to sacrifice time that had been dedicated to core content for more interdisciplinary or generalist studies. Nevertheless it was generally considered that if like-minded individuals, who regard this issue as a priority, could act collectively in advocating an interdisciplinary approach, then progress could be made.

Resource pressures and faculty structures were identified as serious problems. A seemingly ever-worsening resource aspect of higher education—the staff to student ratio, stimulated by a quest for increased efficiency—has been exacerbated by increased numbers of students who can seem almost logistically impossible to organise into interdisciplinary project teams. Such resource constraints inevitably reduce innovation and therefore do not create a climate conducive to a demand being met for extra input and further restructuring. In addition, there was some scepticism that the issue of interdisciplinarity might be hijacked to achieve even more commonality and therefore save money.

Some staff identified faculty structures as encouraging professions to act independently through a professional group system. This was reinforcing the compartmentalisation created by the physical separation of staff accommodation into professional group corridors. Meeting like-minded people from other disciplines in this context was difficult as there was no forum for casual interaction.

Finally, external accrediting bodies were cited as potential barriers. It was suggested that they must change in order to allow a common education programme, or at least one that would dilute the disciplines in order to achieve a greater degree of truly interdisciplinary work. Others considered that the wholesale change that was required would not be possible with impending reviews by professional institutions or funding bodies. However another respondent commented that although professional institutions and funding bodies were often cited as problematic, when they actually visited they often seemed disappointed that schools and faculties did not have more innovative approaches. This view was substantiated by the documented observations of the Higher Education Funding Council for England (1994):

> Many architecture courses are located within a wider built environment faculty, alongside related subjects such as building, planning, quantity surveying, urban design and the various facets of engineering. Effective curriculum links have been established in some institutions ... assessors also found examples of unsubstantiated claims to integration and missed opportunities for the interdisciplinary cooperation that reflects developments in the profession.

Similarly, the consultation document for the current RIBA review of architectural education (Stansfield Smith 1998) comments that 'There are many different models for encouraging multidisciplinary understanding and inter-disciplinary working. Architectural education is in a strong position to lead in the development of such initiatives.'

Taken overall, this final section of the study could be seen as disappointing in view of the radical ideas that had been expressed earlier and the apparently unified belief in the importance of the issue. Fundamentally, there is no consensus on the direction that interdisciplinary studies should take. In practice, this might be as big a barrier to further development as any other identified.

Construction Industry Board findings

It is interesting to compare the views expressed against the recommendations of the Construction Industry Board (CIB 1996).

Looking at course structures, our study raised two options: the radical, favouring some form of foundation programme; and the pragmatic, introducing interdisciplinary working more incrementally into existing courses. The CIB suggested that general built environment degrees would, on the available evidence (not referenced), be heavily undersubscribed. The Cambridge conference in 1991 also concluded that postgraduate collaboration is the way forward, rather than joint courses at degree level (Oliver *et al.* 1994). Hence there are clear signs that the pragmatic or incremental approach has some influential supporters.

Teaching and learning

How do we foster a more collaborative approach to interdisciplinary working—what are the appropriate teaching and learning vehicles? The respondents in our study overwhelmingly favoured multidisciplinary project work, and some were convinced that this must include reflective activity. The majority thought that this type of work should occur at all levels, culminating at higher levels in an examination of current processes and a consideration of alternative approaches and methods.

In contrast the CIB (1996) recommends that students on built environment courses should develop a common platform of skills, but it stops short of specifying when, how and why the outcomes will be achieved. This is disappointing, since the unanimous view of the academics in our study was that common skills and commonality are different aspects of education from the promotion of interdisciplinary working. The proposal for a common platform of skills, reached independently, could be viewed as a dilution of the essence of collaboration.

Barriers

The barriers perceived by the academics in our study correspond, to some extent, with those identified by the CIB, including funding, professional exemptions and staff attitudes as current constraints. While some barriers may be more perceived than real, it seems undeniable that in an increasingly demanding environment the attitudes of the staff of a school or faculty are paramount.

Conclusions

While the views expressed in this study are obviously limited to a select group of staff in a single faculty, they do illustrate a progression of thinking amongst experienced academics. Beginning with an exciting spectrum of ideas, it then moves towards a more convergent reality. Do differences in thinking result, in part, from a lack of clarity in what we are trying to achieve and at what level—foundation, undergraduate or postgraduate?

Further research is required to examine what the future construction industry requires—improved teamworking, a better appreciation of the many facets of design/construction problems, fully integrated solutions, or a common foundation of knowledge. They are not necessarily the same thing or achieved by the same means. Nor are they mutually exclusive, but a greater clarity of aim is required. The terminology must also be addressed more rigorously—interdisciplinary, cross-disciplinary, interprofessional, multidisciplinary and commonality often seem to be used as interchangeable terms, yet there are crucial differences.

In the short term it seems likely that each higher education institution will try to find its own solutions. For instance De Montfort University has recently incorporated interdisciplinary studies at all levels of all built environment courses. Subsequent to our study, a similar approach has been adopted at Leeds Metropolitan University, but this does not currently include architecture and landscape architecture. Such initiatives are not limited to the UK—the Universities of New South Wales and Western Sydney have both formally embedded interdisciplinary studies into the structure of undergraduate programmes.

However, acceptance of the need for this type of working is by no means universal. The University of Central England developed an ambitious curriculum to include interdisciplinary studies across all built environment courses in the early 1990s, only to abandon the entire whole philosophy in 1997. Some universities pay little or no attention whatsoever to the notion of interdisciplinary education. In the longer term we should learn from the successes and failures of these various attempts in order to determine the most effective methods of fostering interdisciplinary working within programmes of study. Without this, minor changes in course structures and learning methods—such as those proposed by the Construction Industry Board—will only result in minor changes in outcomes.

References

Andrews, J. and Derbyshire, A. (1993) *Crossing Boundaries*. London: Construction Industry Council.

Burton, R. (1992) *Steering Group on Architectural Education—Report and Recommendations*. London: Royal Institute of British Architects.

Collier, A., Bacon, J., Burns, D. and Muir, T. (1991) *Interdisciplinary studies for the built environment*, Council for National Academic Awards. London.

Construction Industry Board (1996), *Educating the professional team*. London: Thomas Telford.

Haenlein, H., Brookes, A. and Penz, F. (1989) *Professional Education for Construction: Overseas Comparisons*. London: Department of the Environment.

Higher Education Funding Council for England (1994), *Quality Assessment of Architecture 1994, Subject Overview Report QO 6/95*. London: HMSO.

Kolb, D. (1984) *Experiential Learning: experience as a source of learning and development*. Englewood elitts, NJ: Prentice Hall.

Latham, M. (1994) *Constructing the Team*. London: HMSO.

Oliver, G., Spence, R. and Kirby, P. (1994) 'Charting a New Course—Education for the Built Environment', *The Cambridge Review*, May.

Oppenheim, A. (1992) *Questionnaire design, interviewing and attitude measurement*. London: Pinter.

Phillips, E. and Pugh, D. (1987) *How to get a PhD*. Buckingham: Open University Press.

Stansfield Smith, C. (1998) *Review of Architectural Education—Consultation Working Document*. London: RIBA.

University of Cambridge (1991), *Education for the Built Environment*. Cambridge: Ove Arup Foundation.

University of Central England (1995), *Developments in Education and Training for Professionals in the Built Environment*. Birmingham University of Central England.

Waterhouse, M. and Crook, G. (1995) *Management and Business Skills in the Built Environment*. London: E & FN Spon.

Section 3

Lifelong learning

Developing independence in learning

Section 3 focuses on the development of attitudes and skills that are relevant to lifelong learning in students. In order to cope with the knowledge explosion and the rapid rate of change in society, architects (like all other professionals) need to develop the habit of monitoring, evaluating and managing their own learning and of learning from practical experience. The chapters in this section outline some ways in which schools of architecture might foster in their students the skills for and habits of continuous learning.

Farren Bradley's concern (Chapter 18) is with the current model of architectural education, whereby students spend five years in formal academic study and then two years in supervised practical training. She believes that this separation is artificial and inappropriate for the twenty-first century. Academic study and experience are not separate aspects of learning—they interact and they inform and enrich each other. Farren Bradley explores some alternative models for architectural education.

Cottrell (Chapter 19) describes how personal development plans and negotiated learning contracts are used to support students during their year in practice and as a means of fostering lifelong learning, attitudes and skills. The aim of both these processes is to develop in students the practice of reflecting on and managing their own learning, and to help them integrate their learning from practice with their academic studies (as suggested by Farren Bradley).

Webster (Chapter 20) also describes the development of independent and lifelong learning through negotiated learning contracts, although the focus of her contract is different from that of Cottrell. Webster's learning contracts are used by students to make curriculum choices in relation to the two-year, full-time diploma and to plan their study pathway. Webster provides a detailed description of the stages of the learning contract process and of the associated reflective activities.

White (Chapter 21) describes the organisation and benefits of student-led and peer-supported reviews. A central feature of these reviews is that students learn to evaluate and to comment constructively on their own and each others' designs. This encourages students to take responsibility for their own learning. White provides some data on the effectiveness of these reviews from the point of view of both students and tutors.

18 Learning in practice

A retreat, an opportunity or an imperative?

Judith V. Farren Bradley

The education/practice schism

> The real and substantial effects of the experience of higher educa-
> tion extend over the whole lifetime of graduates and are inextric-
> ably entwined with other forces and the experiences beyond our
> walls' reach.
>
> (Trow 1995, p 21)

The current form of architectural education in the UK is relatively new.
Prior to the Oxford Conference of 1958 the profession had been the
product of a predominantly office-based educational process, enhanced
(or for some disturbed) by an examination system and a variety of educational opportunities to support the candidates. In fact it was not until
the 1980s that the majority of registered architects entered the profession through a combination of five years of full-time education and a
minimum of two years of supervised practical training.

Excellent histories of the architectural profession have been written
(Crinson and Lubbock 1994; Kaye 1960; Saint 1983). In each, reference
is made to an apparent schism between architectural education and
architectural practice, and sociological studies of the profession also
refer to this (Cuff 1991; Gutman 1988). It also forms a not incon-
siderable part of the discussion on architectural education and practice
at conferences and symposia, and in journals and reports (Carolin
1992; Cuff 1996; Gutman 1996; Pressman 1997; Rappaport 1984;
Rowe 1996). Most of these works debate the relative merits or demer-
its of the schism. Cuff commends it as 'a creative tension', while
Gutman decries it as the primary cause of, 'immense frustration
among young architects'. Button and Fleming (1991) and Symes *et al.*
(1995) revealed a similar mismatch in their studies of the profession by
identifying an almost inverse relationship between the time and
importance attributed to activities such as conceptual design and technical and management issues in education, and that attributed in
practice.

Moreover, as a topic for debate it is not restricted to any single country or geographical area. Stevens (1998a) compares the form and consequences of the Anglo-American education system with the more overtly academic/technical European model. This helps to illuminate some of the current tensions, as it is clear that the UK schools find aspects of the European model immensely attractive. Education systems and subsequent expectations in the workplace are intricately linked to the societies in which they operate. The general trend in the UK has been towards creating greater interdependence between universities and industry, rather than offering any incentive for intellectual autonomy. This is not merely for financial reasons, it is also a product of the move towards wider participation in higher education and the recognition of a need for lifelong learning in a highly competitive global marketplace.

Architectural education—a combination of intellectual rigour and professional and practical skill—should be well placed to gain from this trend. Why is it then, that as more academic subjects are embracing concepts of transferable skills and issues of employability, architectural education is in danger of heading in the opposite direction?

The rise of the academic

The original reasons for the development of a predominantly full-time higher education model for architectural education were sound for what were anticipated as the needs of a society entering an essentially technical era. In the 1950s and 1960s the profession was dominated by the public sector and the challenges of postwar reconstruction. The development of a research culture was considered essential, especially in technology and social studies. Existing modes of practice were considered inadequate to meet these needs, and the higher education establishments were entrusted to provide the intellectual and physical resources necessary for the transformation of the profession, and therefore architecture itself. A technological elite would be produced to lead the production of the built environment.

Prescribed academic standards were deemed necessary for entry to architectural education and a prescribed curriculum was devised to be delivered over an extended undergraduate programme. A formal accommodation between practice and education was developed in the MacMorran Report (1955), consolidated after the Oxford Conference, finalised after the publication of *The Report on the Practical Training of Architects* (Layton 1962) and partially implemented as the current RIBA Practical Training Scheme. For over 30 years it has remained an accommodation between a less than convinced profession and educational institutions that are unable and/or unwilling to deal with activities outside standard academic practice.

Carolin's (1992) paper in the RIBA's *Strategic Study of the Profession* states the accepted convention: 'Education is the responsibility of the schools, but responsibility for prequalification training is shared between the schools and practice. Theoretical work is best done in the schools, practical work in practice.' Despite the 'tense and even hotly debated' relationship between architectural practice and architectural education (Rowe 1996), tacit acceptance of this division of labour has developed, which suits the purposes of both education and practice. Each is able to maintain control over and develop its respective territory, unchallenged by 'the other side'. The territory of architectural discourse and production is partitioned between the two sectors, reducing the ability of either constructively to inform the other. It has also allowed an operational difference to become an intellectual schism between the sectors.

From teaching to learning

The traditional view of education is that it is about 'teaching'— through curricula, structures and prescribed activity. However, prompted by research in psychology and neuroscience, a new insight has been gained into the ways in which we learn. This has served to shift the emphasis in education from teaching to 'learning'.

Learning is now accepted as a multifaceted activity. Recent research suggests that each of us has a particular set of learning characteristics that determine the ways and means by which we learn. However these innate learning preferences are almost immediately modified and developed by activity and experience. This continues over time and in relationship to context, through the variety of learning experiences we encounter (Long, 1990; Wolf and Kolb 1984).

One of the strengths of architectural education is that it has always used a range of teaching and learning strategies. Experiential learning, through the studio, has been at the core of these. The project, as a vehicle for 'learning by doing', is recognised as a highly successful mechanism for developing and embedding knowledge and skill.

As an activity the design process, in education and practice, has been used as an exemplar by Schön (1983) and others of how 'reflection in action' operates. The iterative nature of the design process also mirrors Kolb's learning cycle and connects to previously mentioned theories of individual learning styles and preferences (Honey and Mumford 1992, 1996).

As a professional discipline, architecture has required both academic qualifications and practical experience. In current educational terminology, the basic structure of UK architectural education is a combination of institution-based and work-based learning. Architectural education is associated with institution-based activity. Practical training is the description given to work-based activity. This too is promoted as a model for future education. Handy (1989) suggests that this combination of work-based and formal learning will be the most appropriate for the 'portfolio man' of tomorrow. It is also identified as a necessity for the creation of learning organisations. The importance of what Mumford describes as 'negative capability' in the learning process is the ability to allow people to learn 'on the job' from their mistakes in both the academic environment and the workplace.

The greatest contribution any educational establishment can make to its graduates is to provide them with the self-awareness and abilities to learn in whatever context they find themselves throughout their lives. The greatest disservice an educational process can do is to attempt to circumscribe education to the formalised, institutional environment and, *inter alia*, consign any action or educational experience that takes place outside these controls to a position of lesser value and lower calibre.

What's in a name?

The difference in nomenclature between architectural education and practical training has tended to support the idea that these are mutually exclusive and different forms of activity, fulfilling different functions. In the world of the 1958 Oxford Conference this may indeed have been the case.

- Education was assumed to be open ended, exploratory and expansive. Essentially associated with theory, success in this arena was defined in terms of individual intellectual attainment and rewarded by the titles and letters appended to an individual's name.
- Training, on the other hand, was assumed to be restrictive, skill-based and linear in nature—specific to the needs of the task and/or organisation rather than the individual, and achieved through the repetition of specific activities or standardised processes. Essentially associated with practice, success here was rewarded by less prestigious awards and vocational qualifications—those accredited by trade or national vocational agencies.

Consequent to a better understanding of how we learn and how we use learning to inform action, educational theorists have proposed a variety of ways in which education can be reordered. These vary between what might be considered as the distinction between different forms of knowledge production, as in the distinction between 'propositional knowledge' and 'process knowledge' (Eraut 1994), or in terms of outcomes as 'academic competence' or 'operational competence' (Barnett 1994). Eraut clearly interrelates these forms of knowledge, and as his work was generated from a study of professions it is of particular interest to architectural education.

A third definition comes from Gibbons *et al.* (1994), who also differentiate between forms of knowledge production, associating one with the highly controlled activities in educational institutions and the other with the 'multivariant, unsystematic and even anti-coherent' (Scott 1996) nature of knowledge production outside the institution. From this it would be interesting to surmise that there has been a kind of role reversal between the school and the workplace. As modes of working have changed significantly and the speed of organisational and cultural change has increased, the workplace may now offer the greatest educational challenge to the student. In contrast, learning outcomes are much easier to predict and control within the institution. The presumed hierarchy between different forms of knowledge production or forms of competence is therefore challenged. What emerges is that education could and should be inclusive. The boundaries are being redrawn: 'knowledge is no longer seen as being predominantly generated within homogeneous communities of academic peers [but is] produced with heterogeneous networks where producers, users, intermediaries, popularisers co-mingle.' (Scott 1996).

In 1996 the DfEE published *A Review of Work Based Learning in Higher Education* (Brennan and Little 1996). This is a well-researched study and covers not only key academic research on the efficacy of different learning strategies and environments, but also reviews the strengths and weaknesses of work-based learning programmes from more than 30 higher education institutions and across more than 50 disciplines. Brennan and Little set out the case for and against the development and acceptance of work-based learning in higher education. Whilst the advantages of a closer relationship appear considerable for the student and in terms of the development of the discipline, the challenge to higher education institutions and their staff is also considerable. Some of the first work-based learning necessary would therefore be for the academic staff themselves!

Mastering Change: Learning Lessons of the Enterprise in Higher Education Initiative (Hawkins and Winter 1997), is another useful study. It is based on an evaluation of the Enterprise in Higher Education Initiative, which operated over a five-year period (from 1988) across 66 higher education institutions in the UK. What is clear from both publications is that the quality and value of educational experience available outside the academic institutions is as high as that offered within its walls. What is more important is that if it is sufficiently structured, it should be given an equivalence in terms of level of attainment and as a contribution to an academic award.

Society's call for change

A series of studies, including the RIBA's *Strategic Study of the Profession* (1992–95) and *Architects and their Practices* (Symes *et al.* 1995), have documented the perceived strengths and weaknesses of the architectural profession. All the studies identified a profession with considerable potential, but one that has failed to maintain existing spheres of activity and, therefore lines of income; failed to impact on identified potential areas for activity; and failed to maintain the confidence of either commissioning clients or users. Commercial pressures mean that practice is unable adequately to support a Practical Training Scheme that offers it little short-term benefit. Specialisation means that it is more difficult for students to gain all-round experience. Fear of litigation and the requirement for client confidentiality limit information transfer within practices and the opportunities for any 'negative capability'.

Related reports and papers have concentrated on the educational needs of the construction industry as a whole (Andrews and Derbyshire 1993; National Contractors' Group 1989, OST Report 1995). These have consistently challenged the role of all the professions within education and attributed the lack of interdisciplinary understanding and adequate research across the industry to the narrow focus of each professional body. There is, in addition, an increasingly antitrust, antiprofession view in contemporary society. The requirement for a lay majority in the current Architects Registration Board reflects this general trend.

The more general failings of the UK construction industry have been extensively documented, culminating in Egan's *Rethinking Construction* (1998). The place of design and the role of the architect have been challenged in all these reports. Following Latham (1994) and Egan (1998) a combination of new legislation and public procurement procedures have challenged architects to rethink their role in construction (Howarth 1999). Despite these failures, the importance of design and environmental quality is higher in the public's perception than ever before. The work of individual architects is recognised and valued internationally, and practising architects are playing an active and prominent part in policy decisions at the national level.

Changing architectural education

Higher education has seen significant changes since the Oxford Conference. Student numbers have risen by 600 per cent. Funding has been effectively reduced per student by 40 per cent. Education has become part of the all-pervasive performance ethos and is viewed as a major contributor to national economic growth and regeneration

(Dearing 1997). In this environment, architectural education is seen as having potential benefits and disadvantages to parent institutions. As a popular subject, it has been able to recruit well, and as a five-year course it has maintained institutional departments of significant size, commanding capitation fees for all five years. However it remains outside academic norms and its vocational status has proved a problem for some of the older universities. The studio-based culture has become increasingly difficult to defend as student to staff ratios in lecture-based subjects are driven higher with diminishing resources. Part-time staff, the intermediaries between practice and education, are the first victims of financial strictures.

Despite the hopes of the Oxford Conference, education has not become the primary generator of research. Although individual schools have made considerable contributions, the research record of architecture as a discipline remains poor in relation to science and engineering—other resource-hungry areas. Meunier (1987) suggests that the most important theoretical work in both architecture and building in the UK and USA, has been conducted outside universities, or by those only loosely affiliated to universities. Broadbent (1991) argues that deconstruction, one of the more radical areas of recent architectural theory, emanated from practice. Duffy (1998) refers to research as predominantly emerging from areas outside the universities.

Unlike other professions, such as medicine and law, architecture has failed significantly to increase access for women, ethnic minority groups and non-standard entry students. Despite the increased enrolment of women, the percentage drop-out rate for women is higher than for men (RIBA statistics). As student finances tighten, withdrawals and suspension of studies are increasing. Forty per cent of students work during term-time and 30 per cent miss lectures because of employment. Whilst the fee contribution is a factor in reduced applications across all subject areas, the loss of the maintenance grant is the most problematic factor for many students as 50 per cent of their income goes on accommodation.

Graduates face entry into a relatively poorly paid profession with a debt burden in excess of their contemporaries entering law, medicine or even other areas of the construction industry. Inadequate and uncertain career prospects within the profession are exacerbated by the prospect of students leaving a five-year undergraduate education with an apparently vocational but incomplete qualification. They may find themselves demonstrating their abilities to prospective employers via a portfolio of discrete objects whose existence is predicated on an equally discrete dialogue, at best common to architectural discourse and at worst specific to the institution from which they emerge.

Can education and practice become mutually beneficial?

'When the wind blows, some people build walls, others build windmills.' Architectural education as a design discipline, values the ability to learn through and from practice. It must therefore apply this dictum to itself.

There are at least two recognisable and distinct professions within architectural education: the educators and the practitioners. They are not mutually exclusive, but like the distinction between pedestrians and motorists, who may be both at different times, when acting as either they tend to adopt the behaviour and prejudices of that particular group.

One of the characteristics and criticisms of any profession is its tendency to privilege its own view of the world and knowledge base over that of other groups. Educators and practitioners are demonstrating all the boundary conditions and preferences for internally referencing structures described in this criticism. It is therefore not surprising to see that, rather than working together in a mutual aid and support mechanism, education and practice have developed increasingly isolationist attitudes and an increasing lack of vision as to the interdependence of education and practice.

As the emphasis moves from teaching to learning, and outcomes and levels of achievement become the main focus rather than inputs and duration of study, a more flexible and student-centred architectural education can be designed. The academic institution is not the repository of all architectural knowledge or research, and it is not the most appropriate context for particular forms of action learning. By integrating learning opportunities across practices and academic institutions, rather than offering an either/or, in/out situation, students, education and practice can reap benefits. Learning *through* practice, rather than just learning *in* practice, has considerable potential.

By incorporating work-based learning into architectural education programmes, a more varied route to registration could be offered to suit the needs of individual students' learning preferences and their financial necessities. This could widen access to the profession without reducing standards. At the most prosaic level, this would allow students who need to support themselves to 'learn while they earn', in educational programmes devised to benefit both the employer and the student. This is not the traditional part-time model, but one in which full equivalence is given to work-based learning and specific learning outcomes achieved outside the traditional institutional environment.

There is no need to restrict work-based learning opportunities to the architectural profession. There could be no better way for a student to acquire knowledge and experience of integrating environmental engineering into architectural design than to work with engineers. In order to reach a certain level of knowledge and competency in managing people and projects, spending time in a contracting or project management enterprise could be most appropriate. Working with user groups and client organisations would offer other opportunities. If a better understanding across these groups is required, then this must be as valid a strategy as the development of multidisciplinary courses.

The greater challenge

Research has shown that in order to develop successful work-based learning, old prejudices must be set aside and new understanding and skills acquired.

Academic staff must recognise the advantages of spreading the resource base of education and the opportunities that more flexible course provision can offer in widening access, creating attitudinal shifts and providing opportunities for research. Staff will need to be trained to understand and operate these programmes, develop new teaching strategies and provide clear support documentation.

Students need to be adequately supported in work-based learning. By developing learning contracts, students become independent learners and managers of their own educational process. This is the best way to create life-long learners and establish and assess the skills necessary for continuing professional development (CPD).

Those in the workplace must share the vision that even in the most pressured working environment, opportunities for education exist and that by supporting work-based learning for visiting students and current employees, past performance can be better assessed, current operational performance can be improved and future opportunities identified and maximised.

Training and support will need to be given to those responsible for mentoring or supervising students in the workplace. Even this initial work can be used for benefit. It can be used by the profession to speed the development of learning strategies within practices and support CPD.

The acceptance of academics into practice might be expanded to develop and assist joint research projects and allow them to act as facilitators of structured professional and management development plans.

Academic institutions would develop better links with practice and industry, one of the current performance criteria.

A more informed critique of architectural production could be developed and possible innovations tested.

Finally, the profession would have the opportunity to develop a learning culture and a recognition that practice is and must be a primary site for architectural education.

Conclusion

Education has an impact on its recipients not merely in terms of knowledge transfer but also in terms of the acquisition of modes of operation and the creation of attitudinal preferences. This chapter does not suggest that the immediate needs of contemporary practice should be the focus of educational endeavour. Nor does it suggest that competence to practice should be the determinant of academic success. Rather, architectural education—through its structure and content—should nurture in its graduates the ability and self-confidence to challenge the current boundaries of the discipline and contribute to its development. This would reduce the need artificially to maintain 'creative tensions' within and between architectural education and practice.

Dialogue, both critical or supportive, is best achieved through vigorous interaction. Graduates from such a revised architectural education system will create modes and forms of practice appropriate to the future, the details of which it would be impossible and probably unwise to predict.

References

Andrews, J. and Derbyshire, A. (1993) *Crossing Boundaries: A report on the State of Commonality in Education and Training for the Construction Professions*. London: CIC.

Barnett, R. (1994) *The Limits of Competence, Higher Education and Society*. Milton Keynes: SRHE/Open University Press.

Brennan, J. and Little, B. (1996) *A Review of Work Based Learning in Higher Education*. London: DfEE.

Broadbent, G. (1991) 'Deconstruction: A Student Guide', *Journal of Architectural Theory and Criticism*, 2(10).

Button, K. and Fleming, M. (1991) *Architectural Education and Training Needs*. London: RIBA.

Carolin, P. (1992) In Strategic Study of the Profession: Phase 1: Strategic overview, pp. 171–82, London: RIBA.

Crinson, M. and Lubbock, J. (1994) *Architecture: Art or Profession*. Manchester: Manchester University Press.

Cuff, D. (1991) *Architecture: The Story of Practice*. Cambridge, Mass.: MIT Press.

Cuff, D. (1996) 'Celebrate the gap between education and practice', *Architecture*, 85(8).

Dearing, R. (1997) *Higher Education in the Learning Society*. London: HMSO.

Duffy, F. (1998) *Architectural Knowledge*. London: E & FN Spon.

Egan, Sir John (1998) Rethinking Construction: The report of the Construction Task Force, Department of Environment, Transport and the regions, London.

Eraut, M. (1994) *Developing Professional Knowledge and Competence*. London: Falmer Press.

Eraut, M. and Cole, G. (1993) *Assessing Competence in the Professions*. Sheffield: Sheffield Employment Department.

Fisher, T. (1996) 'Three Models for the Future of Practice', in W. S. Saunders (ed.), *Reflections on Architectural Practices in the Nineties*. Princeton, NJ: Princeton Architectural Press.

Gibbons, M., Limoges, C., Nowtny, H., Schwartzman, S., Scott, P. and Trow, M. (1994) *The New Production of Knowledge: The Dynamics of Science and Research in Contemporary Societies*. Beverly Hills, CA: Sage.

Gutman, R. (1988) *Architectural Practice A Critical View*. Princeton, NJ: Princeton Architectural Press.

Gutman, R. (1996) 'Redesigning Architecture Schools', *Architecture*, 85(8).

Handy, C. (1989) *The Age of Unreason*. London: Business Books.

Hawkins, P. and Winter, J. (1997) *Mastering Change: Learning Lessons of the Enterprise in Higher Education Initiative*. London: DfEE/Whiteways Research.

Honey, P. and Mumford, A. (1992) *Manual of Learning Styles*, 3rd edn. London: Honey.

Honey, P. and Mumford, A. (1996) *Managing your learning Environment*. London: Honey.

Howarth, Alan (1999) Interview in *Building*, 2 July.

Kaye, B. (1960) *The development of the Architectural Profession in Britain: A Sociological Approach*. London: Allen & Unwin.

Latham, Sir Michael (1994) *Constructing the Team: Final Report of the Government/Industry Review of Procurement and Contractual Arrangements in the UK*. London: HMSO.

Layton, E. (1962) *The Report on the Practical Training of Architects*. London: RIBA.

Long, D. G. (1990) *Learner Managed Learning*. London: Kogan Page.

MacMorran, D. (1955) 'The McMorran Report', *Architects Journal*, 10 February.

Meunier, J. (1987) 'Paradigms for Practice: A task for architecture schools', *Journal of Architectural Education*, 40(2).

Mumford, A. (1994) 'Effectiveness in management development', in A. Mumford (ed.), *The Gower Handbook of Management Development*, 4th edn. Aldershot: Gower.

National Contractors Group (1989) *Building towards 2001*. NCG/Building. London: The Builder Group.

Office of Science and Technology (OST) (1995) *Progress through Partnership*, report from the Technology Foresight Panel on Construction. London: HMSO.

Pressman, A. (1997) *Professional Practice 101*. Chichester: John Wiley & Sons.

Rappaport, A. (1984) 'There is an Urgent need to Reduce or Eliminate the Dominance of the Studio', *Architectural Record*, October.

RIBA (1992) *Strategic Study of the Profession: Phase 1: Strategic Overview*, London: RIBA.

RIBA (1993) *Strategic Study of the Profession: Phase 2: Clients and Architects*, London: RIBA.

RIBA (1995) *Strategic Study of the Profession: Phases 3 and 4: The Way Forward*, London: RIBA.

Robertson, I. (1999) *Mind Sculpture*. London: Bantam Press.

Rowe, P. (1996) 'Shaping design education', in W. S. Saunders, (ed.), *Reflections on Architectural Practices in the Nineties*. Princeton, NJ: Princeton Architectural Press.

Saint, A. (1983) *The Image of the Architect*. New Haven, CT: Yale University Press.

Saint, A. (1996) 'Architecture as Image: Can we rein in this new beast?', in W. S. Saunders, (ed.), *Reflections on Architectural Practices in the Nineties*. Princeton, NJ: Princeton Architectural Press.

Scarborough, H. (ed.) (1996) *The Management of Expertise*. London: Macmillan.

Schön, D. (1983) *The Reflective Practitioner*, New York: Basic Books.

Scott, P. (1996) 'Governance and Management in Universities', paper presented at the workshop on 'New challenges to Academic Professions', Academia Europaea.

Stevens, G. (1998a) 'Angst in Academia: Universities, The Architecture Schools and the Profession', *Journal of Architecture and Planning Research*, 15(2).

Stevens, G. (1998b) *The favored Circle: The Social Foundations of Architectural Distinction*. Cambridge, Mass.: MIT Press.

Symes, M., Eley, J. and Seidel, A. (1995) *Architects and their Practices*. London: Butterworth.

Trow, M. (1995) *Two Essays in Quality in Higher Education*. Universitetskanslern. London.

Wolfe, D. M. and Kolb, D. A. (1984) 'Career Development, Personal Growth and Experiential Learning', in D. Kolb *et al.*, *Organisational Psychology*. Englewood elitts, NJ: Prentice-Hall.

Woodhall, J. and Winstanley, D. (1998) *Management Development: Strategy and Practice*. Oxford: Blackwell.

19 The role of personal development plans and learning contracts in self-directed student learning

Derek Cottrell

Introduction

Hull School of Architecture has piloted a personal development plan (PDP) process to provide the means for better informing student choice on the Postgraduate Certificate/Diploma in Architectural Practice, which covers the two years of practical training on its professionally accredited architecture programme. The PDP process has now been extended to other courses in the university to guide student choice and foster independent learning.

Our experience suggests that the PDP process is:

- particularly appropriate for vocational courses leading to careers in a rapidly changing profession such as architecture;
- a sound preparation for professional practice where continuing education is mandatory;
- a useful aid in the negotiation of learning contracts between students and their tutor.

My purpose here is to:

- outline the main aspects of the PDP process as it has evolved in the Hull School of Architecture;
- describe its relationship to individual learning contracts;
- review experience of the process in operation;
- describe how operational problems have been addressed.

The context

The Hull School of Architecture has substantial experience of implementing study programmes that emphasise self-directed student learning. The school's philosophy is to favour student-centred learning over a more didactic approach. Accordingly it has, for some years, operated a learning contract system to extend student choice and foster independent learning on its architecture programmes. In the 1970s the school adopted a 'unit' or 'atelier' system of teaching whereby students were grouped in so-called 'workbases', each led by one tutor. The workbase was the focus of all learning. Individual programmes of learning were negotiated between the student and the workbase tutor. A learning contract defined:

- each project brief;
- the intended learning outcomes;
- the basis for assessment.

The introduction of unitisation and subject modularity by the university has since partly eroded the workbase model of learning, but the learning contract remains intact. Indeed the idea of the learning contract gained strength by the change, since the detailed unit descriptions demanded by the university's modular scheme provided a clearer basis for the contract by defining, more explicitly than before, the required learning outcomes, the weight of assessment and criteria for assessment.

As applied currently, students are allowed to negotiate a learning contract as a substitute for any unit of study providing there is:

- an educational rationale for the proposal;
- an equivalence between the outcomes of the contract and the unit it replaces.

The PDP provides the educational rationale, and thereby is a mechanism for retaining and optimising student choice within a unitised curriculum.

The learning contract system has been adapted for other non-architectural programmes in the university, including the Modular Masters Programme and the Masters by Learning Contract. In the Masters by Learning Contract, only the framework of the programme is defined. The whole of the programme's content is based on negotiated learning contracts. This effectively means that participants design their own qualification under the guidance of subject tutors. The Modular Masters Programme was the precursor of the Masters by Learning Contract and is essentially similar, although less flexible as award titles are prescribed. In both programmes PDPs are used to guide student learning.

Although initially the Postgraduate Certificate/Diploma in Architectural Practice (PCAP/PDAP) provided the test bed for the use of a PDP process to guide student learning, the process has now been extended to the postgraduate Bachelor of Architecture programme (recognised by the RIBA for exemption from the RIBA Part 2 examination) and will be extended to the undergraduate programmes in the school.

The postgraduate certificate in architectural practice and the PDP

The Postgraduate Certificate in Architectural Practice (PCAP) is aimed at students undertaking their first year of practical training following their successful completion of the BA(Hons) degree in architecture or other recognised Part 1 qualifications. This is a crucial stage in their education as an architect:

- It is the first of a required minimum of two years' practical training.
- For many students it may be their first experience of architectural practice.
- It is a preparation for the postgraduate Bachelor of Architecture (equivalent to RIBA Part 2).
- It is a chance to broaden the skills and knowledge to practise as an architect.
- It is a time to re-evaluate career options and choices.

All this has to be achieved in locations divorced from the school, in a wide variety of settings with variable levels of office support.

The Hull School of Architecture developed the PCAP to support this year-out experience more effectively.

The programme has a number of components:

- Students are required to attend regular block courses in architectural practice. These are an opportunity for sharing experience, and allow access to the school's practical training adviser (PTA) for advice and counselling.
- The PTA also visits the work placement to meet the office mentor at least once during the programme and prepares a report on the office and the student's experience.
- Students prepare case studies, a practical training record and a personal statement of their experience to consolidate their learning and as part of their assessment.

An incidental but intended benefit of the assessment is the annual snapshot it provides to the school of trends in the construction industry, and feedback on the quality of experience, even the quality of professionalism, in the practices where the students are located. The PDP is prepared by the students at the start of the year to guide their learning during their placement. Eventually it provides the backbone of the personal statement submitted as part of the final assessment for the award of the PCAP. The features and operation of the PDP are described below, but it is important to understand that the term describes both a document and a process. The process is, I would argue, an essential foundation of the Hull School of Architecture's philosophy of self-directed independent learning.

The PDP was developed to address a number of issues. Previously the overall coherence of individual study programmes in the School of Architecture had been monitored through a system of termly portfolio reviews. The review entailed an interview with a panel of two to three tutors, including the workbase tutor. Students were required to present an organised portfolio of their work to the panel and received counselling on their progress and academic aspirations. This process worked well enough for the full-time, undergraduate and postgraduate architecture courses leading to Part 1 and 2 qualifications. However, when the school developed a framework of postgraduate qualifications, including PCAP, covering the periods of practical training, it was felt that portfolio review alone was insufficient as a means for managing individual programmes of study. Particular problems were:

- Reduced contact with students out on placement.
- The variability of student experience of practical training.
- The need to maintain a 'practice-led' curriculum.
- The need to support students moving beyond a conventional architectural career.
- The need to encourage students to diversify.

The solution adopted was to introduce a personal development planning unit into the programme of study.

There were a number of objectives:

- To help students formulate more robust career development strategies.
- To inform tutors more fully of individual student aspirations and general trends.
- To encourage a more reflective approach to the period of practical training.
- To ensure that the taught elements of the programme supported students' practical training.
- To help students prepare for their Part 2 studies.

The PDP process was considered important enough to give it a credit rating equivalent to 60 hours of full-time study over the academic year. Students were supported in their preparation of their PDPs by seminars and tutorials.

The personal development plan process

PCAP students are required to produce and maintain a personal development plan as part of their study programme. The process comprises the following elements:

- a personal appraisal (a 'SWOT' analysis) of skills and experience analysing:
  1 strengths;
  2 weaknesses;
  3 opportunities for personal development;
  4 'threats' to achievement.
- A statement of the student's personal goals and objectives.
- A personal action plan, including a learning plan for at least the duration of the study programme.
- A learning contract for each unit of study.
- Processes to monitor, record and reflect on achievement.
- A review of the personal action plan, possibly resulting in the setting of new objectives for the next stage of learning.
- A personal statement informed by the PDP and providing the basis for a summative assessment.

The whole process takes a minimum of eight months and is supported by peer group and tutor mentoring. Key stages are:

- The PDP, derived from the SWOT analysis, is prepared. It sets out short-, medium- and long-term personal and academic objectives.
- Achievements during the placement period are monitored against the PDP, and if necessary the plan is modified to suit changing circumstances.
- The PDP is used to prepare the student's personal statement to support the final assessment.

The PDP is an ongoing process, not a blueprint. Commenced during the first year out, the plan continues to guide choices during subsequent years of Part 2 study and the final stage of practical training after Part 2. The initial personal action plan is transformed during this period into a record of achievement. This can be used to support a student's presentation at the Part 2 and Part 3 examinations, and if included in the student's personal statement it becomes a component of the summative assessment in Part 3.

The very best students produce documents that are not only valuable in supporting their preparation for job interviews, but in many cases (although this was not intended originally) are suitable for inclusion in their portfolio of work as a design/communication project.

Although the Postgraduate Certificate in Architectural Practice (PCAP) made successful use of the PDP, there was no equivalent RIBA examination. A sterner test for the PDP was the Bachelor of Architecture postgraduate programme, which is recognised as giving exemption from the RIBA Part 2 examination. Here the demands of an accredited award had to be reconciled with the ambitions of the independent learner. The Bachelor of Architecture postgraduate programme, leading to Part 2 exemption, is a mixed mode programme, but predominantly taken full time. Here the PDP has several functions: guiding the choice of studio and project briefs and underpinning the learning contract system, which extends student choice in the Bachelor of Architecture programme.

Evaluation

Evaluation to date is preliminary in nature and has been carried out with the limited purpose of guiding curriculum developments and contributing to normal course-monitoring procedures. The evaluation has led to some relatively insignificant adaptations and refinements to PDP pro formas and induction procedures, and has confirmed the value of the PDP process in guiding students' academic and career choices. Most significant has been a recent change to the architecture programme that has embedded the PDP process in other units, so that it is no longer a free-standing unit. Although largely a response to changes in the university's postgraduate award framework, the change also reflects an acceptance that the PDP is now intrinsic to postgraduate architectural studies at the Hull School of Architecture.

Sources of information for the evaluation were:

- Direct verbal feedback from students gained in seminars during PDP inductions and reviews over several years.
- Quotations of students' views recorded by the PCAP/PDAP course leader in an evaluation seminar.
- External examiners' views over several years, expressed during discussions of submitted PDPs following oral examinations for the PDAP final assessment.
- Views formed by the course leader, myself and other staff involved in using PDPs as a basis for progress reviews and as components of assessment.

A more systematic evaluation, tracking changes in students' responses during their period of architectural studies and beyond into practice, would be desirable and would allow a statistical analysis, but that remains for a future study.

Students' reactions, as might be expected, vary. At one end of the range there are those who see the PDP as a distraction and of little value. At the opposite end there are those who are enthusiastic and regard the process as an invaluable aid to achieving their career and life goals. Examples of positive reactions are that it 'encourages us to think about our future and what we need to do to prepare for it', and 'creates awareness of matters that ought to be thought about'.

Here the critical reactions are perhaps of more interest:

- Some students are reticent about setting out their plans in written form for a variety of reasons, for example:
    1 they have concerns about confidentiality;
    2 they are reluctant to share or, perhaps, even acknowledge secret ambitions;
    3 they feel insufficiently in control of their own destiny to set out firm targets: 'it is impossible to plan ... or define the path to any goal'. Getting a job is difficult, never mind employment which fits into plans;
    4 they fear that the PDP will highlight personal failure;
    5 they regard the PDP philosophy as alien to their personal culture.
- The process is demanding and may seem bureaucratic: '[too many] repetitive answers', 'difficult to complete, not having had to think about the issues beforehand'.
- Many students are reluctant to follow a prescribed format: 'A good thing in theory, but the format and the way it is presented do not generate any enthusiasm'. 'The format should be flexible, allowing freedom to present in the form to suit the individual.'
- The PDP exposes weaknesses in writing skills.
- It is not immediately obvious to the uninitiated that the PDP process expands awareness of the opportunities for choice: 'do not see the point of it, it is a waste of time'.
- Not everyone is ready to take responsibility for their learning: 'questions should be more specific'.

However, writing the contract requires extra effort from the student, so the less committed student will not see this as a benefit.

Observation of particular cohorts over the period of a year suggests that, whatever their initial reservations, the majority of students eventually do see the value of the PDP process in clarifying their career or even life objectives, so that they are more focused on achieving their goals, and by systematically logging their many small achievements, which might previously have been disregarded, they increase their self-esteem and enhance their overall development and growth as an individual. Other feedback is overwhelmingly positive about the principle of the PDP and its value to students who tackle the process conscientiously.

According to the PCAP/PDAP course leader the PDP 'gives increased focus and awareness of what is possible. Students have come to appreciate the need to plan their course, their projects and their employment to prepare themselves [to meet] their ambitions, rather than aimlessly following what seems interesting at the time'.

Feedback from external examiners on the architectural practice programme (covering practical training and work-based learning) is also positive. The PDP is seen as a useful support in the assessment of an individual's competence for practice. As the PDP forms part of the documentation submitted for the final assessment, alongside written examination papers, a case study, a personal statement and a log book, it can provide an insight into another facet of the student that is possibly not revealed by other components of the assessment. It especially highlights students' motivations and interests and their level of commitment to their profession.

Resolution of problems

Previously identified student reservations are now addressed at induction. The confidentiality issue is resolved by limiting the circulation of the PDP to relevant tutors and examiners. The issue of 'secret ambitions' is tackled by counselling students that they are not required to declare all their aims and objectives. They are, however, encouraged to prepare a parallel plan for their personal reference only.

Students are advised that the plan is not a blueprint and its main value is to help them prioritise. Regular changes and updates of the plan are not only expected, but are also desirable to keep them on track to meet their academic, career and other goals. The current plan is only a point of reference or the starting point for the next plan. It is a part of the feedback loop that is essential to reflective learning and later practice.

Students are strongly encouraged to include short-term, achievable objectives for themselves alongside longer term, more ambitious objectives. The subsequent monitoring stage of the process should then focus on achievements being acknowledged. Areas for further development are identified rather than emphasising failures. Cultural antipathy is less of a problem now. This may be partly influenced by students' familiarity with the processes followed in many secondary schools, which issue personal planners and use records of achievement extensively. Also the idea of career and life plans have more currency now than when the PDP was first introduced, so there is wider acceptance of the underlying philosophy. Where the issue does arise, it is debated in seminar groups.

A particular format is not prescribed. The format of the PDP at Hull is being continuously developed as it is applied to new courses, and the value of a diversity of formats to suit particular circumstances is accepted. The standard PDP pro formas are issued as only a guide to the content and coverage of the PDP, and students are encouraged to create their own formats if they wish to achieve a higher quality presentation. The use of word-processing and desktop publishing packages avoids repetitive form filling, and allows the PDP to be used as a platform for displaying a student's communication and design skills. The induction process for the PDP unit now emphasises the purpose and value of the PDP, and there are samples of previous student's PDPs that, subject to confidentiality rules, provide supporting exemplars and case studies.

Widespread recognition of the need for students and practitioners to take responsibility for their own learning is now reinforced by government promotion of lifelong learning.

The school is committed to supporting any learning contract for independent study that demonstrably fits in with course aims and objectives and derives from a well considered PDP. This provides a facility for incremental curriculum change led by student choice, reflecting industry and society priorities, which should help to ensure that the architecture programme is kept up to date and relevant.

Conclusion

Experience in the Hull School suggests that the personal development planning process is particularly appropriate to vocational courses leading to careers in a rapidly changing profession such as architecture. Fundamental to the PDP process is the inculcation of a habit of reflection, goal setting and evaluation of achievements used iteratively to guide students' learning. This approach is now underpinned by the processes adopted by the Royal Institute of British Architects' continuing professional development monitoring mechanisms. The mandatory requirements of the professional body have made effective continuing professional education (CPE) the prerequisite for competent practice in architecture. Architectural practice is increasingly complex and architects respond by becoming more specialised; so it is important for CPE to be tailored to the individual. It is generally accepted that effective continuing professional development depends on clear aims and objectives derived from an analysis of individual practitioner's development needs, which are best defined in a PDP. So I would argue that the PDP process provides an appropriate preparation for professional practice wherever continuing education is mandatory.

As student-centred learning is increasingly emphasised in higher education, it is important to consider what support students need to make sound choices. At the University of Lincolnshire and Humberside, learning contracts offer the means to achieve the widest possible student choice and the PDP process is an essential aid in the negotiation of such learning contracts. As Aldous Huxley said: 'Experience is not what happens to you; it is what you do with what happens to you.' My proposition is that the PDP at the Hull School of Architecture, by informing student choice, is an aid to good learning experiences and inculcates habits that are appropriate to successful lifelong learning and essential for competent professional practice.

20 Establishing and managing a student learning contract

A diploma in architecture case study

Helena Webster

Education for the profession

The RIBA's *Meeting the Challenge—a strategy for architecture and architects* (1999) recognises that there is a crisis facing the profession and sets out a number of goals to be achieved within the next five years. These goals include the redefinition of the key knowledge and competencies required by architects if they are to operate successfully in a complex and rapidly changing world.

Behind this redefinition is the belief that architects will have to acquire attitudes and skills that enable life-long learning, and in particular—if they are to embrace the inevitability of change—develop the motivation and skill needed for self-directed and independent learning throughout life. As the primary professional education for architects takes place in schools of architecture it follows that it will be necessary for course management teams to look at ways to integrate the development of self-directed and independent learning into the curriculum. Additional impetus for curricular development in the area of life-long learning comes from the recent Part 2 RIBA guideline syllabus (RIBA 1996) and from the Dearing Report (1997). The challenge for schools of architecture is how to do this in the face of existing curricula structures that are often considered already 'full'.

This chapter describes how we believe the student learning contract in the Oxford Brookes Part 2 diploma in architecture helps develop independent learning and self-directed learning abilities within a modular course structure.

The student learning contract

The Oxford Brookes School of Architecture, the largest school of architecture in the UK, first adopted a modular structure for its two-year, full-time diploma course in architecture in the late 1970s. The aim was to offer graduate students a degree of choice in the subjects they selected (Table 20.1) and to allow a certain amount of flexibility in the order in which they took them (Table 20.2).

Table 20.1 Graduate diploma in architecture 1998: course components and subjects offered in each component

Design studio—core	Requisite studies—linked to core	Alternative routes—specialism
Unit 1	Construction	Built resource studies
Unit 2	Economics of design	Development practices
Unit 3	Energy and environmental design	Energy efficient building
Unit 4	Structures	Vernacular architecture
Computers and design studio	Practice and management	Major study
Energy efficient building	Research and writing	Urban design
External studies WAAC	Urban design	
External studies SOCRATES	Computer aided design	
Housing studio		
Interior architecture studio	*Options—peripheral*	
Responsive environments Studio	Analysing arch precedent	Connections
Architecture and cultural studies	Architecture and the city	Energy efficient architecture
	Anatomy of Oxford	Identity in design
	Architectural geometry	Landscape and architecture
	Architectural psychology	Leading edge
	Computing	Responsive environments
	Urban architecture	Reclaiming modernism
	Languages	

The structure and content of the course has continuously evolved, but in recent years the course management team has recognised the possibility of building on the preexisting requirement for incoming students to select and manage their individual programme of study to promote self-directed learning. To facilitate this a student learning contract was introduced.

Learning contracts are commonly defined as 'agreements negotiated between students and staff regarding the type and amount of study to be undertaken and the type and amount of assessment or credit resulting from this study' (Laycock and Stephenson 1993). They are frequently employed within a particular subject (or an individual project) to plan the study journey and define what will count as evidence of achieved learning. They are useful as a means of fostering self-directed learning because students have to take responsibility for

Table 20.2 Diploma in architecture: examples of common course routes leading to DipArch and Dip/MA alternative route

	Year 1 (5th year)			Year 2 (6th year)			
	Term 1	Term 2	Term 3	Term 4	Term 5	Term 6	Term 7
Route one	Alt. route	Alt. route	Studio + options	Studio + requisite options + Alt. route	Studio + requisite options + Alt. route	Studio + portfolio options +	Masters (alt. route)
Route two	Studio + options + requisite	Studio + options + requisite	Studio + options + requisite	Alt. route	Alt. route	Studio + options + portfolio	Masters (alt. route)

deciding their own learning goals and tracking their progress against these goals. In our diploma course the student learning contract is employed to assist students to plan the two-year programme of study.

The following description uses Malcolm Knowles' 'four stages of a learning contract' to explain the application of the student learning contract at Oxford Brookes (Knowles 1991):

- Orientating the learners to the process of self-directed and contract learning.
- Negotiating the learning contract.
- Providing support, resources and monitoring the contract.
- Evaluation of accomplishments—examination.

Orientation of the learners towards the process of self-directed and contract learning

At the beginning of the diploma an intensive two-week induction programme introduces the students to the course. It begins with a general introductory session to explain the modular system and the purpose and operation of the student learning contract, emphasising that the students will be personally responsible for their own learning package over the six terms of the course. This is followed by a series of short verbal presentations by course leaders describing the subjects on offer in more detail. Interleaved throughout the two weeks are introductions to the school/university resources and a short design project, which is intended primarily as a group-bonding exercise.

Lastly, the students are issued with the *Diploma Course Handbook*, which provides them with a hard copy of the information they receive during the induction programme.

Negotiating the learning contract

After the induction programme the students are required to construct their individual student learning contracts, with the guidance of a personal tutor (personal tutors are normally full-time staff who teach the core design studio and each tutor is allocated about ten tutees from each year). The personal tutor's role is to help students to identify their strengths, weaknesses and aspirations. This information, together with the course requirements, forms the basis on which to construct the content and sequencing of the students' two-year programme of study (student learning contract). The student learning contract takes physical form in the 2-year plan (Figure 20.1), which has to be finalised by week 4 of term 1. The tutor's role at this stage in the learning contract is to encourage students to reflect on their own learning goals and to discuss and plan their pathway through the

STUDENT NAME: Jane Smith

Course Components   **Code Modules**   **Terms**

             1 2 3 4 5 6

Design Studio

	Code	Modules
Unit 1 Studio (LS)	DS0	2.0–8.0
Unit 2 Studio (JS)	DS2	2.0–8.0
Unit 3 Studio (HW)	DS3	2.0–8.0
Architecture and Cultural Studies (MF)	DS15	2.0–8 0
Computers and Design Studio (PA)	DS6	2.0–8.0
Energy Efficient Building Studio (SR)	DS7	2.0
External Studies WAAC	DS8	3.0
External Studies RMIT	DS9	2.0–3.0
External Studies SOCRATES	DS10	2.0
Extreme Environments Studio (TA)	DS11	2.0–8.0
Housing Studio (RH)	DS12	1.0–2.0
Interior Architecture Studio (TP)	DS13	2.0–8.0
Responsive Environments Studio (GPS)	DS14	2.0–8.0
Portfolio Review	DS16	1.0

Requisite Studies

	Code	Modules
Computer-Aided Design	RS8	0.5
Construction	RS1	1.5
Economics of Design	RS2	0.25
Energy and Environmental Design	RS3	1.0
Structures	RS4	0.5
Practice and Management	RS5	1.0
Research and Writing	RS6	0.5
Urban Design	RS7	0.25

Figure 20.1 Example of completed two-year plan—the formalised student learning contract.

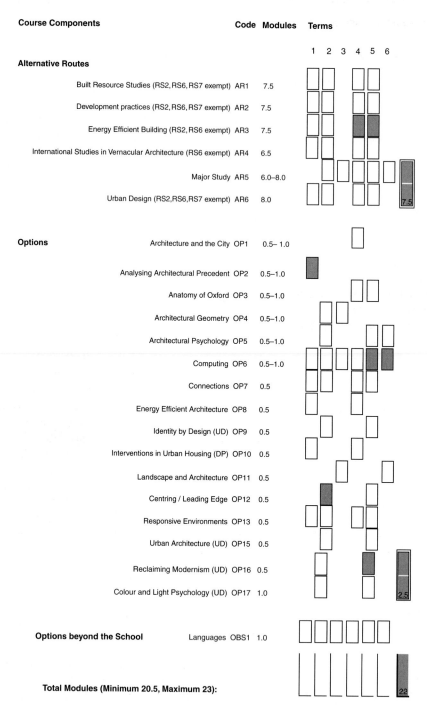

Course Components	Code	Modules	Terms

Alternative Routes

			1 2 3 4 5 6
Built Resource Studies (RS2, RS6, RS7 exempt)	AR1	7.5	
Development practices (RS2, RS6, RS7 exempt)	AR2	7.5	
Energy Efficient Building (RS2, RS6 exempt)	AR3	7.5	
International Studies in Vernacular Architecture (RS6 exempt)	AR4	6.5	
Major Study	AR5	6.0–8.0	
Urban Design (RS2, RS6, RS7 exempt)	AR6	8.0	7.5

Options

Architecture and the City	OP1	0.5–1.0	
Analysing Architectural Precedent	OP2	0.5–1.0	
Anatomy of Oxford	OP3	0.5–1.0	
Architectural Geometry	OP4	0.5–1.0	
Architectural Psychology	OP5	0.5–1.0	
Computing	OP6	0.5–1.0	
Connections	OP7	0.5	
Energy Efficient Architecture	OP8	0.5	
Identity by Design (UD)	OP9	0.5	
Interventions in Urban Housing (DP)	OP10	0.5	
Landscape and Architecture	OP11	0.5	
Centring / Leading Edge	OP12	0.5	
Responsive Environments	OP13	0.5	
Urban Architecture (UD)	OP15	0.5	
Reclaiming Modernism (UD)	OP16	0.5	
Colour and Light Psychology (UD)	OP17	1.0	2.5

Options beyond the School   Languages   OBS1   1.0

Total Modules (Minimum 20.5, Maximum 23):   22

Figure 20.1 (Continued)

diploma, the goal being to get students to take responsibility for their own choices and the direction of their learning.

Support, resources and monitoring progress

Once the individual 2-year plans are formally submitted to the chair of diploma the data is entered into a computer database. This allows the data to be manipulated and reordered to produce termly lists of students taking each course area, for both staff and student information. Personal tutors are available for counselling throughout the 2-year period of study. The course handbook makes it clear that students are allowed to change their initial 2-year plan as they go through the diploma, but that any such changes must be discussed and negotiated with personal tutors. In any discussion/negotiation, personal tutors require students to reflect on their learning experience before making changes to their programme of study as well as ensuring that the revised course of study continues to satisfy the course requirements. Requiring students to reflect on their learning experience before altering their programme of study again encourages students to analyse and reflect on the reasons for their decision-making.

Evaluation of learning outcomes

Evaluation of the development of self-responsibility in learning through the student learning contract procedure is currently made in the final term of the course. A mark is attached to the compulsory portfolio module—a module introduced in 1998 in recognition that a physical 'portfolio' is the primary means by which students present their personal profile to the external examiners, in a 40 minute *viva voce*, for the final examination. Preparation for this is a two-stage process. At the beginning of the final term the student's portfolio is looked at by his or her personal tutor, in conjunction with the student, with a view to how well it represents the student's learning experience and individual profile. The student then agrees on additional work that might improve the portfolio's effectiveness. Again this requires the student to reflect on his or her progress in relation to the overall learning goals, but it also encourages the student to identify gaps between progress and goals and to determine what has to be done next in order to close that gap. This self-assessment of progress is critical for the fostering of self-direction in learning.

A second review takes place just before the final examination, at which a mark is awarded for the work carried out for the module. Additionally, student and tutor discuss the way that the student intends to present his or her portfolio in the *viva voce*. In some cases a 'dry run' is attempted, with the personal tutor playing the external examiner. Subsequently both tutor and student reflect on the performance, paying particular attention to the clarity of the verbal communication. Both stages of the portfolio review are both backward and forward looking. This helps to develop reflective patterns that are important for the cultivation of self-responsibility in learning.

Reflecting on the learning contract

The present student learning contract procedures were put in place well before the call from the profession or higher education for architecture courses to include the learning of attitudes and skills necessary for life-long learning. It is timely, therefore, to reexamine the present diploma procedures for strengths and weaknesses. Arguably, the key strength of the student learning contract is that it provides students with a framework that encourages them to take some responsibility for their own learning. By selecting their own programme of work, students are helped to take more responsibility for their studies and to be more enthusiastic and committed to what they learn, because it is meeting their own learning goals. This accords with Malcolm Knowles' (1991) premise that 'adults learn best when they have responsibility for their learning'.

However it is clear from the annual student feedback returns that the support mechanisms, especially the induction period and the personal tutor support procedures, are critical to the successful development of independence in learning. It is vital that the information about the modules presented to students during the induction programme should be full, accurate and clearly presented, so that students can base their learning contracts on as full an understanding of the course options as possible. Beyond this, an obvious addition to the induction programme would be workshops to help prepare students for self-directed learning, particularly those who in the past have been subject to a great deal of teacher-directed learning. For example students could be asked to compile a personal profile of their present knowledge and competencies and their future learning aspirations. This would encourage a deeper analysis by students of their own learning goals, which could be compared against the learning goals of the modules during the selection process. Creating a profile in this way would also help students recognise and value their own abilities. This would be the first step in getting students to think for themselves and take control over their own learning. A workshop of this type is being planned for inclusion in the induction programme for the 1999–2000 academic year.

Another key to the success of the learning contract procedure is the role adopted by personal tutors, who help the students to clarify their needs, goals and aspirations at the beginning of the course and subsequently help them to construct a 2-year plan. The tutors then follow the students' progress through the two years of the course and are responsible for helping the students to present themselves and their portfolio of work for final assessment by the external examiners. To encourage self-directed learning, the tutors must show respect for the students' ability to analyse their own learning needs and also encourage their active participation in all aspects of the negotiation process. In summary the tutors and the students must enter into the process in good faith and with a clear understanding of their individual roles and reponsibilities.

Being supportive whilst at the same time remaining non-directive can be difficult and some students have noted that some personal tutors do not really want to take on the role. Indeed some academic staff have been reluctant to do so, perhaps because of confusion over how the role of personal tutor differs from that of course leader. These issues will be addressed in future years by strengthening the induction process for personal tutors to make sure they are clear about their roles and responsibilities, and by creating a more formal structure for tutor–student meetings, including a timetable of key dates for personal tutor–student contact.

A further improvement will be the development of a code of practice to include in the staff diploma guidelines, which will detail the roles and responsibilities of personal tutors in the learning contract process.

Next steps

The 1999/2000 academic year will see the revision of the portfolio module into a six-term, long, thin learning contract module, giving a formal structure to the reviews of students' work and to that aspect of the personal tutor–student relationship (Table 20.3).

At present it is proposed that the learning contract module will assess the term 6 portfolio work. However this may be extended so that the module creates a framework for monitoring and giving credit to the students for demonstrating self-directed learning skills, such as goal analysis, periodic review, reflection on personal development and self-evaluation. Its success will rely on broad opportunities for feedback on learning in the early stages of the diploma course so that students acquire the confidence to be self-directed. This will make it possible, later on, formally to assess some aspects of independence or self-direction in learning. This module might also involve students in keeping a reflective journal of their learning experiences throughout the two years of the course, thus encouraging them continuously to monitor any gaps between current progress and the learning goals they have set themselves.

Table 20.3 Structure of the learning contract module, as defined in the *Staff Diploma Guidelines* manual

Date	Purpose of meeting
Term 1, weeks 0–4	Meeting with individual tutees to discuss 2-year programme. Tutor to arrange by E-mail
Term 3, week 10	End of year review of progress and 2-year programme update. Tutor to arrange by E-mail
Term 6, week 1	Meeting to look at overall portfolio and agree on additional presentation work to be carried out for the final examination. To be recorded on a review sheet as a 'learning contract'—copy to student. Tutor to arrange meeting by E-mail
Term 6, week 8	Meeting to mark work carried out to the portfolio during term 6. Marking to be carried out by personal tutor and another member of staff (preferably the compound project tutor) and should reflect how well (both quantity and quality) the student carried out the work scheduled in the learning contract. Mark and comments to be recorded on the learning contract Review Sheet and submitted for filing into student file, with copy to the student, by Thursday of week 8 at the latest. Tutor to arrange by E-mail

Note: If a tutee wishes to see her or his personal tutor at times other than those defined in the portfolio module, this is by mutual agreement/arrangement.

Developments will be monitored over the next year as part of a pedagogic research programme carried out by the course chair in association with the Oxford Brookes Centre for Teaching and Learning.

References

Dearing, R. F. (1997) *Higher Education in a Learning Society*, the report of the National Committee of Inquiry into Higher Education. London: HMSO.

Knowles, Malcolm (1991) *Using Learning Contracts*. San Francisco, CA: Jossey-Bass.

Laycock, Michael and Stephenson John (eds) (1993) *Using Learning Contracts in Higher Education*. London: Kogan Page.

Royal Institute for British Architecture (RIBA) (1996) *RIBA Guidelines for Architecture Courses Leading to Examination at Part 2*. London: RIBA Publications.

Royal Institute for British Architecture (RIBA) (1999) *Meeting the Challenge—a strategy for architecture and architects*. London: RIBA Publications.

21 The student-led 'crit' as a learning device

Rosie White

Background

The crit or review system, as a context for critical analysis of the studio design project, can provide a broad learning opportunity for both students and staff and offers an important celebration of the student's hard work. However it is widely recognised that there is scope in the current crit system for negative qualities to suppress the positive, thereby eradicating much of the potential of the crit as a learning experience:

> The architectural jury system [or crit] fails when it lowers the students' self-esteem, permits verbal abuse of students ... teaches students to be defensive about their work ... is poorly organised and does not allow equal time for each student's work ... jurors offer nothing constructive or positive
>
> (Rossi 1997)

One of the priorities of CUDE's work was the promotion of teamworking and communication skills. In this context, the traditional 'crit' or review was seen as a central, underexploited resource for the development and practice of such skills. The student-led review was developed as an experimental alternative with three primary objectives:

- To increase student participation.
- To encourage skills in presentation and asking for feedback.
- To encourage students constructively to criticise their own work and that of others.

> The review would draw on learning methods that are rooted in the theory of collaborative learning, which asserts that learning is a mutual endeavour undertaken by students and faculty, embracing various active learning approaches that value the voice and contributions of all participants
>
> (Matthews 1996)

Methodology

Two student-led reviews were run, each including feedback and evaluation activities. They were run at the interim review stage of second-year design projects involving the whole year of 70 students. While their structure was prescribed, responsibility for running them, including their time-keeping, was handed over to the students. The tutors' role was restricted to facilitating the process. Seats were arranged in a single-line semi-circle around the presentation area, with the tutors seated behind the students, thereby psychologically reinforcing the principle that the session was student-led.

The students were put into groups of 12–15, comprising three panels of four to five in each group. The first panel made individual presentations of their schemes for five minutes each to the other two panels, who adopted the role of critic. Each of these two panels then spent 15 minutes privately discussing the schemes and presentations they had seen. Then a spokesperson from each panel presented the key points raised, making sure that all schemes were addressed, and any specific requests for feedback that had come from the presenters were responded to (all students had recently attended a preparatory workshop to introduce methods of developing presentations and offering and receiving constructive criticism). Finally the presenters were asked to summarise/paraphrase the feedback that they felt they had received from the panels, and explain how they planned to proceed.

Evaluation method

At the end of each session the students and facilitators were asked to complete a feedback form, giving a score from 1 (not at all) to 5 (completely) according to their judgement of how successful the crit had been in achieving the three primary objectives. Space was left after the scores for comments relating to each of the three aims. The students and facilitators were then asked to note anything they particularly liked about the session and any suggestions they might have for improving it.

Analysis of student feedback

Increased student participation

A total of 81 feedback forms were returned by the students after the two sessions. The overwhelming majority felt that the sessions had been successful in increasing student participation (Figure 21.1). Many of the comments suggested that the students had enjoyed the process, a typical comment being: 'I actually had fun listening to my friends speak and address not only the tutor but also all the rest of us'.

Some of the comments indicated that tutors can be seen as intimidating and the cause of poor student participation: 'It worked really

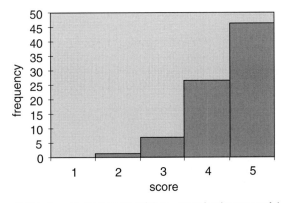

Notes: 1 = not at all successful; 5 = completely successful.

Figure 21.1 Student feedback: increasing participation.

well—everyone got involved, less intimidating with other students critting.' The students also felt that they had received some useful and constructive feedback from their peers: 'It was a useful exercise to justify/discuss ideas/approaches with your peers rather than simply seeking tutor approval', and 'colleagues can sometimes be the best critics'.

Taken overall, such comments reveal a great deal about students' attitude towards crits. They suggest that the traditional crit is not viewed as a learning opportunity, but rather as an opportunity to judge the reaction of the tutor to one's ideas. The difference is subtle, but highly significant.

The students acknowledged that they had had to pay attention in order to take part in the discussion and feedback process. They had been fully involved in the crit and as a result it had been 'less boring' and 'people actually stayed awake'. Feedback also suggests that both the presenters and the individuals offering constructive criticism felt that their work and opinion had been valued: 'It's very positive having feedback from colleagues because you feel like people actually are taking what you think into consideration'.

Encouraging skills in presentation and asking for feedback

The comments on presentation skills were mixed (Figure 21.2). Some felt that such skills had not really been developed or improved; others felt that they had been encouraged to put more time into preparing the presentation and that they had benefited from this. The earlier preparation session had played a particularly important role in this aspect of the student-led crit process. By drawing attention to the importance of the presentation and the crit as an opportunity to ask for feedback, the students had been encouraged to think about presenting concisely and with clarity, and about what they wanted to get out of the crit.

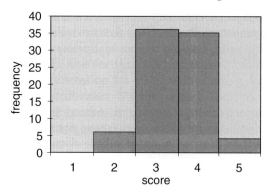

Notes: 1 = not at all successful; 5 = completely successful.

Figure 21.2 Student feedback: improving presentation.

It is interesting to note that by playing the role of the critic some students had been made to appreciate the tutors' view and had begun to understand some of the advice they had previously been given: 'It does make you consider points that tutors have been telling us for two years!'

For many, the relaxed atmosphere had helped the presentations themselves. One student raised two important broader issues, suggesting that if some of the presentations had been poor it was because they were not being marked, and that people had not asked for feedback because they lacked trust in the worth of comments from 'unqualified individuals'. However, more representative of the general student opinion was the comment that it is 'easier to present when ungraded and to those who actually know all the problems of the task set'. Such comments highlight one of the fundamental dilemmas in the generic review process: are we to use the crit as a learning device or as an opportunity to assess students' work? This raises a further question: will there ever be room for both objectives in the same review session?

Encouraging constructive criticism of one's own work and that of others

It was noted that the criticism had been much more constructive than usual. This was partly because students acting as critics had been aware that they would soon be receiving criticism themselves, and partly due to the fact that the critics had been through the same design processes as the presenter. The feedback suggests that most students had been happy with the criticism received from their peers (Figure 21.3) and felt that it had been helpful. Some were sure that the process had been better without the input of tutors: 'The whole thing seems to work a lot better without a tutor (sorry).'

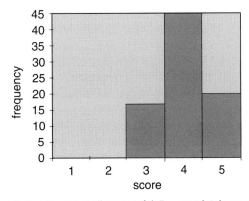

Notes: 1 = not at all successful; 5 = completely successful.

Figure 21.3 Student feedback: constructive criticism.

Others, however, felt that some tutor input in addition to student criticism would have been beneficial. It is not clear whether the students really felt that they had not received sufficient feedback or whether they were simply worried that they had not been given the opportunity to hear the opinions of the tutors who would ultimately be marking their work: 'Criticism from other students was helpful, but more participation from tutors would be helpful as they are more knowledgeable and mark the work.'

The students had enjoyed the opportunity to develop their own critical analysis skills, offering comments with great enthusiasm; some of the people who had spoken had never participated in the past. The students had also enjoyed receiving the varied opinions of many people rather than just one or two tutors, and the student crit panels had enjoyed being addressed directly rather than the usual scenario of the presenter talking only to the tutor.

Analysis of tutor feedback

Increase in student participation

The tutors concurred that participation had increased (Figure 21.4): The 'students stayed alert and attentive as they expected to participate in the criticism.' It was felt that there had been a tendency at times for students to feel they had to say something at the expense of content. However it was appreciated that the time created after the presentations for discussion in crit panels had allowed the students (and tutors) to study the drawings and read them properly.

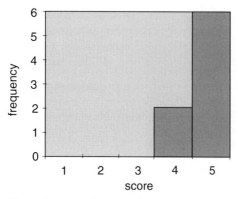

Notes: 1 = not at all successful; 5 = completely successful.

Figure 21.4 Tutor feedback: increasing participation.

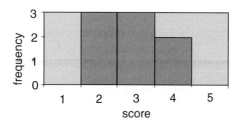

Notes: 1 = not at all successful; 5 = completely successful.

Figure 21.5 Tutor feedback: improving presentation.

Encouraging skills in presentation and in asking for feedback

Here the responses were mixed (Figure 21.5). Taken overall, it was felt that the student presentations had not been noticeably better than in the traditional crit. Some presentations had been less structured than usual, perhaps because the students had not felt as though they would be judged by their peers. It was felt that there had been a need for more guidance in verbal and graphic presentation. Time-keeping had been good on the whole.

Although the students had taken the opportunity to ask for specific feedback, as suggested, some tutors felt that such requests for comment had often been only in very basic areas that never really progressed beyond 'What do you think of ...?' or 'Do you like ...?' They had also tended to be made as an afterthought at the end of the presentation.

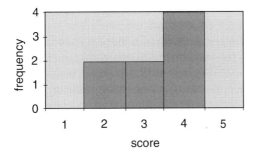

Notes: 1 = not at all successful; 5 = completely successful.

Figure 21.6 Tutor feedback: constructive criticism.

Encouraging constructive criticism of your own work and that of others

The tutors had much to say about this final aim of the crit, but again the responses were mixed (Figure 21.6). Whereas tutors usually sit at the front, concentrating very hard and nodding in all the right places, in this review they had been left to entertain themselves at the back. As one participant put it, 'tutors need a chance to say something to stop us sitting at the back, chatting, smoking and making paper planes'.

The responses suggest that the tutors had been frustrated by not being able to make comments about issues that they felt had been missed by the students: 'I felt that the students were constrained by their own inexperience in engaging with the design process ... often dealing with specific planning issues, rather than debating wider conceptual/urban/architectural ideas or taking a holistic approach to the design.'

It was felt that while some students had still had a defensive mode of presentation, many had been noticeably less defensive than usual and had been able to accept the constructive criticism of their peers.

The presence of the tutor was seen as useful in enforcing the crit structure, ensuring that it did not loosen. However it was noted that the more responsibility that is given to students, the better they seem to use it.

Discussion

Factors influencing the effectiveness of the student-led crits

In summary, the sessions proved to be most effective in increasing student participation. Perhaps more important is the fact that the students and tutors felt that this participation was beneficial. As one student commented: 'We stayed totally awake and interactive for three hours ....

Constructive, interesting and useful—I felt I learned a lot from other people's crits too.'

It is acknowledged that there are many factors that could have contributed to the effectiveness of the sessions, including the time structuring, preparatory sessions and the small group size achieved by breaking down the year into parallel sessions; the importance of the latter cannot be overstated.

Potential for development

Many tutors felt that the students would have benefited more from the crits if tutor input had been allowed. This has to be read against the general student feedback, which suggested that the absence of the tutor voice had probably been the most significant contributor to the success of the crits in terms of participation levels, asking for feedback and encouraging constructive criticism of work.

The introduction of tutor comment, therefore, must not be at the expense of the other clear benefits arising from the student-centred approach. It was suggested that tutors might be allowed to 'mop up' after the students have said all that they want, however this can present its own difficulties. This method was subsequently chosen for a third student-led crit at Sheffield, but feedback revealed a danger that students might expect the 'real' comments to come later, thus rendering their own discussions unimportant. One student pointed out that it also felt very artificial having the tutors 'waiting' to speak. However, had the tutors participated throughout there would have been the traditional danger of suppressing student participation and stifling initiative and discussion.

The question of what exactly the tutor's role should be in this type of crit is perhaps the most interesting. Further research is needed in this area to find an effective balance. Perhaps, in essence, the role must be one that students can see as reinforcing and building on student involvement, rather than—implicitly or explicitly—diminishing or dismissing the student voice. We should not discount the possibility that the crit might not be the most suitable place for tutor feedback if critical analysis skills are to be developed. Roberta Matthews (1996) adds to this debate in her work on collaborative learning:

> We need to stop asking perjoratively 'How much content must be sacrificed in order to do collaborative learning?' That assumes collaborative learning and content coverage are not compatible. Rather we need to start asking, how can collaborative learning be used to help students understand what it means to study the essential content of this discipline?

While we continue to presume that content must be sacrificed in order to allow the crit to be a student learning experience, certain conflicts remain unresolved, for example student participation versus tutor comment, and assessment versus the receiving of constructive criticism. If, however, the crit were to become a forum reserved for student discussion and debate, it could become a healthy breeding ground for peer group learning.

Opportunities

As budgets shrink and student numbers soar, the educational environment inevitably becomes more impersonal and alienating. In this climate, collaborative learning becomes all the more necessary. The balance of student–tutor input explored in this collaborative crit technique needs further examination. More research is required to discover the value of the student-led crit approach at various stages of training. However, if the student-led emphasis is retained, the role of facilitator could be taken by, for instance, diploma students.

Despite revealing some pedagogical conflicts, these experimental crits clearly present an opportunity to support and enhance course content by encouraging students to

> use what they are learning and integrate it at a deeper level; identify for themselves and discuss with their peers the important elements of their learning; to actively contribute what they already know and to enrich content discussion with dimensions that may be beyond the experience of the instructor; to feel valued and engaged in learning (Matthews 1996).

The student voice at Sheffield is clearly saying that it would like to see the adoption of the student-led approach to crits.

References

Matthews, R. S. (1996) 'Collaborative Learning: Creating Knowledge with Students', in R. J. Menges (ed.), *Teaching on Solid Ground*. San Francisco, CA: Jossey-Bass.
Rossi, J. (1997) 'Is the architectural school jury system valuable or destructive?', *ChapterLetter*, May/June. Newsletter of the Boston Society of Architects.

Section 4

A new professionalism

Embedding change in
schools of architecture

Learning in architecture is not only influenced by what happens in the design studio, but also by the learning climate within the school and the interactions that occur between the school and its wider communities. The chapters in this section focus on what the schools themselves and outside agencies (that is, RIBA, those in practice) might do to help students develop as professionals.

Milliner (Chapter 22) examines the role of the Royal Institute of British Architects (RIBA) in regulating architectural education and entry into the profession in the UK. She links some of the problems in the profession (for example client dissatisfaction) to the schools, and argues that it is the social practices within schools (for example crits, long hours, competitive culture) perhaps more than the content of courses that determine how students subsequently conceive and act out their professional roles. Milliner outlines how the RIBA might influence both the formal educational processes and the informal social practices in schools so as better to meet the needs of the changing profession.

Gutman (Chapter 23) describes how schools in the USA have adapted and responded to the needs of the profession in recent years. For example some schools specialise in teaching specific approaches (design, environmental behaviour, architectural management) and/or in experimenting with new teaching methods (interdisciplinary studios, charrettes on site). Some schools also encourage students to study liberal arts subjects before concentrating on architecture as a way of broadening their education. Gutman argues for a strengthening of academic–industry partnerships.

The next two chapters explore the role of the school in creating a supportive environment for the development of professional skills in students. Potts (Chapter 24) presents a case study of coordinated change across a whole school of architecture. A central feature of the approach is the 'vertical studio' arrangement. Students from different years learn and study together in the same design studio—the idea is to foster collaborative learning both within and across years.

Potts gives a detailed account of the organisational and management changes in teaching that are necessary to support these vertical studios. Henderson (Chapter 25) discusses the difficulties encountered and the progress made in another school as it tried to change its strategy to give more importance to the development of students' professional skills. The difficulties discussed include resource constraints, problems associated with changing staff attitudes towards the teaching of professional skills, and providing staff with the pedagogic competence needed to implement changes in student learning.

Vowles (Chapter 26) discusses a specific example of how the wider social context influences student learning. She examines the tacit social processes inherent in the architectural review (or 'crit') and their influence on learning in the schools, and on the values and ways of thinking and acting that students carry into professional practice. She argues that if those in the profession would acknowledge that current practice is 'socially generated' (starting in schools) then it would be easier to construct different models of education for practice.

The last two chapters are concerned with how tutors might be prepared for and supported in their teaching roles, and with how to help foster a professional attitude towards teaching. Weaver, O'Reilly and Caddick (Chapter 27) describe a tutor training programme in one school for new architects entering teaching. The programme is based on experiential learning, mentoring arrangements and shared discussion of teaching practice and of research on student learning. The aim of the training course is to develop reflective studio tutors. The writers identify issues that might be of interest to others thinking of setting up a programme to prepare and support architecture tutors. Cowan (Chapter 28) describes a variety of ways in which teachers might gather information from students, and from other teachers, in order to improve teaching and architecture courses. Most of the techniques suggested are quick and easy to implement; and many have the added benefit that they lead to improvements in student learning as well as in teachers' teaching.

22 Delight in transgression

Shifting boundaries in architectural education

Leonie Milliner

Dirt is never a unique, isolated event. Where there is dirt there is a system. Dirt is the by-product of a systematic ordering and classification of matter, in so far as ordering involves rejecting inappropriate elements.

(Douglas 1966)

The role of the professional institute

The Royal Institute of British Architects (RIBA) represents 32000 architects in the UK and overseas. Since its establishment in 1837 it has been the location for the production and reproduction of the architect.[1]

As Schneider (1992) has noted, the jurisdiction of the architectural profession over the occupation of architecture is maintained by a series of codified practices and quasimonopolistic positions. The regulations that govern professional life—such as the *RIBA Code of Professional Conduct and Standard of Professional Performance* (RIBA 1997)—are contested and controlled in an extensive system of committees and subcommittees at the RIBA's headquarters in Portland Place, London. Most of these documented procedures seek to define a set of ordered relations that can include or exclude ideas, styles, people and practices according to their appropriateness to professional needs.

We know from Smith and Morris (1992) that the defining characteristic in any profession or self-regulating body is its ability to reproduce its collective norms. By prescribing long, formal university training with tightly controlled professional entry qualifications, the architectural profession seeks to influence not only what areas of knowledge a trainee is inculcated with, but also how that abstract knowledge is applied through techniques learnt by experience.

Architectural education, the key transmitter of the 'culture' of architecture, not only imparts objectified rational knowledge in the form of calculations and techniques, but also transmits less obvious social practices in the form of confessional critiques, design tutorials and intense studio culture (Stevens 1998). For instance one is identified as belonging to the profession not only by the letters after one's name, but also by the clothes one wears and the language one uses: 'Intelligence, in any absolute sense, is not a major factor in the production of distinguished architecture. Arrogance, coupled with a sense of competition and a pleasure in the fashionable and exotic are much more important' (ibid.).

The boundaries of professional control in architectural education are therefore at once seen and unseen, the undefinable and unclassifiable codes of taste and cultivation being as influential in demarcating the boundaries of architectural education as the objectified and rational codes and procedures produced by the Royal Institute of British Architects and the Architects Registration Board (RIBA 1995; RIBA/ARB 1997).

Shifting boundaries of influence

The only element of monopolistic control within the profession's jurisdiction is its ability to regulate the formal qualifications required to enter the profession. In other words, those areas of abstract knowledge considered relevant for professional training and entry, and the appropriate method for charting the application of that knowledge in practice through work experience.[2]

The traditional concept of professionalism promoted by sociologists such as Eric Freidson (1983) was one founded on the idea of a market monopoly—of professionals dominating a particular occupational area for financial and social gain, and offering clients the benefit of their skill, accrued through years of rigorous education. Freidson identifies four defining characteristics of a profession:

- A monopoly over the profession's work, granted by the state—a protected field of occupation.
- A set of self-regulating codes and associations to control work and safeguard clients' interests.
- Protected fees scaled to ensure the financial stability of the profession and prevent competition.
- Long, formal university education coupled with tightly controlled professional entry qualifications.

However, as Duffy (1992) points out, at no point has the architectural profession exhibited all four characteristics simultaneously. In the UK we have no state-regulated monopoly over the practice of architecture—only of the title 'architect' (which arose from the concept of consumer protection rather than professional self-regulation). Of the

44 services defined in the standard form of appointment for an architect, 39 could now be undertaken by specialists in other fields. Mandatory fee scales no longer exist, having been swept away by the government through the findings of the Monopolies and Mergers' Commission in 1981.

In 1962 the RIBA Plan of Work codified a standard method of practice against which an architect's services could be measured and fees calculated. This normalisation of architectural practice tended towards an exclusion of activities/services that did not fit into a mainstream definition of what an architect's duties should be, such as cost estimation or town planning. Nevertheless this Plan of Work was used in 1998 as the baseline document in the development of the recently establised national vocational qualification (NVQ) level 5 in architectural practice. This despite the fact that in 1992, 20 per cent of architects' fee income was generated by services described as 'other' (that is, other than mainstream).

Yet despite the decline in professional influence and the perceived reduction in our field of occupation as architects, we maintain a sophisticated set of procedures to restrict both formal entry into our profession and penetration of our knowledge base. This policy of exclusivity is demonstrated by RIBA education statistics: the number of students passing RIBA Part 3—the examination leading to corporate membership of the RIBA—declined steadily from 892 passes in 1982 to 707 in 1998.

Broadening the mainstream

Following the so-called 'Burton Report' in 1992, the architectural profession encouraged education to broaden the first three years of an architect's training (Part 1), and thereby provide a springboard for students to move into other careers, rather than inevitably proceeding to Part 2. However the dropout rate (a highly subjective term) between RIBA Part 1 and 2 has continued steadily to decline. At the same time it has increased between RIBA Part 2 and 3. For example, of the 2125 students who entered Part 1 in 1990, 705 passed Part 3 in 1997—a notional dropout rate of 66 per cent. It would seem that, for many students, completing RIBA Part 2 chartered status is perceived as either an irrelevant or an impossible ambition.

The profession not only excludes, it is generating the conditions for its own self-selection.

The activities of the 4700 'almost' architects who have passed their RIBA Part 2 since 1997 but failed to progress to pass RIBA Part 3 are just as influential on the culture of the architecture as those who made it into the club. Many activities that constitute architectural expression—such as writing, researching, teaching, acting as a client or an exhibition curator—sit uncomfortably outside the architectural profession when they could so easily enrich the mainstream. This is compounded by the low number of women and ethnic minorities in education and as members of the RIBA. Whilst in comparable professions, such as law and medicine, women are making good progress in achieving the numerical critical mass needed to effect change, in the architectural profession the number of women filtering through to chartered status is still astonishingly small—rising from 147 in 1989 to 176 in 1998. The statistics on the recruitment, retention and participation of ethnic minority students and those from low socioeconomic backgrounds in architectural education are unknown. As Wigglesworth (1996) notes, the absence of the excluded in the profession—as corporate members of the RIBA, as council members, as president, on building sites and in drawing offices—has allowed the phallocentric nature of our profession to remain unchallenged for too long.

Recasting the role models

The most compelling and most completely flawed vision of the modernist architect is Ayn Rand's hero, Howard Roark, in the book *The Fountainhead* (Rand 1947). This image of the male, white, middle-class, ruthless architect, single-minded to the point of pawning his last possession and concerned only with the creation of 'his' building, is still promoted in architectural practice and education. The famous quote, 'I have clients in order to build, I do not build in order to have clients', demonstrates Roark's disinterest in client needs or user expectations. For Roark, collaboration is compromise—an unacceptable concept in the quest to build taller, more beautiful buildings. The story climaxes when Roark is persuaded to take a holiday during the construction of his biggest project (it is no coincidence this temptation is offered by a woman). In his absence, his great design is so altered by weaker men that on his return he razes it to the ground.

One might extract from this role model three key attributes to being a great architect:

- Never be distracted from your goal.
- Never be seduced by an easy life of commercial gain, social recognition or family demands.
- Be prepared to manipulate a client's desires in order to satisfy your own creative ambition and sacrifice everything, everything you possess to achieve greatness.

This model is problematic. Client satisfaction levels are falling (Prince 1992). The profession is failing to meet the needs of the construction industry in terms of leadership and construction management.

Architects perceive their role to be increasingly impoverished within an exceptionally demanding environment (ibid.)

Working within a model of the profession founded on the idea of the 'star' architect—where collaboration and compromise ultimately signify mediocrity—and in the absence of the traditional professional framework that could have secured pay and prestige, the reality of the contemporary architectural profession is founded on the sole practitioner (ibid.) These architects, with highly generalised skills, are operating in a fiercely competitive market where profit margins are declining and work is falling away to other competing professionals.

The strengths and weaknesses of the profession were clearly identified in the *Strategic Study* (RIBA 1992, 1993, 1995), as were the pressures that demarcated either an expanding or contracting professional jurisdiction over architectural practice. The options outlined in the report were clear, but failed to be embedded because of a level of inaction in architectural education and the profession.

Three options were identified: to equip individuals to operate as specialist architects, or as managers of specialists, or as general practitioners with a low specialist input. This required three strategic moves from the profession:

- To consolidate the architect's role as designer by focusing on meeting client and user requirements.
- To strengthen the architect's ability to deliver design services at the required level of quality, to time and to budget.
- To be prepared to provide a wider range of design and management-based services.

In order to deliver these strategic moves, the profession needed the commitment of architectural education. At that very moment, however, the RIBA was defending architectural education in the High Court to prevent a reduction in funding of courses from five to three years.

Education is the key

Education is the profession's lever over its own future. The profession controls the production and reproduction of the architect through a series of formal procedures and informal social practices. These codes operate in architectural education to determine the profile and membership of the profession, to legitimate its activities and regulate its practices. The *Strategic Study* (RIBA 1992) outlined a compelling argument for change in the skills and knowledge base of the profession. The primary mechanism for this change in the profession is architectural education.

Equally, the work of the RIBA in education, through its involvement in the validation of architectural courses, is the profession's most powerful lever over education. It exerts a wide influence over architectural education, working alongside other key stakeholders to influence the way in which architecture is taught, practised and experienced in the studio, lecture theatre and drawing office.

The most powerful document the Royal Institute of British Architects produces is its outline syllabus (RIBA ARB 1997). This document codifies the minimum standard for the validation of architectural courses. It describes the educational threshold for entry into the profession and prescribes the baseline competencies that practitioners need to maintain throughout their working career. It is the mechanism for ensuring that entry to the profession is consistent, comparable and competent for general practice. Widely regarded throughout the world, the outline syllabus is the basis for the RIBA's extensive validation programme, encompassing courses at nearly 100 schools of architecture in the UK and overseas.

If change needs to be embedded into architectural education, it will have little effect unless it is prescribed in this documentation. However the curriculum alone cannot support change in architectural education. Surrounding its implementation is a complex mechanism of visiting boards and panel members. There are procedures for authorising changes to existing courses and approving new courses, of making recommendations via the Joint Validation Panel (JVP) to the RIBA and the Architects Registration Board (ARB) for decisions regarding validation and exemption from the RIBA's own examination. To embed change one not only has to effect the written codes in the syllabus document, but also to review the manner in which evidence is gathered and examined on visits, the training that visiting board members receive to interpret this evidence, the questions they need to ask and the procedures that need to be followed. It is in its implementation that the maximum leverage of these codified desires is exerted over architectural education, and hence the profession.

The new RIBA Part 3 Professional Practice Syllabus, agreed by the RIBA Council in March 1999 (RIBA 1999), attempted to address the concerns of the profession by concentrating on generic management theory and up-to-date business management and communication skills in a manner that would not prescribe either geographical location or time. As with RIBA Parts 1 and 2, each section is described through a series of learning outcomes—defined levels of achievement that students are expected to demonstrate at least at a minimum pass standard. Each learning outcome is described at one of four levels of achievement: awareness, understanding, knowledge or ability. For example students are expected to demonstrate 'an ability to communicate effectively with the full client body' and 'an understanding of legislation on health and safety and its implications for design and construction' (ibid.)

The RIBA does not prescribe the mode of delivery or the form of evidence required to meet these learning outcomes. This is to enable schools of architecture to develop innovative programmes and teaching methods and to allow course providers flexibility in developing an approach to learning that is relevant to their environment.

Recasting the profession

Revision of the codes and a reformulation of the charting of practical experience are the tools. But embedding the change in architectural education and steering the profession towards the model outlined in the *Strategic Study* (RIBA 1992) will require a diverse membership backed by proper briefing and training.

The profession also influences change by providing an educational framework that can adapt over time to satisfy the competing demands of the varied stakeholders in architectural education: the government, the heads of schools of architecture, academics, students, researchers, regulatory and professional bodies, parents and teachers.

The RIBA Review of Architectural Education, established in 1997 and chaired by Sir Colin Stansfield Smith, is currently trying to solve this problem by offering a new vision for architectural education that will provide valid academic and professional exit points in the long slog to become an architect. The review has acknowledged that national educational frameworks will become increasingly irrelevant in a global marketplace. It has gone further to recommend the establishment of a postgraduate second qualification—as a specialist base to a professional career and as a platform for research—and an academically assessed Part 4 to try to solve the lack of career structure within normative architectural practice.

Conclusion

So many assumptions about the way architecture should be practised, in a conventional sense, are learnt in education:

- The long hours in the studio are replicated in the office.
- The importance of the lone designer, lauded in the classroom, is manifest in the profession.
- The lack of equality reinforces a common perception of the profession—one with a liberal and broad public image but with little space or time for women or ethnic minorities, either physically or symbolically.

Although recruitment to architectural courses fell by only 1 per cent in 1998, the architectural profession cannot be complacent. Other professions saw admissions fall by as much as 30–40 per cent. Long working hours and poor pay simply do not equate with the thousands of pounds students now have to pay for their education.

Each year the RIBA hosts conferences and workshops and presents prizes and awards to encourage and support innovative teaching and learning, to challenge conventional philosophies and disseminate best practice. This ranges from international prizes for student design work to continuing professional development (CPD) sessions for external examiners. However the profession has to question how far the RIBA, as the key membership body of architects in the UK, can represent positions that are beyond a normative view of either architectural practice or education.

The institute must also question how it can maintain its relevance to education and the profession in its ability to embrace new and innovative practices that exist at the margins of its occupational territory. Such questioning will test the limits of the codified boundaries outlined in this chapter and their potential for adaptation into a new professionalism.

Notes

1 See also J. Hill, *The Illegal Architect*. London: Black Dog Publishing, 1998.
2 The standard pattern of architectural education in the UK is five years full-time study or equivalent plus 24 months practical training in an architect's office, 12 months of which are usually taken after the first three years of study (RIBA Part I) and 12 months after year 5 (RIBA Part 2), prior to the final examination (RIBA Part 3).

References

Burton, R. (1992) *Report of the steering group on architectural education*. London: RIBA.

Douglas, M. (1966) *Purity and Danger, an analysis of the concepts of pollution and taboo*. London: Routledge, p. 36.

Duffy, F. (1992) 'Part A—Strategic Overview', in RIBA, *Strategic Study of the Profession, Phase 1: Strategic Overview*. London: RIBA Publications.

Freidson, E. (1983) 'The Theory of the Professions; State of the Art' in *The sociology of the Professions*. London: Dingwell & Lewis (eds), Macmillan, pp. 19–37.

Prince, W. (1992) 'Delivering Added Value' in RIBA, *Strategic Study of the Profession, Phase 1: Strategic Overview*. London: RIBA Publications, pp. 26–39.

Rand, A. (1988) *The Fountainhead*. London: Grafton Books (first published 1947).

RIBA (1995) *RIBA Practical Training Scheme—Objectives and Rules; Guidance Notes for Employers of Students*. London: RIBA Publications.

RIBA (1997) *RIBA Code of Professional Conduct and Standard of Professional Performance*. London: RIBA Publications.

RIBA (1999) *RIBA Outline Syllabus for Part III Programmes in Architectural Practice*. London: RIBA Publications.

RIBA/ARB Joint Validation Panel (1997) *Procedures and Criteria for the Validation of Courses, Programmes and Examinations in Architecture*. London: RIBA Publications.

Schneider, E. (1992) 'Segmenting a Diverse Profession', in RIBA, *Strategic Study of the Profession, Phase 1: Strategic Overview*. London: RIBA Publications, pp. 123–34.

Smith, G. and Morris, T. (1992) 'Exploiting Shifting Boundaries', in RIBA, *Strategic Study of the Profession, Phase 1: Strategic Overview*. London: RIBA Publications, pp. 61–77.

Stevens, G. (1998) *The Favored Circle*. Cambridge, Mass.: MIT Press, p. 201.

Wigglesworth, S. (1996) 'Practice; The Significant Others', in McCorquodale D., Ruedi K. and Wigglesworth S. (eds), *Desiring Practices*. London: Black Dog Publishing, p. 227.

23 Schools and practice in the United States

Robert Gutman

The changing context of practice

Professionals are increasingly confused about their task. We see this in medicine. Doctors are no longer responsible just for the diagnosis and treatment of their personal patients. More of them are in the business of providing general management of patient care that involves the coordination of many new specialisations, including preventive medicine, home care, aftercare and data services for tracking health outcomes (Hirschhorn 1997:2). It is also true of the legal profession: lawyers are now taking on the role of accountants and management consultants, while firms in these professions have in turn begun to hire lawyers and offer legal services. The five big international accounting firms are now among the largest law firms in the world. Individual lawyers and doctors are asking themselves where they fit in the new systems that are emerging.

Architecture has been following a similar path, and it is not surprising that many architects are wondering about their future too. It becomes more difficult each year to define what an architect does. Some are builders, many are now graphic designers, including designers of web sites, others specialise in facility management or serve as consultants on the handling of property portfolios. Architects in the USA are now employed by large firms of accountants. I know of architectural firms that run their public relations department as a separate profit centre, selling its expertise to other businesses. Several large American practices now include strategic planning departments. I remember first discovering this development when I was talking to the head of the New York office of a prominent international firm during the recession of the early 1990s. With the interests of my students in mind, I asked whether he had begun to hire again. He told me that they had, but not architects. 'What then', I asked 'Management consultants', he replied.

How is one to describe in one word or short phrase what architects do now, what the scope of the profession's role is? I do not think one can. Certainly it is true that fewer architects in the USA limit their activities to making designs and supervising the construction process. In some respects their control over projects has been expanded, for other jobs it is much reduced compared, say, with the authority now given to construction managers (Gutman 1988:35–6). The process leading up to the present confusion about roles and purposes has been evolving and is likely to continue. There is greater ambiguity in being an architect today than ever before. It is not surprising to see the profession in the USA searching for a new definition of its role in the building industry. Many firms have begun to group themselves into strategic alliances with specialist offices in other fields connected to building. One of the first such groups, the Global Design Alliance, now includes 15 firms, including specialists in environmental engineering, water resource design and management, acoustics and noise control, real estate brokerage, and project control and management. The alliance has it own chief executive officer, who was formerly the marketing partner of a well-known international practice. I regard the new emphasis on design (invariably spelt with a capital D), and the identification of a category of so-called 'signature' architecture, as another type of response to the ambiguity. Signature architects are choosing to practise at what they consider the pinnacle of professional activity, the terrain in which, presumably, there is less competition from other building professions. The strategy has been working, as shown by the number of important jobs given to design architects, and the tremendous publicity Michael Graves, Frank Gehry, Daniel Liebeskind and Zaha Hadid receive from the media. In the struggle to resolve the identity problem, I do not know of anyone who has suggested that the name of the profession should be changed to indicate the new roles of architects. Yet landscape architects in the USA played with such an idea during the 1970s, when many leaders of that profession advocated changing their name to 'environmental designers' to reflect more fully the range of their new tasks and to distance themselves from landscape gardeners. Fortunately for architects, the traditional name seems to accommodate their new functions, leaving them with whatever advantages can be obtained from their elite lineage.

The response of the schools: new courses and programmes

The education system in the USA has been remarkably responsive to the changing roles of the profession and the demand for well-educated men and women who are intelligent enough to cope with the new tasks. The success of the schools in this respect is partly made easier because there are so many of them: 105 accredited schools, plus several new schools that are considered candidates for accreditation. There is at least one school in almost every state. In addition, 11 schools enrol 500 or more full-time candidates for professional degrees, leaving aside those who concentrate on building construction, planning or landscape, which would swell the number twofold (Edwards 1998). These conditions enable individual schools to specialise in teaching specific approaches to architecture, some focusing on design, others on environment behaviour studies, technology or architectural management. The large number of schools and the size of some of them provides wide latitude for experimentation with approaches such as team teaching or studios, in which other specialists beside architects join. There are schools, for example, that put all their students through collaborative studios, in which they work on projects jointly with students concentrating on urban design, planning and landscape architecture. There are still other schools, such as those in Michigan and Washington, where most students participate in so-called 'charettes', in which the teams meet at the project site and include not only students but also community leaders, developers and prospective building users.

The adaptability to the needs of the profession is especially interesting because in the USA the profession has had very little control over the schools compared with the influence of the RIBA on professional education in the UK. The separation of the schools and the profession has been characteristic of American architectural education almost from the schools' inception, largely because they were installed in universities, from whose intellectual independence they benefited. Even one hundred years ago it was common for the profession to complain that students spent too much time on historical studies and writing essays (Oliver 1981:42–3). Despite the lack of direct connection, the schools have often anticipated developments in the profession. I am not sure how to explain this phenomenon, other than to say it is consistent with the marketing mentality of institutions of higher education in the USA. It cannot be explained by saying that more practitioners have been teaching in the schools because the fact is there are fewer than ever before. Many studios are currently led by faculty members who have no practices or very limited practices. This has been especially true of schools located far from cities, which is still the standard situation for the public universities in the centre of the country.[1]

Even the schools located near big cities, which are centres of architectural practice, now find it difficult to recruit practitioners to teach, because in the current building boom they cannot spare the time and do not need the additional income. Another factor contributing to the decline of practitioners in faculties is that the schools have had to become more rigorous about teachers' qualifications. This is a price the schools have paid for becoming more integrated into the academic culture of the universities. Design faculty members are reviewed by committees from other disciplines; they must be truly distinguished to receive long-term appointments.[2] Architectural history, formerly a sideline activity of design teachers, is now taught by faculty members who have doctoral degrees in architectural history.

The responsiveness of the schools is very conspicuous with respect to computer instruction. Almost every school now has computer installations, and there are a great many schools where the hardware is state of the art and continuously upgraded, and faculty members are experts in the subject. Of course instruction in computer aided design is a very costly undertaking, but schools have profited from the fact that other academic disciplines as well as administrative functions are computer-dependent.

As recently as the mid 1990s it was a standard complaint among practitioners that the schools were not sufficiently emphasising computer instruction. The complaint came mainly from the smaller firms, which recognised the importance of developing competence in this technology if they were to compete with the largest offices. We should remember that in 1990 firms such as Hellmuth, Obata and Kassebaum, and Skidmore, Owings and Merrill had already developed their own design software and were selling it to other practitioners. But the situation has reversed now. Students coming out of the schools are now far more sophisticated in the use of computers than is the case in the average office. Indeed this has become a problem for small firms that cannot afford the advanced hardware and software that graduates expect. In these circumstances it is not surprising that graduates choose to follow other careers—in film making and animation, in the advertising industry and in Silicon Valley—where they can exploit their computer skills. These career choices have the added advantage that the remuneration is two to four times that for entry level jobs in architecture. I have been told that similar trends have emerged in the UK.

The schools have also been unusually flexible in developing degree programmes that serve the emergent needs of the profession. This effort began right after World War II, when several reports sponsored by the American Institute of Architects (AIA) and the Association of Collegiate Schools of Architecture advocated two very important changes in architectural education (Consortium of East Coast Schools of Architecture 1981, Appendix 2). The first of these was to extend the length of formal schooling from five years to six or seven years, with the actual length depending on the student's previous experience in design and building subjects. These reforms continued a process that had begun with the establishment of the first American schools in the 1860s, when architecture instruction had lasted three years and classes in design were often not introduced until the final year. The extension to six or seven years was clearly a recognition that the boundaries of architectural knowledge were expanding, and that it would necessarily take longer for students to master the relevant subject matter.

The second important structural change in the professional curriculum since World War II has been to insist that students spend more time acquiring a general background in liberal studies, including the social sciences, literature and philosophy, before concentrating on architecture. In the best versions of these programmes today, the liberal studies component is very strong; although as the recent Carnegie Endowment report on architectural education points out, this unfortunately is not the case throughout the USA (Boyer and Mitgang 1996). The reason for the focus on liberal studies was partly to make architectural education more like the education of lawyers and physicians, who start their professional education only after completing a bachelor's degree in liberal studies or science. But another reason, surely, was to enable architects to be better informed and therefore better able to talk intelligently about matters outside the realm of architecture, especially in their encounters with clients.

Education for research

A further innovation introduced in American schools since the early 1980s are research-oriented programmes of one or two years' duration, leading to a master of science or master of arts degree in architecture. These programmes were introduced to address the needs of practising architects who wished to improve their knowledge in specific areas that were regarded as relevant to the conduct of practice. Forty of the 105 schools offer such programmes now, providing advanced training in design theory, preservation, programming, environment behaviour studies, computer aided design and real estate development. Sometimes the graduates of these programmes go on to new careers, say in teaching or research. The large majority return to practice, thus the name by which they are often known: mid-career programmes. Twenty schools now also offer doctoral programmes, of which all but three grant the Doctor of Philosophy degree (PhD).[3] The overwhelming majority of students who go through the doctoral programmes end up teaching in universities or working in research institutes.

An ancillary consequence of the new degree programmes has been the stimulation of research activity in schools of architecture. Most of the research currently follows the tradition of humanities research, with the emphasis on the history of architecture. This in itself is an innovation, because research in architectural history was traditionally the province of art history departments. Considerable research activity is also done on technical subjects, such as computer aided design, structures and environmental control systems, and a small amount on programming studies. The big problem the schools face with research is lack of funding. The software and building materials industries and the National Science Foundation support some investigations, but these studies are mainly in the technology area. Indeed the absence of funding sources is a major issue for the schools because, in some universities, deans and department heads are under considerable pressure to increase the amount of outside support, which is generally less for architecture than any other discipline. At present the building industry, the software industry and architectural firms probably do as much research as the schools, except obviously in the humanities area. On the other hand it has been often noted that, among industries, the building industry spends a smaller share of its income on research and development than any other major industry. For a number of years the research centres of the schools organised themselves into the Architectural Research Centers Consortium, an organisation largely intended to lobby industry and federal granting agencies to expand their support for architectural research. Other organisations in the field have now joined in this undertaking, which is presently known as the Initiative for Architectural Research. Although it has had limited success in achieving its financial objectives, the Consortium and the Initiative have provided a valuable forum in which the small proportion of faculty members committed to research can exchange ideas and colaborate on projects.

The transition to practice

From the time that architects began to attend schools for their education rather than depend exclusively on the apprenticeship system, practitioners complained that graduates were poorly prepared to step straight into practice. Although one still hears this comment, it seems to fluctuate depending on the state of the architectural economy. With the current building boom in the USA the criticism has become muted. The big worry in many firms now is shortage of staff, almost regardless of their qualifications, particularly men and women in their late thirties and early forties. This was the generation that was turned off architecture by the recession in the late 1980s and early 1990s.

Even before the recent boom, however, dissatisfaction with the schools was diminishing. As most practitioners began to be drawn from the cohorts of students who were better educated because of the reforms in the postwar period, there was greater appreciation that the purpose of the schools was to *educate* rather than merely to *train* architects. One often meets practitioners who are nostalgic about what they remember as the less stressful life of a student, when they had the time to think about the ideals of the profession. Of course, sometimes envy turns into criticism, but for the most part practitioners have come to terms with their gripes. Indeed they seem increasingly to acknowledge their obligation to assume responsibility for the professional development of their employees. Their new concern is kindled by the requirement, as of 1998, that *all* practitioners must participate in continuing education programmes as the condition for maintaining AIA membership. The relatively new AIA requirement universalises a standard earlier imposed by the licensing boards in 13 of the 50 US states that architects engage in a self-study programme to maintain their licenses.[4]

Since 1979 the responsibility of principals to oversee the further training of entry-level personnel has been institutionalised through a programme known as the Intern Development Program (IDP), sponsored jointly by the AIA and the state licensing boards. The programme is intended to upgrade the existing statutory requirement in all 50 states for novice architects to have three years of work experience in an office before they can sit for the licensing examination. The IDP programme adds to this requirement a definitive specification of the practical skills that novices should acquire, and that the firm has a responsibility to teach. It includes such skills as programming, code research, building cost analysis, document checking, construction administration, office management and community service. The programme was modelled on the internships available to physicians, but it failed to recognise the significance of the differences between the resources of teaching hospitals and architectural practices. The difference is that few of the 18 000 architectural firms[5] in the USA have the capacity to oversee the learning process. Few firms have enough projects going on in the office at one time to enable a young architect to experience the range of skill situations called for in the IDP protocol, nor can the offices spare the staff and time to mentor and instruct the candidate.

The next debate

One of the important challenges in architectural education in the next century will be to find ways to make graduate trainee programmes more effective. The licensing boards, practices and schools, which are critical to the success of the IDP programme, have been reexamining its operation, largely in response to discussion of its shortcomings, which is one of the principal conclusions of the Carnegie Endowment study. The outcome of these investigations is unclear. Any recommendations will take years to implement, given the many constituencies—the AIA, the state licensing boards, the organisation that accredits the schools, the school faculties—that will have to approve regulatory changes. The new system that will emerge is likely to require the schools to be more directly involved with the trainees, perhaps building on the fact that many of the schools now offer the courses through which licensed architects and AIA members fulfil their continuing education requirements.[6]

The format of the transition to practice will, in my judgment, constitute the next topic of debate on architectural education in the USA. It will probably also require financial and staff contributions from the large firms, which are the only group of practitioners with the resources to endow the programme, and from the schools themselves. It is one of the ironies of the history of architectural education that the schools are now the most powerful and best endowed constituency in the entire community of architectural organisations in the USA. Their staff have the most secure jobs, the demand for their services continue more or less independently of fluctuations in economic conditions, and their budgets are reasonably well protected from year to year. They can well afford to help out with this important mission.

Assuming some development along these lines, architectural education will have come full circle. In its American version, it began in the late eighteenth century with a union of education and training functions in the architecture office by means of the apprenticeship system. The establishment of architectural schools at the end of the American Civil War, in the 1860s, led slowly to an uneasy and not totally satisfactory division of labour. The schools were eventually defined as mainly responsible for communicating new knowledge and general principles, and the offices were laden with the task of helping novices to apply these general ideas to practical problems. There was continuous tension and argument between the two parties until fairly recently, but now they seem to have more or less agreed on what the schools and the offices can each do best. The acceptance by the offices that they are responsible for the training of graduates is the latest sign of the agreement. If there does indeed emerge a new partnership between educators and practitioners to strengthen postgraduate training through the office, it will restore some of the attractive features and simplicity of the apprenticeship system. But it will be in a manner that acknowledges the great progress that has taken place in education and architectural knowledge in the twentieth century.

Notes

1   This is especially interesting because the second school established in the USA in 1868, was that at the University of Illinois. For many years it had the country's largest enrolment, yet it was located in the centre of the farm belt.

2   A few schools, by establishing 'professorship in practice', have begun to address the problem created by competing demands on practitioners who teach. The Graduate School of Design at Harvard has taken the lead. Its appointments of this type are half-time tenured appointments, which are subject to the same university review as full-time tenured appointments. Persons who hold these chairs must have a practice in the Boston area. Rem Koolhaas, the Dutch architect, occupies one of these chairs. At the University of Pennsylvania and MIT there are similar arrangements; in these schools the appointment is for a five-year term.

3   The three doctoral degrees that are not PhD degrees are called Doctor of Architecture or Doctor of Design. In order to grant a PhD (doctor of philosophy) degree, the course of study for the degree must be approved by the graduate faculty of arts and sciences. Presumably this did not happen in the three schools perhaps because they wanted to emphasise their degree's connection to professional, that is, applied endeavour.

4   Since August 1999 the licensing boards of 11 more states have been considering the imposition of this standard.

5   Ninety per cent of the firms are solo practices or have one to five employees.

6   Representatives of the different organisations met in April 1999 to formulate proposals for the redesign of the graduate trainee programme. A committee has been formed to consider the proposals and develop procedures for their implementation. One proposal is to incorporate the training into the period of formal study (some schools have had such an arrangement for 70 or more years). Another is to establish a 'teaching academy', in which graduates would continue to study while working in an office. For both types of arrangement, school faculty members would be expected to take an active role.

References

Boyer, Ernest and Mitgang, Lee (1996) *Building Community: A New Future for Architecture Education and Practice*. Princeton, NJ: The Carnegie Foundation for the Advancement of Teaching.

Consortium of East Coast Schools of Architecture (1981) *Architecture Education Study*, vol. I, *The Papers*. Cambridge, Mass.: Consortium of East Coast Schools of Architecture.

Edwards, John (ed.) (1998) *Guide to Architecture Schools*. Washington, DC: Association of Collegiate Schools of Architecture.

Gutman, Robert (1988) *Architectural Practice: A Critical View*. NY: Princeton Architectural Press.

Hirschhorn, Larry (1997) *Reworking Authority: Leading and Following in the Post-Modern Organization*. Cambridge, Mass.: MIT Press.

Oliver, Richard (ed.) (1981) *The Making of An Architect, 1881–1981*. New York: Rizzoli.

24 The design studio as a vehicle for change
The 'Portsmouth Model'

Wendy Potts

Context

Studio teaching is central to the pedagogy of architectural education. However it is also frequently seen as the most expensive and least understood component of architectural education, prompting such questions as 'Is it expensive in terms of space and staff time?', 'What does it achieve that cannot be achieved in other ways?', 'Do we fully understand it, can we explain it and can we quantify its benefits?', 'How do we maximise these benefits?'

These were some of the questions we asked ourselves in Portsmouth. In the early 1990s the School of Architecture at the University of Portsmouth was facing challenges to the *status quo* on a broad front. Housed in poor accommodation, its imminent new premises were to have 40 per cent less studio space. Student numbers were rising—doubling from a first-year intake of 55 in 1992 to 110 in 1994. The staff were becoming demoralised, trying to maintain previous studio teaching methods in the face of such radical change. There were major staff losses throughout 1992 and those staff lost to early retirement could not be replaced if the school was to remain viable. It was clear that all teaching methods would need to be reviewed.

Our common belief remained that studio teaching was central and special. But in uniting to protect this fundamental of our pedagogy, we had to understand what we meant by it and learn how to communicate it. In *The Design Studio*, Schön (1985) argues that 'in order for the lessons of the [design] studio to be made accessible to other professions … studio masters must be willing to examine what they already know how to do', but cautions that 'We take for granted that which we are confident we can do, and the defensive attitude implicit in a process that requires subjective judgement inhibits our desire to communicate its mysteries but also its benefits to others. Perhaps for these reasons even the vocabulary for communicating the process and its outcomes is defensive, limited and confusing.'

The debate that followed centred on studio teaching and the specific interests and beliefs of full-time colleagues: What were we good at? How would we ideally like to teach design? Could we define the methodology of vertical and horizontal studio teaching in relation to other methods?

At that time Portsmouth had a core of full-time staff with tenure that we would supplement with part-time staff—some from practice and some offering particular areas of expertise that were not available amongst the core staff. Our proposed new model was to allow for individuality in the studio but with commonality in the overall intention via the existing year programmes. Thus early on we were aware that continual balancing/tuning would be needed to maintain the effectiveness of the system and that, to achieve this, despite Schön's pessimism, our ability to communicate studio teaching techniques would be critical.

To help set this in a larger context, a three-day symposium—'Educating Architects' (Pearce and Toy 1995)—was organised to take place in February 1994. This enabled us to discuss broader issues and to test our proposals against fresh ideas. Concurrent with discussion and preparation for the symposium, we were able to agree our first set of objectives.

- To reinforce, support and develop studio teaching.
- To enable individual members of staff to develop their own interests/passions, and to develop their own teaching techniques within a framework that would ensure that all students had equal studio tutoring.
- To encourage cross-school communication between students (and years).
- To maximise the benefits of the new accommodation.
- To agree a programme to implement changes.

Throughout the 1993 and 1994 sessions we worked towards the introduction of 'vertical' studios—across all years, from first to final—which would run 'horizontal' design programmes. Working in small groups with students and studio teaching representatives, all non-studio components were reviewed and their relationship with studio programmes examined and questioned. At this point the methods for delivery of non-studio-taught subjects were much debated:

- Which areas of the curriculum could be delivered as formal lecture courses? Did they need new visual aid input, and if so, what? How could this be developed? Which areas of the curriculum did students find difficult and would need contextual reinforcement? For example, even though students had received all the construction information they needed to create a solution to a design problem, they often appeared unable to use it.

- Were there different, more appropriate methods: demonstrations, seminars, workshops, parallel studio projects specifically designed to enable students to test their knowledge?

As a result of this work, most non-studio courses were substantially rewritten and new methods of delivery explored and tried. In the summer of 1994 the results of the new course inputs were discussed and reviewed, and as a result new design programmes were written that emphasised the integration of the curriculum horizontally whilst clearly articulating the vertical development of students as they proceeded through the course.

We became convinced that all colleagues—from the history specialist to the construction specialist—had an equal, albeit different, important contribution to make in the studio—an environment where such information could be explored, expanded and tested. This marked a fundamental change in attitude and meant that studio activity could no longer be seen as an exclusive activity and that the development of studio programmes therefore needed to be inclusive and their progression clearly articulated (Lawson 1990).

At this stage, two demands of the new system became dominant:

- We would have to run all lecture and design programmes to a common time scale for the 'beginnings and ends' so that colleagues would have the flexibility to move across years and across studios.
- If all design programmes were to be taught by all colleagues, communication of aims, objectives and requirements would need to be explicit.

Finding a common direction

Concurrently, two fundamental questions had to be asked:

- What is the 'shape' of the school?
- What does it want to be?

Working with three visiting architecture professors bringing different perspectives from practice, we derived a second set of objectives:

- Every perspective of architecture has a value that can only be assessed by an evaluation, which requires open discussion and debate.
- Specialisation adds breadth to the debate.

- Students are individuals and it is our duty as educators to expose them to as many areas as we can rigorously inform. At this point we identified our particular passions as a school: architectural education (design, technology and professionalism) and environmental issues (urban and sustainable).
- If individualism is encouraged, it must be supported and informed. Students must learn to respect the contribution of those outside their personal sphere of interest and to be confident when communicating their own contribution—they need to become team players.
- Studios serve to reinforce all these values.

In October 1994 the studio system was prototyped. Teams of studio tutors moved to work across all years, having now chosen particular design programmes to develop. Students from each year were equally divided between all studios. A system of 'three weeks on/three weeks off' studio/lecture blocking was instigated to maximise studio contact time. Each full-time staff member became a 'studio master' and would have autonomy in the way in which design programmes were taught in the studio—taking responsibility for all students in their studio regardless of year. The design programmes would parallel the students' abilities as they progressed through the school, taking into account the content and setting into context the knowledge gained through the lecture and workshop programme. The responsibility for writing the design programmes and communicating the strategic 'year' objectives through teaching notes for each design programme fell to 'year coordinators'. All design programmes were agreed across each year and then across the whole school in a series of meetings and discussion groups held before the start of the academic year.

Our new model had been driven by two primary forces: management and academic needs.

Management

We were facing a period of rapid change, including:

- Financial: increased pressure arising from fewer staff and increased student numbers—this required us to include all colleagues in our review and evaluate the efficiency of all existing teaching methods.
- New accommodation: we had to ensure that large, multipurpose spaces were commissioned to enable future flexibility.
- Changing management systems: the need to embed the management system with academic objectives—studio structure.
- Demoralised and disenfranchised staff: we had to enable colleagues to question and inform future direction, include administrative

and technical support colleagues in all discussions, and divulge budgets to the academic, support and student bodies. This was to achieve 'transparency'.

Academic

- There was a lack of support and understanding by the institution of the major pedagogical delivery method—studio teaching. This required the development and celebration of studio successes— for example the improved results, the winning competition entries.
- Adjustment to unitisation in a creative programme, requiring us to make explicit the academic development/progression through clarification of the studio programmes' aims and objectives.
- The RIBA's curriculum rewrite (Tarn 1993) was used as an opportunity to define and refine the syllabus and reduce workloads by reevaluating the delivery methods.
- The debate surrounding education related to and affected by uncertainties in the profession (Latham 1994) provoked fundamental discussions of the school's strengths and weaknesses, and led to agreement on future directions/passions of the school that would maximise and acknowledge colleagues' inputs.
- The changing role of architects in the construction team caused us to reinforce generic roles such as teamworking (Andrews and Derbyshire 1993).
- Internalised perceptions—the early symposium was initiated to broaden the debate.

The model

The new, reduced, studio accommodation divided most easily into 11 definable areas. Colleagues and students were to use studios in different ways, but originally each had six drawing boards, four computers, 10–12 tables and an adjoining staff office. A model-making room was shared by adjoining studios. In addition, within the overall faculty there was a faculty learning resource centre that contained the architecture, technical and map libraries, reprographics and further computer facilities, and a serviced workshop with larger model-making equipment. There was access to five lecture theatres, ranging from 90 to 220 seats.

The design programmes are now set by year coordinators and run horizontally, whilst tutoring takes place in vertical groups—studios— that contain students from all years. The school is organised into 12 studios. Each has its own permanent geographical base and in general is run by one full-time member of the teaching staff with part-time teaching support. Students from all five years are allocated to each studio to give a mixture of students at different levels of the course and with different educational/cultural backgrounds. They are allocated for a period of one semester, after which all the studios are reorganised. This ensures that students can have the benefit of being tutored by up to 10 of the possible 12 studio tutors over the full five-year period.

In contrast to the unit-based system, the educational programmes are set for each year cohort and organised by a year coordinator, who liases with each studio tutor in respect of the educational objectives and methods for the projects. However it is accepted that each individual tutor will bring her or his own personality and flavour to the student's learning experience through the studio. Important to achieving parity whilst maintaining variety is the recent development of clear guidelines on assessment criteria being made available to the students, as well as written feedback on reviews.

Each tutor teaches across the undergraduate and postgraduate schools, thus integrating the studio base, comprising students from all five years. Each of the studios has approximately 36 students, and is staffed for three days a week by one full-time and one part-time member of staff, working 30 hours between them. This means that every student can have a minimum of 40 minutes of one-to-one tutorial time per week.

Student allocation

First-year students are placed in studios based on their entry qualification, educational background, sex and nationality, so that all studios have a cross-section of students. In the second and third years, students are placed according to their portfolio results so that an even mix of strengths/abilities is achieved across all studios. For the first semester of their diploma course, students are allocated according to their degree classifications, so that a mixture of abilities across studios is maintained. In their second semester they choose 'electives', offered on a first/second/third-choice basis, again to retain an even distribution across studios. In their final year, students choose a studio master for each semester—almost all receive their first choice.

Organisation

The new studio system has been made possible by an elaborate system of programming. A master programme is drawn up well before each semester, then issued for comment and corrected. Rooms are booked, guest reviewers and external lecturers are booked and so on. Each week, events lists are extracted from the master programme, issued for comment, corrected and added to. The master programme is also used to produce studio-teaching diagrams for each studio, showing the general teaching commitments of each member of staff.

All design programmes are looked at as a 'line' that begins in the first year and ends in the fifth year. They are a progression—building towards an integration of the knowledge and skills gained and enabling students to test their own understanding and development through the course. Students also question and hypothesise about their personal development in the design thesis. Before the start of each academic session, a two-day meeting considers all the proposed design programmes and discusses their requirements against the requirements of the 'line'. Possible studio teaching methods to reinforce and expand those requirements are identified. Although studio masters will be defining and refining their own preferred methods and interests, this is also the point at which the areas for their integration across the years is addressed, beginning with highlighting the teaching and learning requirements for each year.

While the typical work on group projects with other students enables the students to get to know their cohort, this, in itself, is not enough. Students are helped by understanding the extent of their development against the other years—to see where they have been and where they are going. Therefore in each of the three years one of the design programmes takes the form of 'precedent' project: the first year exploring architectural ideas (architectonics), the second year researching the work of contemporary architects using the language of the first-year precedent project to articulate the ideas, and the third year researching, using and exploring the ideas of the 'greats' of the modern movement in order to design a building as a paradigm of the master.

There is added learning value in such a model. For instance if the first year help the second year to research the work of contemporary architects, the first year will learn how to use the library and what they may be looking for. Meanwhile the second-year students are able to reinforce the knowledge they gained in their first year by informally helping the new students to find examples for their architectonics paradigm. Both years are now interested in the work of the other. When the final review takes place the first and second years will normally attend each other's reviews—the former thereby understanding where they are going and the latter reflecting where they have been. For the third-year students, one of the requirements of their presentation is to communicate the relevance and importance of the ideas they have researched and to make them explicit to the second-year students. Thus the third-year students demonstrate and reinforce their ability to understand, analyse and communicate.

Students in their final two years form part of the studio review teams on the reviews of the work of the first three years. Mentoring then occurs through the younger students asking for help from the older students who reviewed their work. This process is not yet formalised, but we are debating whether it should be. We see that the sense of responsibility and the vital skills developed by the final years is important in their development and will be useful to them when practising, but it may be enough that it remains part of the ethos of the studio and is not formalised.

This form of cross-fertilisation takes place across many of the design programmes. It is helped structurally by the fact that numbers are small: of the 36 students in a studio, approximately 10 are first-year, 9 are second-year, 8 are third-year and 10 are fourth- or fifth-year. It is helped academically by the fact that a studio master and part-time assistant are responsible for the academic development of all 36.

Assessment

Initially, most assessment took place within each full studio and moderating the results was very time consuming. We therefore sought to establish an acceptable but clearer methodology that would enable smaller reviews to take place in the studios without losing the benefits of the cross-fertilisation, and at the same time formalise the feedback and results of reviews. Five stages were agreed:

- Pin-up: an informal review of progress as part of the studio design/tutorial process. No feedback will be recorded.
- Crit: an interim review of the current design programme by the studio master and one other, who may be a senior student. Feedback will be recorded. A guide mark will not normally be given, but if it is it will be unmoderated, will take into account any potential for development and will be unrelated to cross-year standards.
- Jury: final review of the design programme by the studio master and one other, who may be a 'guest juror'. A guide mark will be given. It will be moderated, will not take account of any potential for development, will be related to cross-year standards, may be changed at portfolio examination and will be for guidance only.
- Portfolio review: a review of all the work of the current academic session in the portfolio. Advice may be given for additional work and entered in the feedback record.
- Portfolio examination: final examination of all design work in the portfolio by the current studio master and year coordinator. All guide marks given at this stage may be changed to take into account the work in the overall portfolio. No feedback will be recorded. The final mark will go to the board of examiners.

A simple system of coloured feedback records was also agreed because it is important for studio masters to have an overview of students' abilities as they move into their studios at the beginning of each semester.

Evaluation

For students, it would be difficult to produce concrete evidence that the system is better than the previous one, partly because it is still evolving and changing and partly because the students currently in the school know no other system. However, indicators of success include the fact that although the student numbers have increased but staffing has not increased comparably, the percentage of students gaining firsts and upper seconds has marginally increased, not fallen.

It is also clear that students have taken ownership of, understand and support the system. There are two examples of this. The first was a problem of 'studio hopping'. Some students felt they would benefit from having as many tutorials as possible a week, and one group was seen going from one studio to another seeking further tutorials. The tutors felt the problem would be resolved naturally when the students saw their results, because their work would be confused and incomplete. However, before this, student representatives at a weekly lunch meeting saw this behaviour as a threat to the system and decided to speak to the other students to ensure it would not continue. Secondly, current students volunteer to speak to prospective students on open days about the Portsmouth model. Clearly their enthusiasm for it is a significant factor in the strong student recruitment that the school enjoys.

The model has increased the level of pastoral care at the studio tutor/student level. The early dropout rate has decreased. There is a consensus among both students and staff that the studio system has been working well academically and socially, and final-year students claim that the school is more united than it has ever been before. This despite the fact that the school is twice the size it was when they started their studies.

Students in the early levels of the course have clearly benefited from association with the more senior students in their studios, and the in-studio reviews have seen students from across the school engaged in architectural debate. Certainly they are now aware of the need for communication skills, and at their request an actor has been appointed to coach them in these skills. Senior students have responded well to their new responsibilities in the studio and enjoy the opportunity to test their critical skills. However work is needed to develop these skills and senior students have requested help in mentoring. This raises the question of how formalised the relationship between junior and senior students should be. It is interesting that the mature students are requesting this because they see it as a necessary professional skill.

Tutors are becoming more confident about developing their own new methods for studio teaching. There is more discussion about studio teaching methods, and two studios often join together to develop new methods. At the weekly lunches, studio masters who are less successful have perceived the need to change and are generally supported and helped by more confident colleagues. There remains, however, a problem in that not all studios are seen as equal by students—there are 'preferred' studios. Clearly this is a management problem and needs to be addressed, but solving it should not be difficult because the problem is visible and can be shared.

Part-time tutors have expressed their enthusiasm for and enjoyment of being part of the studio team, and this has attracted some particularly bright and able young practitioners. They feel that working with a studio master across years is an invaluable experience and gives them good educational experience of many tutoring techniques. Again there is discussion about whether this teaching experience should be formalised, and work is underway on a masters programme in architectural education based on the studio teaching experience.

Most studios are now exceptionally busy and vibrant. The lack of dedicated workspace has only occasionally caused problems. When groups have wanted a quiet space in which to work together they have been allowed to annexe a seminar or model room for the period they need. The students accept that the studio is a resource base—it has interesting people, good debate, moral support and good equipment on offer. The students have become as flexible as the space they occupy, and perhaps this too will be a useful professional preparation.

A further studio has been set up to reduce the total number of students in each studio to 36 in the face of rising student numbers. In 1998–9 the number of students in the studio increased to over 40, and although the staff hours were increased it became clear that the studio masters were under too much pressure. However, because the system needs transparency in planning and resources to operate, it is easy to produce the statistical evidence necessary to justify additional resources. For example the staffing cost per student architect in this model is half that required for a student of civil engineering.

Conclusion

To run the studios in this way we had to develop new studio-teaching methods and learn how to share these with the new and part-time colleagues who joined us. We had to rethink the ways in which design programmes/briefs are developed and communicated, and we had to define and clarify mechanisms for assessment.

Since its inception the staff to student ratio has doubled and the studio space has halved, but our new model has survived and now, after five years, we have identified unexpected benefits that we are beginning to build on and develop.

To date our model appears to have increased both staff and student accountability and responsibility, and individual staff strengths and interests are better recognised. Hence we have achieved many of the objectives first set. We have also learned that good communication and continual evaluation is vital to retain the 'balance' between the cult of the individual and the collective pedagogy. Finally, and perhaps most importantly, we have gained enough confidence to know that to continue to change and evolve is healthy.

References

Andrews, J. and Derbyshire, Sir Andrew (1993) *Crossing Boundaries*. London: Construction industry Council.

Latham, Sir Michael (1994) *Constructing the Team*. London: HMSO.

Lawson, B. (1990) *How Designers Think—The Design Process Demystified*. London: Butterworth.

Pearce, M. and Toy, M. (eds) (1995) *Educating Architects*. London: Academy Group.

Schön, D. (1985) *The Design Studio—An Exploration of its Traditions and Potential*. London: RIBA Publications.

Tarn, J. (1993) *Syllabus, Guide and Regulations*. London: RIBA.

25 Embedding change

A case study of the CUDE experience

George Henderson

Background

This chapter is a narrative. It tells the story of a school of architecture that decided it wanted to embed a new professionalism in its students, describes some of the difficulties it encountered and gives an account of progress to date.

Running architecture courses in today's academic environment requires trying to resolve the conflicting demands of university, external validators and an increasingly hybrid student body (vocational, non-vocational, home and overseas). Staff are expected to recruit and teach more students in less time, as well as perform well in research and generate external income. In addition, the environment into which students are emerging at the end of their formal courses is changing rapidly and a range of government and professional reports over the last decade have identified a need for a change in the professional culture to enable the construction industry to operate more effectively (DOETR 1998; Latham 1994; RIBA 1992–5; 1999). Education must play a part in promoting that change as well as reflecting changes that are already taking place.

However, within such a context—one of external pressures and rapid change, beyond the control of staff—it is understandable that some staff are resistant to change in areas still within their control—the teaching domain. Coping with external pressures also leaves little time to consider more appropriate ways of teaching and learning. Teachers frequently hold on to the old ways, the proven methods, the tested techniques. And yet if they do not adapt, both in terms of course content and teaching, it is likely that graduates will not acquire the range of skills required of today's professionals, whilst academic staff will wear themselves out using old techniques in new situations.

CUDE provided a unique opportunity for the Leicester School of Architecture (LSA) to take stock—in particular of the way in which its students were learning how to communicate effectively with lay clients and users, and other professionals—and to develop teaching techniques that would emphasise professional and personal skills. We also sought to create a learning environment for staff and students in which educational objectives would be given greater clarity.

A vocational school

Courses in architecture at the LSA have always emphasised the development of the practical skills that are essential to working practice—drawing, designing, report writing and management. The history of the school explains its strong practical and vocational tradition. It began its life in the Art and Technical Schools in Leicester towards the end of the nineteenth century. Developing in response to the needs of local architectural practices, it provided part-time formal tuition for articled pupils who were being trained as future architects. Alongside the School of Architecture was a School of Building, providing craft training for building operatives. Inevitably, early classes at the school centred on developing drawing skills provided by the Art School, and a knowledge of construction provided by the School of Building.

The LSA is now part of De Montfort University (DMU)—a 'new university', formerly Leicester Polytechnic. The strong craft tradition and understanding of how buildings are made—the 'art of building'—has endured to the present day. So too has the close relationship with practice. The LSA is one of very few architecture schools in the UK still providing a part-time route for students working in practice, who have weekly day release.

However, despite being located in a university that actively promotes new learning methods and the development of personal skills, and within a school with a strong vocational tradition, courses in architecture at the LSA have been remarkably resistant to the recent changing needs of practice. Two underlying factors can be cited. Firstly, DMU's commitment to new methods of learning and the development of personal skills have been underresourced and have not enjoyed wide take-up across the faculties. Secondly, the belief amongst some architecture staff that 'we're doing what is needed'—as evidenced by the fact that our graduates are in demand by good practices and get good jobs—has led to some complacency and a resistance to change.

The CUDE initiative

DMU's involvement with CUDE was based on the rationale that the LSA offered great potential for cross-disciplinary collaboration since the architecture department was at that time based in the School of the Built Environment (comprising surveying and construction study programmes). Here was an opportunity to place greater emphasis on 'people' within the design process by developing cross-disciplinary working. This focus, it was thought, would inevitably lead to a broader definition of design and create a new professionalism in students. We defined this as possessing those skills which are not just about presentation to but also collaboration with a range of professionals, clients and users. It is an issue that is being slowly recognised by all professions, and involves fostering attitudes and skills to promote less perceived arrogance, more effective teamwork, effective cross-disciplinary working, better communication and designing for others with others.

Implementation

LSA's initial approach was to tap existing staff interests by asking for suggestions and proposals. Inevitably this process of self-selection was rather hit and miss, and led to the adjustment of existing projects rather than a fundamental reassessment of the teaching and learning culture. Initial progress was also slow, due to resistance by some staff, together with muddled communication within the school and the various layers of management overseeing the project.

Most importantly, it took some time for us to realise that staff who had offered to develop projects with a CUDE component did not necessarily have the educational theory needed to follow through to the required conclusion. Staff reskilling became a key focus and this process took time. It was clear that all the staff needed both to understand and to endorse the philosophy behind the CUDE project. This rethink had to be done in a strategic framework within which the specific skills to be developed in students could be identified, as well as when and how they should be introduced into the design programmes. The undergraduate programme was refashioned to accommodate specific projects that allowed the cumulative development of new communication skills over the three-year undergraduate architecture programme. In all, it took around 18 months to create a truly strategic approach that could effect a real change in the learning culture.

Now that the first, three-year phase of the CUDE project has been completed it is possible to reflect on its achievements at the LSA. Initial inertia gave way to a more positive readiness to change and the second half of the three-year project has seen considerable progress. Initial tinkerings with existing projects, involving a limited number of staff, have now been replaced by a more strategic approach that involves a healthy level of staff commitment and participation.

In the case of the undergraduate course a strategic framework has been agreed, identifying projects within which specific personal and professional skills will be developed. This includes the provision of focused workshops to develop skills in brief-making, teamworking, oral and verbal communication, talking to lay clients and users and working with students and practitioners from associated disciplines. Professional educators are brought in to pass on learning techniques to resident staff.

There has been a complete reassessment of the review process. The traditional crit has been examined and ways of making it more effective proposed. A sociologist came into the school to appraise a variety of crit situations with resident staff, and identified a range of potential opportunities for enhanced learning (Wilkin 1999). The undergraduate course is now restructuring the evaluation process in response to her observations and analysis of student questionnaires and staff interviews (see Chapter 10).

A greater variety of crits has been introduced, where learning is emphasised and specific communication skills are developed (IT presentation, poster presentation, conference format, lecture room format and so on). Separation of the crit—with its educational opportunities for reflection and feedback for development—from assessment—where the student's work is evaluated—has been reinforced. Clarification of the activity has ranged from consideration of room layout to overtly expressed educational objectives.

The graduate school potential

Although the graduate school was not involved in the CUDE project, its staff have reflected on ways in which the existing course can build on the new professionalism that is being developed in the undergraduate course. The course already offers significant opportunities for group working and multidisciplinary activities, along with the development of skills and making judgements under pressure of time:

- Professional studies is taught both in the lecture theatre and in the design studio context. Students are asked to solve, jointly, typical problems faced in practice and present proposals.
- The year out in practice between the undergraduate and graduate years is seen as an integral part of the graduate course. It involves close monitoring of students in practice and a number of 'recall' days, when students return to the school to relate and reflect upon their experiences and take part in structured design exercises.
- At RIBA Part 3 level (the professional practice examination) an office-based exam is run. This is a regional initiative that currently involves three schools of architecture: Leicester, Nottingham and Sheffield. The examination is 'owned' by the architectural

profession and run by the schools. External examiners set the practice scenarios, which are examined in the office context. They mark the work and conduct the final professional interview.

Overall, at the school level the LSA has rewritten its strategic plan, emphasising the school's commitment to the needs of clients, users and society within a broader definition of design. There is a declared wish to embed a new professionalism in the school (with its courses in architecture, building surveying and architectural design technology and production), which involves the development of life-long skills rather than short-term knowledge.

Critique

Despite the apparently receptive environment at DMU and the LSA there was initial inertia with regard to developing the opportunities presented by CUDE. Why was this so? One reason might be that higher education in general, and schools of architecture in particular, have witnessed considerable change over the last decade. Most have increased their student intake and reduced the number of tutors, and are trying to retain the same academic standards in a much shorter academic year. Restructuring the academic year into two semesters has resulted in a lack of continuity due to the disruption caused by traditional holiday periods. Modularisation has led to further fragmentation of integrated subjects such as architecture. It has also required teaching to become much more quantifiable and emphasise learning processes rather than teaching input. Teachers are expected to reduce student contact time in order to maintain a cost-effective staff–student regime.

This climate of change in higher education has produced particular difficulties for design courses such as architecture. A strong design ethic persists, involving problem-solving design exercises. The studio culture is seen as sacrosanct and central to learning by the act of practising designing buildings. Traditionally this has involved one-to-one tuition, which many schools can now ill afford. The design focus is self-absorbing and time consuming and its evaluation involves assessing the designed artefact rather than the student's academic progress.

Most teachers in schools of architecture have not received formal teacher training. They generally come straight from practice and tend to replicate their own student experiences whilst learning on the job, and therefore tend to lack understanding of the theory of educational processes. This makes it difficult for them to be objective about defining explicit teaching and learning outcomes within the holistic teaching environment. Moreover they inherit a tradition that relied on high levels of teaching, but which is now considered to be 'over-teaching'. When asked to teach less, develop a culture of learning and retain traditional definitions of design quality while broadening the definition of design, the resulting inertia is perhaps unsurprising. Such inertia can be further exacerbated by the ageing profile of untrained teachers who are distant from current architectural practice. Links with practice are made even more difficult by the high demands placed on them by the current requirements of higher education. Part-time teachers, based in practice, can ameliorate this situation, but they often see their teaching as an escape from the constraints of office life and have no wish to follow a strategic approach to embedding professional skills.

Conclusion

Embedding new professional skills within a crowded curriculum is a challenge that now faces architecture and related disciplines. However the call for a new professionalism in architecture courses has yet to result in a discernible change of culture in schools of architecture. The recognition that such skills can and must be taught and tested in a structured way will only take place if teachers can be trained to identify and develop these skills.

For the LSA, the CUDE experience brought mixed blessings. Embedding change was initially met by staff resistance, progress was slower than expected and some divisiveness was encountered. The ambition of CUDE was, through its additional funding, to release busy staff from their heavy teaching commitments, thereby enabling them to develop new educational initiatives. But not all staff were willing to let go of their normal teaching duties, even though external consultants and tutors had been afforded by the CUDE project. Similarly the ambition to increase cross-disciplinary activity has not yet been fully realised—even in a multidisciplinary school there is clearly residual resistance to change.

Genuine success in changing staff and student attitudes must have a life beyond the duration of the CUDE project. Only time will tell, but the signs are positive. There is now a clear strategy for staff—both full and part-time—and students in terms of embedding a range of professional skills. Staff are being reskilled and trained to carry on the work that was introduced by external consultants.

What started as a desire to improve vocation—considering clients and users in the design process—has now become the pursuit of new professionalism—embedding different skills and attitudes. There is a genuine desire to move from confrontation to creative partnerships in education, which in turn, it is felt, will feed through into practice.

References

Department of Environment, Transport and Regions (DOETR) (1998) *Rethinking Construction: The Report of the Construction Task Force*, the Egan Report. London: HMSO.

Latham, Sir Michael (1994) *Constructing the Team: Final Report of the Government/Industry Review of Procurement and Contractual Arrangements in the UK*. London: HMSO.

Royal Institute of British Architects (RIBA) (1992) *Report of the Steering Group on Architectural Education*, the Burton Report. London: RIBA.

Royal Institute of British Architects (RIBA) (1992) *The Strategic Study of the Profession—Phase 1: Strategic Overview*. London: RIBA.

Royal Institute of British Architects (RIBA) (1993) *The Strategic Study of the Profession—Phase 2: Clients and Architects*. London: RIBA.

Royal Institute of British Architects (RIBA) (1995) *The Strategic Study of the Profession—Phases 3 and 4: The Way Forward*. London: RIBA.

Royal Institute of British Architects (RIBA) (1999) Vision: Stansfield-Smith Review of Architectural Education. London: RIBA.

Wilkin, Margaret (1999) Reassessing the Design Project Review in Undergraduate Architectural Education with Particular Reference to Clients and Users. Leicester: De Montfort University.

26 The 'crit' as a ritualised legitimation procedure in architectural education[1]

Hannah Vowles

Introduction

When I first started teaching architectural design some years ago, I found that I learnt a great deal very rapidly. Teaching can, of course, be a very effective kind of learning too. This was the first lesson: taking different roles produces different learning. I also realised that if students are to produce *good quality* work they have to be able to learn to recognise criteria of judgement, which entails an understanding that criteria are constructed and are therefore susceptible to testing and challenging. And one of the best places to do this is amongst a community of others similarly engaged, who collectively—through doing, observing and critically analysing each other's work—develop their skills as designers. This was the second lesson: criteria of quality are socially produced within a community.

In any discussion about 'the crit' or jury in architectural education we quickly find how slippery is the object of scrutiny, in that the crit is a sophisticated social event that is traditionally both an assessment of representation (the individual student's presentation of his or her project) and a reproduction of the social relations in the architectural profession. Here the former is as socially grounded as the latter, since judgements based on the relatively explicit and formal criteria of quality of content, such as planning, analysis, communication and so on, are inextricably interwoven with those based on largely implicit and thus untaught criteria of form, which occur as often unconscious judgements of students' taste and performance—their degree of success in constructing themselves (also often unconsciously or by trial and error) as designers in the prevailing image of 'the architect'. These criteria of quality are socially produced within the architectural community and are circumscribed by the way in which that community constructs its self-image as a social body within the wider context of society, legitimating some criteria at the expense of others.

Architectural design as a social process

Architectural design, even by an individual, is, I contend, a social process from the outset: communication with others is at the heart of
design just as it is central to teaching and learning. And in architectural design, *drawing*—whether with a pencil, a camera, modelling
materials, a computer or whatever—is a key tool of communication;
communication first of all with yourself, or between codesigners, and
then with partners, colleagues, clients, students, users and, of course,
with a public, real or imagined. Drawing, like writing, externalises
thought, gives form to concept, facilitating the invaluable shock of
surprising yourself; and it enables a dialogue to develop between
designer(s) and project. Drawing entails a process by which it acquires
a measure of independence from conceptual intentions. It becomes an
object of dialogue positing an audience (actual or potential), a collective subject or constituency that includes the author(s).

And design is also a form of mapping—a kind of cultural anthro-
pology of the present that, rather than producing hierarchical or
goal-oriented knowledge, is process-oriented, ongoing and *always
incomplete*. I think this is where there is a link to the idea of maintenance, both practical and philosophical—a mapping of change, of ageing and decay, of remaking and repair, of the 'ruin', both literal and
metaphorical. And, by implication, when a building is 'finished', its life
has only just begun. Architectural practice occurs within an existing
environment—the complexity of everyday lived experience in its constructed context of structures and meanings—restoring it and interven-
ing in it, altering and converting it, destroying and reconstructing it.
Yet at present both the drawing and the project, built or not, tend to
be treated as divorced from their embeddedness in a continuum of
change, attempting to fix them as timeless, aestheticised and autonomous objects, mirroring the professional as disembodied expertise.

The interface between a concept and its representation is not transparent—this is not a mimetic relation, it is indirect and unpredictable.
The drawing is not an illustration of a concept, but is more like a
translation of it into a medium of communication, a kind of language.
Nor should the activity of drawing be mistaken as an unfettered field
of creative freedom. As a medium of communication it is subject to
convention, hierarchy, codes, methods and, of course, fashion. And
any language, having conventions of use, is a 'ruin' of the concept,
a model of *imperfection*. The language of architectural drawing has its
own history and brings with it a whole subset of codes and inherited
ideological positionings that mediate the repertoire of possible meanings and forms.

'There is first the whole area of shared meaning of interpretation of
drawings that the student must come to acquire. And not only what a

certain physical representation on paper means in architectural terms, but also what is *allowable* within this domain.'[2] This is to say that representation is part of the process in architecture of the social construction of meaning. In architectural education at present, representation tends to be taught primarily as a matter of practical skill, as if it were a transparent and neutral means of communication, combined with self-expression and creative flair. Architectural drawing is a rich body of knowledge within the field of representation and visual literacy, with a strong tradition of reinvention and renewal through cycles of legitimation and of competing positions and constituencies. Thus representation as part of the taught curriculum in architecture should be treated as a historical and theoretical, as well as a practical subject.

In theorising drawing and design as a social process, the design project as the principle vehicle of architectural education inevitably comes under scrutiny too. Treating it only as a means for the individual student to acquire professional competencies is to overlook its potential as a vehicle through which the academic institutions can build up a body of original research about sites, users, representational techniques, building appraisal, the process of design, working practices, theoretical models and so forth as a means of producing a profession equipped to diversify its constituencies.

The sedimentation of value and ritualised legitimation: becoming an architect

The development of the architectural profession, its taste culture and its system of education, flows from its historical foundations—the mysteries and secrets of ecclesiastical building traditions and the practices of gentlemen draughtsmen, craft guilds and master builders; and also from the rise of the professions themselves, producing standards of entry as a means of protecting their members and the public from the claims of practitioners perceived as quacks, charlatans, impostors and amateurs encroaching on the turf of the qualified. This kind of history inevitably produces a complex and often contradictory layering or sedimentation of various values and traditions, resulting in ritualised practices that are far from transparent, especially to initiates. As such, we are all symptoms of the present manifestation of this historical process and thus cannot always view it objectively.

'Will it not be found that what is beautiful is harmonious and proportionable; what is harmonious and proportionable is true; and what is at once both beautiful and true is, of consequence agreeable and good?'[3] Following Shaftesbury's neat equation of the good, the true and the beautiful as a conflation of ethics and aesthetics, moral worth reflected as 'good taste', design taste cultures tend to invoke implicit and universal values that perpetuate social and cultural models in a generalised and untheorised manner. These assumptions are supported by the uncritical adoption of untransformed art historical notions, of univocal authorship, inherent meaning and natural creative talent, or even genius. Thus that which is deemed to be bad, false and ugly is taken as a reflection of 'bad taste' and is just as resistant to reasoned analysis. The crit or jury in architectural education is the renowned occasion for the ritual slaughter of unselfconscious displays of bad taste.

At present the crit is primarily constructed on the model of the grande finale, the final crit, in which competence is a prerequisite. Tutorials and interim reviews will have sorted out the basic requirements of the project as students come to understand that in the final crit they cannot expect to be rewarded for meeting any stated criteria. The completed project, reviewed by invited representatives of the profession, confirms the students' status as embryonic architects in two ways. It looks both forward and backwards. It is an occasion retrospectively to legitimate the course and (possibly) the students' work, and to flatter fellow academics and practitioners; and it initiates the student into the profession via the approval of acknowledged representatives of the prevailing taste culture. Invited critics thus play a crucial part as role model: cultured and widely read, and highly experienced in reading into and out of projects and setting the debate about them in an impressively catholic historical and cultural context—the architect as virtuoso. This in turn reinforces the project as the means of producing socially significant meaning, as defined by the unstated current taste culture of the profession, and positions the student as the favoured pupil. In providing an ambitious and sophisticated project, refined in its cultural referencing and conceptual rigour as a vehicle for critics to display their wit and erudition, the student demonstrates that he or she is becoming an architect. Successful initiation is thus a form of immaculate conception. This is often most graphically and tragically revealed by the plight of students who fail this rite, and who fail to see why.

Different models of practice

I am suggesting here that uncritical acceptance of the inherited legitimating procedures of representation and professional initiation rituals of architectural education helps to reproduce a model of architectural practice and of the role of the architect as a self-selecting elite of immaculately conceived creative individuals. This model is increasingly anachronistic and inappropriate to today's technocratic society, let alone to any idea of society as open and flexible, multicultural and democratic, in which specialist knowledge is accessible.

The incursion into the academy in the 1960s and 1970s of an influx of ideas drawn from the newly emerging academic studies—literary, media, social, ecological, postcolonial, political, feminist, to name but a few—which gradually became identified as 'theory', momentarily shook up the established history of philosophy and the authority of history. These ideas generated alternative approaches that seemed to offer the possibility of resituating architecture in relation to rapidly changing everyday life. The initial impact was little short of explosive. Postmodernism derailed the certainties of explanatory doctrines on all sides, firmly putting them in their place as competitive narratives of persuasion. Architectural students, academics and practitioners—a significant proportion of them—after a period of dismissive ridicule, enthusiastically embraced these conceptually interrogative and critically analytical cultural strategies. What revolutionised content and disciplinary boundaries, however, was to be speedily steered away from a parallel critical analysis of form—the enthusiasm did not extend to the deconstruction of one's own legitimating procedures. Nevertheless, like the contents of Pandora's box, once released these contaminating attitudes fester away, producing contradictory doubt.

The architect as virtuoso soloist who has always masked a team of collaborators is slowly being displaced by company names and acronyms, and by self-styled, loosely collaborative group identities. Changes in employment practices, epitomised by Norman Tebbit's call to get 'on your bike', together with the recognition that survival strategies such as specialisation and diversification demand flexibility, mobility and cooperation, have rendered impractical, if not provincial, the model of the profession that architectural education, as typified by the crit in its present form, helps to sustain. Moreover, with the expansion of higher education, not only are the pedagogic practices of academia as a whole being questioned, but also students entering academia are increasingly representative of a greater diversity of ethnicity, culture, class, age and gender and are now a potential source of a more cosmopolitan social exchange, a resource in the conduct of research into and the creation of new constituencies for architecture.

If the profession is not to retreat into a rearguard defensive position but to enter into a real engagement with these challenges as opportunities to cast a more critical eye over its own practices and assess their contradictions, the knowledge that current practice is socially generated should make the construction of different models a real possibility.

The crit as a social event and a central pedagogic strategy is unique to art and design education. If it is to be relevant for today's world it must be reviewed for its appropriateness in all three respects: content, form and procedure. In what ways can the project be reconstructed as a vehicle by which a body of research might be produced? How can

the format of the project and the crit explore different working practices that are more characteristic of already emerging tendencies,
particularly group working, in which the student becomes familiar
with a variety of roles and the kinds of learning that ensue, including
designer, critic, teacher, chair, spokesperson, user, audience and so
on? How can the inherent intensity of the crit as an event be har-
nessed to dramatise the excitement of active participation in design
(and learning) as the social construction and contestation of meaning?
What other forms of this social event may be used to explore design
and the criteria of its development and judgement—for instance the
student led review, peer assessment reviews, research presentations
for information exchange?

Conclusion

I have attempted in this chapter to map out the peculiar and contradictory terrain and tradition colloquially known as the crit, as it is
practised in architectural education. I have argued that it is a tradition
that has become a mystified ritual. Perhaps idealistically I have also
argued that the crit as an event is nevertheless social because it
demonstrates clearly that architectural meaning is not inherent in
the project (or the building for that matter) but is produced by its
audience, which includes its author(s); and that the project is social,
and therefore potentially public property, just as a building is, and
can function as a vehicle for socially produced meanings open to
contestation.

Design in architecture is in need of an open-ended testing ground
for the production of differentiated cultural meaning and social
models of practice. In the co-option of the crit as a social event and
the project as a generator of researched knowledge and creative risk-
taking, we have the potential resources for engendering a spirit of
cooperation, collaboration, competition and criticality in a learning
group that can posit other meanings, values, roles and role models
for architecture and architectural education.

Notes

1 I would like to thank Margaret Wilkin, Jeremy Till and Glyn Banks for their
   invaluable suggestions and criticisms during the writing of this chapter.
2 Margaret Wilkin in an unpublished letter to the author, April 1999, emphasis added.
3 The Third Earl of Shaftesbury (1671–1713) quoted in *The Romantic Ethic
   and the Spirit of Modern Consumerism* by Colin Campbell (Oxford: Basil
   Blackwell, 1987), p. 150.

27 Preparation and support of part-time teachers
Designing a tutor training programme fit for architects

Nicholas Weaver, Dave O'Reilly and Mary Caddick

Introduction

While much has been written about the education of architects (see for example Boyer and Mitgang 1996; Pearce and Toy 1995; Schön 1985, 1987), relatively little has been said about the preparation of teachers of architecture. No doubt this is in part a reflection of the lack of training for lecturers in higher education generally, which has been the norm until recently. As Kevin Rhowbotham (1995) has remarked:

> It is customary among practising architects to assume that those who have achieved some degree of experience are automatically equipped with all that is necessary to teach. Nothing could be further from the truth. The skills which are required to teach successfully cannot be acquired in the context of practice. Teaching is a separate order of things, tied to practice certainly, but by analogy, not by stricture.

It may also be that some colleagues in architecture fear that any form of training might stifle the creative spirit of design tutoring, leading to mediocrity and uniformity. For a discipline with its own long-established discourses on education, it is not unreasonable to be wary of developments foisted upon it from outside.

Yet the climate of learning and teaching is changing, and architecture stands aloof at its peril. In the UK, the Dearing Report—*Higher Education in the Learning Society* (Dearing 1997)—moved learning and teaching firmly up the political agenda. This was followed by the Booth Report (1998), which paved the way towards the professionalisation of teaching in higher education, which is essentially the remit of the Institute for Learning and Teaching, which was inaugurated in June 1999 and will open its accreditation service fully from January 2000.

The funding councils too are responding to the call. Amongst other initiatives, the HEFCE (the Higher Education Funding Council for England and Wales) established a Fund for the Development of

Teaching and Learning (FDTL), open to bids from departments that had achieved 'Excellent' ratings in the teaching assessment exercise. The establishment of the tutor training programme discussed in this chapter grew out of a three-year programme, funded by the FDTL, to disseminate best practice in the form of the teaching methods already used in the School of Architecture at the University of East London— the atelier principle in teaching (APT).

In sketching out the broader context of change, one further initiative is worth noting. Even before the Dearing Report, new methods of staff development and accreditation were being developed by SEDA (the Staff and Educational Development Association). Such programmes are now well established in many UK universities, old and new, as well as in some universities overseas. Typically they involve the individual tutor compiling a portfolio of evidence to demonstrate competent teaching (however that might be defined locally) in his or her own subject area. While some critics may feel there is still too much emphasis on generic, as opposed to subject-based, methods and models in the SEDA approach, it goes some way towards allaying the fear of imposition of an alien and stultifying pedagogy. The atelier tutor training programme at the University of East London (UEL) is designed to be compatible with the university's Post Graduate Certificate of Competence in Teaching in Higher Education, which currently conveys SEDA accreditation and is expected to fulfil the requirements of associate membership of the ILT.

Within the broader context of change outlined above, this chapter wishes to argue that architecture, as a discipline and a profession, is well-placed to develop creative models of tutor training that will serve to enhance learning. We offer one such model for consideration here. However we shall first consider the particular situation and role of the part-time tutor in the academic system, and the typical informal modes of induction and support for that role.

The role of the atelier tutor

Much of the knowledge and skill inherent in good design tutoring remains tacit, in the sense identified generally by Polanyi (1967) and delineated in the design studio by Schön (1985). Moreover, much of the actual practice of design teaching takes place in the relative privacy of the design studio. Many aspects of design teaching thus remain barely articulated. One of the first tasks of the dissemination project was, therefore, to attempt to conceptualise the unit system used in several schools of architecture, including the UEL, as the 'atelier principle in teaching' (APT) (Weaver 1997).

The UEL's aim in educating its students is seen as developing the imaginative, conceptual and practical skills necessary for students to identify human needs and aspirations, and to be able to meet or express these in space and form. Defining abilities in this way distinguishes 'thinking like an architect' from thinking like a lawyer, for example, or a dentist, whose fields of activity are different in terms of what kinds of problem they will look at and what kind of solution they will offer. The task of the design tutor at the UEL is to develop these abilities. As in many schools of architecture, and especially those operating the unit system, most of the studio teaching at the UEL is carried out by part-time tutors who are also practising architects. Usually working in pairs, they are on fixed-term contracts, one or two days a week, for three years.

The school operates a unit system that gives design tutors considerable autonomy in devising the educational programme. The tutors have the explicit responsibility of advancing the art of architecture in their own way, as well as developing the potential of each student for whom they are responsible. Thus they must have an architectural agenda as well as an educational one. They have been drawn into teaching because they want to learn. The unit is an educational device for taking risks: it is in the nature of the atelier principle for the tutor to be exploring unknown territory with the students for whom he or she is responsible (O'Reilly *et al.* 1999b).

Yet none of them is trained as a teacher. Once upon a time they could perhaps have relied on memories of their own education, in which, however hit-and-miss the tutoring, the student was carried along by the traditional design project. Such traditional briefs are no longer the norm, and as an educational device, it could be argued, they would scarcely provide the necessary basis for current practice. Yet for all its deficiencies, the traditional design project, often derived from a public authority brief—with clear aims and unambiguous room schedules—was a very powerful means of 'self-education' because it offered students an open-ended problem with which to wrestle. Comprising both analysis and synthesis, the aspiring architect could practise finding out what was going on and what was required, then make a proposition. All this makes learning a lively, dynamic, fluid experience The relation of the teacher to the student acquiring this skill—in the slow, painful, iterative process called design—has been well described by Donald Schön (1985, 1987), who captures what makes architectural education so absorbing for teachers too.

Induction for the new teacher

How, then, are teachers traditionally prepared for their new responsibility? At the UEL the new, inexperienced teacher was firstly inducted by 'twinning' in the unit with a more experienced teacher who, in an informal way, acted as a mentor. The new teacher then shared responsibility for the unit for at least a year, during which time he or she would experience the full round of the academic year, from the bewilderment of the introductory projects, through the doldrums of early spring, to fruition in the final portfolio. Only then would he or she go on to set up a new unit of his or her own.

Such twinning can benefit the mentor as much as the mentee. It is a way of bringing new ideas into the school—an old dog can learn some new tricks. It is also a way of exploiting the potential of individual teachers—a new unit may be formed, for example, by crossing a talent for imaginative construction with a talent for planning.

However, as higher education has expanded in the UK, staff–student ratios have worsened and the leisurely, apparently hit or miss methods of the past, which relied on more favourable resourcing, have been called into question. At the same time there has been increased pressure to account for the quality of provision and a move to professionalise teaching.

Tutor training course

The idea of setting up a tutor training programme for architects wishing to teach was first conceived simply as a method of getting the APT better known to people in other disciplines and institutions, through placements in the School of Architecture at the UEL (At the time of writing we are about to take on the third cohort, comprising trainees from outside the school, as well as some ex-students of our own RIBA Part 2 programme, who have been in practice a year or two and whom the school would like to draw into teaching at the UEL.)

The course grew out of the existing informal mentoring system, outlined above, and the unit system itself, as well as the particular experience of the APT course leaders—only one of whom was an architect. The aim of the course is to enable practising architects to become reflective studio teachers, able to define their educational aims, choose appropriate methods, implement a programme, and reflect on what has been achieved, with a view to refining their practice in the light of experience.

Trainees attend one day a week for a year. Essentially, what the course offers is mentored placement in a unit, supported by structured reflection on that experience in a weekly seminar. In the first term the trainees observe what is happening in the unit; in the second they contribute under supervision to the teaching; and in the third term they take more responsibility. At the end of the course they produce a proposal for a unit of their own.

In many ways the course is modelled on the atelier principle of the unit, with trainees and their teachers wrestling with the question 'How should we teach architecture?' As in an architectural design, it involves a movement from analysis to proposition. Because of the many tacit elements in design studio teaching, this is not a simple question of transmitting received wisdom—the course team recognised from the start that they did not know how architecture should be taught. Rather, what the course offers is the experience of observing and then participating in the way in which architecture is taught at the UEL, with the intention that trainees should have the opportunity to develop their own ideas about teaching on the basis of this experience. It borrows from the version of architectural education, exemplified by the unit system, that explicitly recognises that the most fruitful educational problems are open-ended and teachers do not know all the answers. The programme relies heavily on experiential learning. Indeed the participants are introduced at an early stage to the notion of learning through an iterative cycle of doing, reflecting, conceptualising and experimenting—the well-known 'experiential learning cycle' (Kolb 1984).

The course process may also be seen as an example of 'situated learning', which Lave and Wenger (1991) have argued is actually the way that most professional learning has traditionally been acquired. Situated learning exists in an apprenticeship, described as follows by Marchese (1999:13):

> Apprenticeship has typically been a cohort activity. That is, there were often two or three masters and a whole set of apprentices, rather than a simple one-to-one arrangement. The master was both taskmaster and mentor. Among the masters and apprentices there was always a rich conversation about what it is they were learning ... the important knowledge was tacit, seldom written down, and had to be learned by doing and talking. Very importantly, too, care was always undertaken that the young person understood the context, the real life meaning of each lesson or step ... the classic example is from stonecutting, where the apprentice knew the stone had to be absolutely square to fit just so in the wall of the cathedral.

Through the apprenticeship the learner is granted 'legitimate peripheral participation' in a community of practice, with the aim of eventually achieving mastery him- or herself. For the trainee atelier tutor, the raw data of teaching experience lies in the placement. What happens in the studio will not be perfect and may sometimes be chaotic, but it is what the students in the school are experiencing as their education.

The first obligation of the trainee is to observe. This is not easy: trainees find it hard to hold back from action and only gradually recognise that it is an unusual privilege simply to be present.

Throughout the year, each trainee keeps a factual log of what happens in the unit each week, and a reflective journal in which to ruminate on the experience.

The weekly seminar then offers the opportunity to reflect on that experience. The seminar is highly structured as an instrument for reflection and is modelled on an atelier. The members commit themselves to the group for a year, during which time they work out individual solutions to a common problem—how to teach. The group meets regularly once a week. Each week one member of the group presents a paper she or he has written for discussion. In the first term each trainee presents one paper reflecting on his or her own education and another on some significant event he or she has observed in the students' experience in the unit, the material for which is drawn from the journal. In the second term the focus is on contextualising the teaching of architecture within current models of professional knowledge and theories of learning in higher education: the trainees write a paper discussing a particular text and a second paper reflecting on students' experience of crits and reviews. In the third term the trainees write a paper on their observation of staff and student experience of assessment and its practice at UEL. Throughout the year other staff are invited to the seminar sessions to talk about aspects of the school or wider educational issues.

How quickly trainees are inducted into active teaching in the unit depends partly on the attitude of the mentor in whose unit they are placed—some are more relaxed about this than others. It also depends on the style of teaching—some will invite the trainee to tutor independently from early on, others will be wary of letting them speak at all till they have understood the unit's agenda. However one can generalise that most trainees will have begun teaching under supervision by the end of the first term, and be relatively independent by the third term. In the second term, after discussion in the seminar and negotiation with their mentor, each trainee runs a workshop for his or her unit on a topic of concern to him or her. This gives the trainees experience in taking complete responsibility for orchestrating an educational experience.

During the third term, on the basis of all this experience and reflection, the trainees develop a proposal for a unit of their own. This will have an architectural agenda fused into an educational agenda—'thinking like an architect'. The development of the proposal is tutored rather in the way that a design project is tutored, and the proposal evolves through a number of stages, which are discussed with the group at the seminar. Again, like any design project, the proposal would be considered incomplete without an analysis of the problem and a rationale for the solution proposed. The proposal for a unit in its final form is then publicly presented to the whole group.

At the end of the year the trainee collects all the written material generated, together with a commentary and feedback from the mentor, into a portfolio. This forms the basis upon which the trainee is assessed. The assessment panel comprises the three members of the course development team and the head of school. The assessment is moderated by an external examiner for the university's Certificate in Learning and Teaching. Upon successful completion of the course, trainees are eligible for part 1 of the teaching certificate and each also receives a letter from the school of architecture recognising them as competent to teach on the atelier principle.

Lessons from the tutor training programme

Embedding change

An important feature of the training course has been the extent to which it has built on to what was already happening in this particular school. At the UEL the customary way in which inexperienced staff were inducted was to twin them with an established teacher. The course then supported this relationship through the seminar programme, which offered a structure to reflect on that experience. The implication for anyone seeking to set up a training programme elsewhere is to consider the particular strengths, characteristics and culture of the institution in which they are working.

Mentoring: strengths and weaknesses

Because of the circumstances in which the course was set up—initially as a way of disseminating the atelier principle to other institutions—it was offered to outsiders rather than existing staff. The mentors had not been trained as teachers, and we underestimated the demands of such mentoring. Consequently the experience of mentors and mentees has been mixed. The relationship of trainee to mentor is quite intimate: to be successful the mentor must be prepared to expose the workings of the unit and the choices open at each stage. Whether this degree of disclosure is congenial, or even possible, has depended on the character of the trainee and the mentor. Some of the trainees have found their role in the unit difficult to define or negotiate— they were there to learn to be good teachers, but being an observer is difficult. Does the observer affect what is observed? Since none of the existing staff had ever been trained, some were uneasy about the boundaries of their responsibility as mentors. At first, some were suspicious of what exactly was going on in the seminars—were the trainees really management spies? It soon became clear that the mentors themselves needed regular support through a more explicit structure for feedback.

Mentoring is often seen as a private relationship between two consenting adults and as lacking a group dimension: mentees teach on their own and discuss problems afterwards with their mentors. A great strength of our system is its ability to counter that tendency, firstly (through the placement) by integrating the trainee as an individual into the unit, and secondly (through the reflective seminar) by enabling the individual to become one of a group of people learning about learning.

Summary

Because of its external (FDTL) funding, the course had the luxury of developing experimentally. It started like an amoeba—a single nucleus in a fluid cell, flowing this way and that in response to the emerging needs of trainees and mentors. Over the two years of its existence, it has evolved into a more sophisticated life-form with a more bony structure. The trainees' experience can now be formally validated and the model has become transferable to other institutions.

The way in which the course has evolved owes something to the very different backgrounds of those who run it. Mary Caddick—a fine artist with a grounding in art teaching and psychotherapy—derived the model of the placement and seminar from her experience of psychoanalytic training, which combined an emphasis on active attention with the containing function of the seminar (O'Reilly *et al.* 1999a). Dave O'Reilly—a researcher in educational development with a particular interest in experiential learning and different ways of knowing— had taught in the School of Independent Study at the UEL, where a framework for student autonomy in learning was pioneered (Stephenson 1988). Lastly, Nicholas Weaver—the only one educated as an architect—has a senior management role in the school, which made it much easier to embed the training course in the school than is often the case with staff development initiatives that are seen to be imposed from outside.

The course is demanding. Trainees have reported that preparing coursework for the reflective weekly seminars occupies, on average, four to six hours a week. Trainees' enjoyment fluctuates over the year, not only because of what happens in the school, but also because of the pressures of their professional work outside the school. However the consensus is that the course has been very valuable. The trainees feel they have learned about teaching, and they have also learned about how they learn themselves. For some the experience of the course has fed directly into their professional practice. For most, the discipline of observing before springing into action has been the most valuable experience of all.

References

Booth, C. (1998) *Accreditation and teaching in Higher Education: Consultation Paper*. London: Committee of Vice Chancellors and Principals.

Boyer, E. L. and Mitgang, L. D. (1996) *Building Community: A new future for architectural education and practice*. Princeton, NJ: Carnegie Foundation for the Advancement of Learning.

Dearing, R. (1997) report of the Committee of Inquiry into Higher Education. *Higher Education in the Learning Society*, London: HMSO.

Kolb, D. A. (1984) *Experiential Learning: Experience as the source of learning and development*. Englewood Cliffs, NJ: Prentice Hall.

Lave, J. and Wenger, E. (1991) *Situated Learning: Legitimate Peripheral Participation*. Cambridge: Cambridge University Press.

Marchese, T. J. (1999) 'The New Conversations about Learning' at the New Horizons for Learning website: http://www.newhorizons.org/lrnbus_marchese.html.

O'Reilly, D., Weaver, N. and Caddick, M. (1999a) 'Developing and delivering a tutor training programme for problem based learning: a case study in architecture', in J. Conway, D. Melville and A. Williams (eds) *Research and Development in Problem Based Learning: Volume 5*. University of Newcastle, NSW: Australian Problem Based Learning Network, pp. 194–202.

O'Reilly, D., Weaver, N. and Caddick, M. (1999b) 'Disciplining interdisciplinarity: pedagogic tensions within architectural education', proceedings of the 7th International Symposium on Improving Student Learning, *Improving Student Learning through the Disciplines*. York: University of York, September.

Pearce, M. and Toy, M. (eds) (1995) *Educating Architects*. London: Academy Editions.

Polanyi, M. (1967) *The Tacit Dimension*. London: Routledge.

Rhowbotham, K. (1995) *Form to Programme*. London: Black Dog Publishing.

Schön, D. A. (1985) *The Design Studio: An Exploration of its Traditions and Potentials*. London: RIBA Publications.

Schön, D. A. (1987) *Educating the Reflective Practitioner: towards a new design for teaching and learning in the professions*. San Francisco, CA: Jossey-Bass.

Stephenson, J. (1988) 'The experience of Independent Study at North East London Polytechnic' in Boud, D. (ed.) (2nd Edition), *Developing Student Autonomy in Learning*, London, Kogan page, ch. 13 pp. 211–26.

Weaver, N. (1997) 'The Atelier Principle in Teaching', in M. Knudsen and T. S. Vinther (eds), *Project Work in University Studies*. University of Roskilde, Denmark. Reprinted in Olesen, H. S. and Jensen, J. H. (eds) (1999) *Project Studies—a Late Modern University Reform?* University of Roskilde Press: Roskilde, Denmark.

28 Evaluation and feedback in architectural education

John Cowan

Prelude: one picture of teaching and learning

Many years ago I heard an Indian academic—and sage—explaining that in his subcontinent they saw teaching as an activity that brought together two people, one of whom was rather more of a teacher and the other of whom was rather more of a learner, this being an activity in which teaching and learning took place for both. It will be clear from the examples below that I am firmly in favour of just such a joint approach to teaching and learning, and the enhancement of teaching quality, through the types of communicative collaborations I call feedback and formative evaluation.

Introduction

At the time of writing this chapter, the world of higher education is greatly changed from that of even 20 years ago. In the past it sufficed to be an enthusiastic teacher, picking up odd ideas from the good practice of others and maintaining a warm rapport with students. Now we operate in an environment where it is the norm for feedback and evaluation to be carried out systematically, and for the findings to be analysed and acted upon. In the past we hoped to form an accurate but subjective impression of how to help students to learn, based mainly on our own experiences of teaching and learning, and on discussions with interested colleagues. Now there are some at least in our discipline who speak of 'pedagogy', and who find ways to tell us about how they apply the theories and researches of educationalists in their own teaching.

What are we to make of this? In particular, how can we make judgements about how well we are, and might be, doing our job of teaching students of architecture? How can we build upon these judgements to bring about developments in our own practices as teachers? In these few pages I shall try to address these questions in practical but rigorous terms, as someone who taught architects over a period of more than 20 years, and who now speculates about how he would operate if he returned to an activity that he left 10 years ago to teach social sciences. How would I establish two-way communication with my students about the nature of their learning, and of the learning experiences for which I am responsible, in a manner that would enable me to build upon that to the advantage of all concerned?

The meanings of the key terms in this chapter

I am aware that, in education, few words have a generally accepted meaning. For that reason I shall begin, rather pedantically, by explaining precisely the meanings I shall be attaching to the key terms used in this chapter.

Assessment will denote judgement of the quality of a student's work. That judgement can be expressed as a grade, a mark, or perhaps a decision. When we grade a presentation of a student's design proposal, that is an assessment. It is an assessment when we rate an architect's ability to research a brief and gather and collate information.

Evaluation will denote judgement of the quality of educational provision. Student ratings of teaching are evaluations, as is the published judgement of a course by a body charged to monitor educational quality. Evaluations are generally expressed in qualitative terms, as in the case of the teacher whose explanations are rated 'extremely clear and helpful', or the course whose methods are 'somewhat old-fashioned, and out-of-date'. But they may be expressed numerically, or on a pseudonumeric scale, such as the module that averaged 4.1 when students were invited to rate it on a 5-point scale.

Feedback means any activity in which learners feed back, to the teacher or the institution, information about their current experience. It is to be hoped that this happens in time for some remedial action to be taken for the benefit of the current class, if and when all is not well; but that is not essential. It is feedback when a student representative informs the course committee that there is an unacceptable overload on the available resources, making it virtually impossible for the students to complete their coursework on schedule. It is feedback when a questionnaire return identifies a particular library assistant as especially helpful.

Let us look, without more ado, at how these activities (other than assessment) can usefully occur in our teaching programmes. It is simplest to explain this by giving some examples of what we, as teachers, can do. Further examples can be found in the handbook by George and Cowan (1999).

If I were to walk into a design studio tomorrow, what then would I do—other than teaching—to keep myself informed about the learning and the learning experience?

Obtaining feedback and evaluation from 'stop/start/continue' sheets

Early in the course I would explain to the students that I cannot be an effective teacher unless I know how the learning is going for them. I need to know which of my messages are getting through, which are creating problems for the students, and what questions are troubling them. I would make it clear that I would welcome informal feedback at any time, and I would arrange for them to do that through a class representative. But more importantly, after four to five weeks, in which time we should have come to know each other and each other's styles, I would ask them to complete a 'stop/start/continue' sheet. On this they would tell me what they wanted me to *stop* doing, and they would explain why they wished me to desist. They would similarly tell me if there was anything that I was not doing that they wanted me to *start* doing, and they would again explain their reasons for that suggestion. Finally, I would hope that they would find some of my practice to be helpful and acceptable; where this was the case, they should encourage me to *continue*, and again explain why they offered that feedback.

This activity can be applied, of course, in almost any learning context. For example it could be used by a tutor within the unit system to get students' reactions to a new design studio programme; it might be used at the end of an early review or crit session to find out what would make the design review a better vehicle for student learning; or it could be used by tutors to find out how students react to, and learn in and from, one-to-one meetings.

When I have used this feedback method I have learnt, for example, that there are some students who prefer my constructive comments to concentrate on their strengths, and that, similarly, there are others who much prefer me to work with them on their weaknesses. Since such feedback may be distinctly individual, it is probably best for stop/start/continue sheets to come back from identified individuals; but you, and your class, may also see advantages in conflating responses for the entire group, and thus preserving anonymity.

Feedback and evaluation from dynamic lists of questions

I would encourage all my students (including postgraduates) to get into the habit of noting down—before we begin either formal or informal activities—the questions for which they hope to have an answer by the time the activity is complete; and then to check off questions as they are answered, one way or the other, while at the same time adding any supplementary questions the activity provokes.

Students might follow this procedure as we prepare before their research for a design project or before they go to meet a client to find out their needs.

The questions may be about the particular task—what questions should I ask this client, in this particular situation? Or they may be about tackling tasks of this type—how should I go about deciding which questions to ask of a client?

I call this approach the 'dynamic list of questions', because the list should shorten but it may also take on additional items—dynamically as the activity progresses. It is one of the most successful combinations of feedback, evaluation and structured teaching and learning I have devised and used.

For when the activity is (virtually) complete, the outstanding questions on the list can be used for both mopping-up unsatisfied needs and evaluating the effectiveness of the activity. Lists with many deleted questions indicate an effective and well-focused activity. Lists on which a fair number of valid questions still remain imply that the activity could have been more effective for the students concerned. The raw initial lists of questions provide informative feedback on expectations. And if I devote effort to answering specific questions (about which questions to ask, for example) with general advice (how to decide what questions to ask), then the activity concentrates neatly on generalisable activities, and hence develops in students the habit of reflecting on how to tackle common tasks.

Feedback from reflective reviews, used as teaching and learning activities

Much of the learning in the design studio is about learning how to do things—tackling a great variety of tasks, of varying complexities and levels of demand. We teachers are quite good—after all those decades of educational tradition—at planning activities in which our students can use such abilities, and be assessed in their use. But there is all the difference in the world between using an ability that has been and is developed serendipitously, and the purposeful and planned development that we can reasonably call learning from teaching. It is like the difference between attending a swimming session and taking part in a swimming class.

Much of the development of educational practice in the past 20 years has concentrated on the development of abilities. Without going into the accumulated evidence of successes under this heading, suffice it to say that we can be fairly confident that if we assist students to be aware of the mental and interpersonal processes they are using, then they will become more competent in these processes. Consequently, from a teaching and learning point of view, it is well worth taking time to get them to stand back from the immediate action and think about how they are doing it—whatever 'it' is. The students should improve in consequence, and in turn we will know what their starting points and approaches are, and can plan our teaching and responses to their needs more appropriately.

I recall asking my architectural design students in a particular situation to summarise the process they were following. We took a short time out after the first iteration, and I asked the students to describe, step by detailed step, precisely how they were designing. This again made a contribution to learning and teaching, as well as serving an evaluative function. It informed my colleagues and myself of the processes that were being followed—or in some cases not being followed. For instance I noted with concern that most students delayed their thinking about the structural behaviour of their optional schemes until a point at which it was too late to do other than make retrospective adjustments to their design plans. Consideration of the need for expansion joints, for example, figured late in the sequence, with the result that many elegant buildings were carved into sections by the late provision of joints, which often left central sections unable to withstand lateral wind forces. In consequence, where my colleagues and I had originally been trying in our teaching to bring about a sounder appreciation of structural behaviour, we switched as a result of this indirect feedback to encouraging a sounder approach to the entire design process, in which salient factors were considered at a stage when they might properly influence the design concept.

Asking students to declare how they do things opens up discussions between them, enabling them to profit from the good ideas and practices of classmates. I point out to them that the Zulus have a saying to the effect that there is nothing wrong with taking an idea from someone—because you do not take it away from them, they still retain it for their own use. I find that in this type of activity, which I describe as analysing the processes they use, students often discover to their surprise that their classmates have better or other ways of doing 'it', or part of it. I have frequently found, for example, that students' enquiries with clients and experts are poorly structured and focused, and that time out to consider process can lead to informed tuition and conscious development of ability. Such reflection can be deepened if the fine detail of how questions are chosen and framed is explored at useful length.

Evaluation by detached observers

Another useful source of data for formative evaluation can be a colleague, briefed on what interests or concerns you, and quietly sitting in a corner, making notes accordingly—preferably as objectively and non-judgementally as possible. The observations may be of you, or of the students, or both. It is probably best if they report merely what they saw or heard—and refrain from expressing judgements, leaving that to the persons observed.

In my early days as a teacher I invited such observation during a one-to-one tour around a studio, and learnt that I took, and responded to, a higher proportion of questions and requests for advice from students whose work was relatively undeveloped; and that my questions about and discussion of what the students proposed to do next were more common with those whose work was well advanced. On reflection, and after discussion with more experienced colleagues, I moved to asking more questions of all students about their intentions. The observer also noted body language indicative of discomfort when I took time before responding to a question that caused me to ponder; on enquiry, the observer learnt from the students that they misread my pondering time as criticism, and an implied suggestion that they should think again about their question. Again, I have modified my style to avoid giving an inaccurate impression.

In my work with groups, the observer noted that I gave those to my left distinctly more eye contact than those on my right, a tendency to which I have subsequently given attention. He also noted that our student groups tended notably to disregard pertinent questions by one of their number, while tending to pay attention to the same point made without a direct question. This led us to encourage the students to engage in rudimentary analysis of the 'transactions' within their groups and discuss their effectiveness—to good effect. Such evaluative observations are formative in that they suggest where improvement is needed, and often how it can be achieved.

Evaluation by paired interviewing

One of the most fruitful exercises I have engaged in, in recent years, has been to work in pairs with a colleague to interview students to declared questions. Each of us (neither being the student's teacher), having warned the students accordingly, contacts perhaps two students individually after a teaching and learning activity. This is a useful activity after a series of one-to-one sessions around designs or following a review or crit session. The enquirer asks questions that have been declared *before* the teaching and learning activity, so that the students are forewarned of what is expected of them. We have used such questions as:

- What were the most important outcomes of that exchange for you?
- What was it that the teacher did that most contributed to bring that about?

- What was least effective for you?
- Can you pinpoint why this may have been so?

The enquirer then asks parallel questions of the teacher, before reporting back to the teacher (with the permission of the students) what the students have provided, and comparing that with the teacher's responses.

If more than two teachers are interested in engaging in this type of enquiry, then pairings can be varied, which enriches the exchange. The outcomes for the teachers are that they identify scope for improvement in their own practice (formative evaluation), gain immediate feedback upon which they can take speedy action, and gather often remarkable information about the nature of the learning experience—and perhaps especially and surprisingly about the affective aspects of it, which can be of noteworthy importance to the learners.

Feedback from interpersonal process recall

I have often used this technique in a person-to-person situation, perhaps involving me with a student in the design studio, discussing his or her project, or in tutorial work with one or more students, when I have been asked to explain something.

A video camera is aimed at us, with me as the main subject. There is no operator. We work as near as possible to our norm, which becomes simple once the method is moderately familiar. I recruit the assistance of a colleague as an enquirer.

After the tuition is complete my colleague picks a short section of the recording, perhaps at my suggestion, and goes off with the student to replay it. The enquirer sits beside the video recorder, with a hand near the pause button. The enquirer pauses the replay whenever he or she notes from the facial expression of the watching student that vivid recall is occurring; or at a natural break in the recording; or when the student says 'Stop'. Always the enquirer asks the same opening question: 'Does that remind you of how you were feeling or what you were thinking at the time?' Subjects find this experience an exciting revelation, for they discover that it enables them, even after a short break, to recall thoughts and feelings in detail utterly inconceivable in comparison with an immediate interview, for example. After the initial recall question the enquirer may then ask follow-up questions to amplify the original response.

The enquirer then repeats the same sequence with the tutor and compares the two accounts, either with the tutor alone, or with both tutor and student. It is rare for this enquiry not to extract a shattering mismatch between reality and the impression of one of the two subjects. In my own case I recall working with a student who 'switched off' when we were through with her first query to me. It was apparent that I had said something offputting—perhaps even strongly politically incorrect. I wracked my brain to think of the best way to allow her to opt out without embarrassment. Should I perhaps suggest a coffee break, from which she would probably not return? When this section of the aborted tutorial was unpacked by the student and myself, it transpired that the student's recall was of a blinding revelation: 'That's it, now I understand. I just need to work out the implications of that. I hope he'll be quiet for a minute or two while I do that—and then he can go on to my next problem.'

From that feedback I learnt and have often recalled to good effect that I do not have the ability to read from people's faces what they are thinking or feeling; and that, as a tutor, I should enquire, or find some way to enquire rather than deduce how we are progressing.

Feedback from identifying criteria and standards

This chapter is not the place to extol the merits of self-assessment in higher education. However I feel it fair to mention as a possibility for formative evaluation the merits of asking students to spell out in detail the criteria and standards by which their work is judged—and to get assessors to do the same, and then to compare the results. I recall a student who was genuinely surprised to discover that the architectural lecturers who were assessing his work would put a significant (negative) weighting on the fact that he had produced a structure that would not stand up in a modest wind, and in which one main column terminated abruptly at first-floor level without support. I remember another whose design was aesthetically pathetic, and who felt that what was needed to improve it was to 'tart up' (*sic*) the presentation. Students who do not know what they are trying to achieve are unlikely to make good progress, other than by chance. It is highly informative and useful to discover that, or whether, some students have no conception of what they are striving to achieve.

Assessment and evaluation both entail the making of professional judgements, which should be done in a defensible and objective manner. That implies the conscious selection of criteria, which are amplified by statements of standards that describe the difference between 'excellent', 'very good', 'good', 'acceptable', and 'not acceptable'—or some such gradings. Performance should then be able to be identified and described in the same terms as those used to spell out the standards, from which it is a straightforward step to define the way the judgement is to be reached.

Sadly, many professional judgements are made on the basis of little more than gut reaction, which the judge is usually unable to distinguish from indigestion. It surely behoves us, as university teachers, to develop in our students the ability not only to evaluate their performance in classwork—which evaluation we conventionally call assessing—and to proceed from there to the development of that evaluative ability which is the supreme cognitive demand.

Letters

Arrange an activity in which you can ask your students, as a class, to write a letter to next year's students, telling them of the trials and tribulations and joys and rewards to be met in this year of studies. Ask them to offer advice about how to get the most out of the year. Promise that the letter will indeed be passed on to next year's students. Leave them on their own for 30–40 minutes, popping your head round the door occasionally to ensure moderate absence of conversation and adherence to task. Read the letters yourself and thus obtain feedback and data to inform your formative evaluations. But adhere to your promise, and pass on the letters to next year's class.

At the same time, perhaps, ask the class as a whole to write one letter to you, with the useful anonymity of class response, offering you advice on how to make the experience more effective for next year's cohort. Set up a session in which, with a student chair, they assemble bullet points for this letter on flipcharts. Seek a volunteer to compile a draft letter, which can go on the notice board with an invitation to suggest editorial changes. These the student writer will incorporate. Again, expect a major exercise in formative evaluation of your teaching.

Closing comments

I hope it will have become apparent that I am more interested in making improvements in my teaching than in judging it. In terms of the vocabulary of education, I am more concerned to evaluate formatively than summatively, and I believe these two forms should come in that order. For if there is scope for improvement in my teaching and in my students' learning, I want to find out where and why, and to be doing something about it before anyone judges me. I have found that when the time comes for me to answer questions about the effectiveness and acceptability of my teaching, the feedback and evaluations I have described have accumulated sufficient evidence upon which to base a reasonable and convincing claim.

You may have noted that in a number of my examples (such as the dynamic list of questions) there was a tendency for evaluation to influence the structure of a teaching and learning activity, and become a natural part of my plan—contributing evaluative data and producing a good outline for teaching and learning. For that reason

I feel it fair to suggest that some of the most effective evaluation methods soon or eventually become a natural part of the teaching and learning process, rather than a separate activity

It will be clear, I hope, from my opening anecdote and my examples that I am firmly of the view that a joint approach to the enhancement of teaching quality is to be preferred, because the best way to improve both teaching and learning is for teacher and learners to work together on the challenge of development.

Finally, I will just remind you that I am a teacher, first and foremost. I have suggested nothing in this short chapter that has not served me well, either as a source of feedback or in formative evaluation, in my search to develop as a teacher, and to help my students to develop as professionals. I hope that some of my suggestions may help you, if you are that kind of teacher of architecture, to make progress that you will value.

Reference

George, J. W., and Cowan, J. (1999) *A Handbook of Techniques for Formative Evaluation*. London: Kogan Page.

Appendix Workshop plans
Teamwork

The following is an edited example of the tutor support packs developed by the CUDE initiative.

Introductory notes

Who this pack is for and what it contains

This pack is written for design tutors who plan some teamwork during their course and want to increase the likelihood that students will have a positive experience of this way of working. Tutors can significantly improve teamwork by getting students to attend to *how* they work together, in addition to achieving the set tasks. Encouraging them to experiment with different ways of working together—for example to research information, generate and select ideas, evaluate options and decide courses of action—increases motivation and can improve learning.

The pack outlines some simple teamwork processes. It suggests ways in which these can be explicitly and sequentially introduced to students in short workshop sessions run during the course of design projects. A script has been provided for three types of workshop:

- Introducing teamwork.
- Developing and selecting ideas in teams.
- Running a review of the effectiveness of teamworking.

Each outlines what the tutor does, what the students do and what the outputs are at each stage. Suggestions for back-up visual material and notes are also included. The intention is that a tutor will be able to use the material—as it stands and with limited preparation—to experiment with a new way of working with students, later adapting and extending it to suit his or her own specific context.

Guiding principles

Introduce teamworking very early in the course

Getting students to work in teams early on means they get to know each other more quickly, establish themselves, share in a common activity and find something to which they can belong in the early stages of the course when everything is unfamiliar.

Introduce team skills as part of project work

Teamwork skills are best introduced during the course of students' work on the design project rather than as a separate activity. For example a workshop on how to generate and select ideas in teams can be used to help students decide the questions they want to put to clients and users on a forthcoming project. Skills introduced in this way are immediately put into practice. They are seen to be effective and students are therefore more likely to use them in other situations.

Make team skills explicit

Some students argue initially that team skills are 'natural'—you either have them or you do not. CUDE's feedback showed that, almost without exception, students felt that when they tried the processes introduced in the skills workshops, their teamwork became more productive and enjoyable. They said how much more they were able to achieve when they used the team to generate a whole list of ideas *before* discussing them, rather than rubbishing each other's ideas as they were suggested and setting up a vengeful hostility in the team.

   For the tutor, making skills explicit means being able to describe clearly the team processes you want students to adopt and the reason why you want them to do this. It also means having very clear aims for each workshop session and making sure the students understand what these are.

Appropriate tasks

Some tasks are better adapted to teamwork than others. Researching information is a good team task—the number of people involved allows a wider field to be explored. Building something together allows division of labour, shared pride in the product and the useful realisation that different people have different and complementary skills.

Team size

Five to seven works best, allowing everybody to contribute. Teams with fewer than five members have the potential for two against one splits, and can fall apart if one member does not attend. Bigger teams are much harder for the students and tutors to manage—students can get 'lost' without anyone noticing.

Student allocation

CUDE's experience shows that teams work better if students are allocated to them by tutors, rather than allowing them to select their own. Some mix of academic background, previous experience, gender and nationality enriches the potential of the team as a learning resource and goes some way towards creating the 'balanced team' described by Belbin. Whilst self-selection may result in some very strong groupings, a large proportion of students may be left out of this.

Workshop plans

1   Introducing teamwork (Timing: 2 Hours)

Learning objectives

- To prepare students for teamwork on a forthcoming project.
- To alert students to the importance of teamworking both in education and at work.
- To enable students to recognise the value of having explicitly agreed ways of working together, rather than leaving this to chance.
- To encourage students to review regularly how they work together so that their skills in teamworking develop.

Students' output

- Each team produces an agreed plan of action for the project (what will be done, when, how and by whom).
- Each team agrees a simple team contract: a written set of rules outlining how they will work together.

Running order and script

Time	What the tutor does	What the students do	Notes
5 mins	Outline the aims of the workshop (planning the project and agreeing a team contract) and how the time will be divided between the tasks. Allocate students to teams, if this has not already been done (5–7 in each). Very briefly summarise the importance of teamworking, both for an architectural student and as a practising architect. (A sample page from an architect's working diary is included in the back-up material to make the point about teamworking.)	Join teams. Listen; ask questions.	Check students have understood all the aspects of the briefing. It is useful to invite one or two students to paraphrase what they have heard. (Paraphrasing to check understanding is a key skill to use in groupwork and it helps if the tutor 'models' it for the students.) It is important to show why spending time developing group-working skills is relevant.
10 mins	As a warm-up, invite students to think about and then share their previous individual experience of effective teamwork. Explain this is a way of starting to think about the *how* of teamwork and that their output will be used later in the workshop.	Spend a couple of minutes thinking individually about the experience of effective teamworking. Share that experience with the team using *headline* form, such as by completing the phrase 'Teamwork is . . . ' All comments should be noted down on an A1 sheet by a	It is important for motivation to get everyone to contribute early on. The device of getting students to make individual notes first makes sure everyone thinks. Contributing these to the group using a common format (the headline 'teamwork is . . .) and having them all written down

		designated team scribe for later reference.	confers equal value on the contributions. Gets the team off to a good start.
15 mins (More time may be needed for complex projects)	Introduce the team project, with additional material as necessary. Use projector to summarise what the students are expected to produce during the project. Brief students to work together to produce the project plan. They have 30 mins for this and the plan should be written up on a large sheet.	Listen; ask questions.	Check understanding as above.
30 mins	Circulate to ensure students have understood the task and are working on it. Observe how the teams approach the task, but do not comment at this stage. Remind students how much time they have for the task. Encourage students to circulate and inspect other teams' plans. (The students' 'raw' team experience will be reviewed in the course of agreeing the 'team contracts'.)	Student teams sit round tables and work together to produce draft project plans. Each team should appoint a 'scribe'. Teams pin up plans when completed.	It is important to keep students to the task at this stage, reminding them how much time they have left and what the required output is.

5 mins	Brief students to start work on 'team contracts'. (Suggestions for what to think about when producing a team contract form part of back-up notes. Tutors may want to give copies to the student.) Recommend that they do this in four stages (use projector to reinforce instructions). 1. Discuss the experience you have just had—in what ways did the team work well? What would you want to see done differently. 2. Look back at the list of effective teamwork experiences you made earlier. What can you do to ensure that these are a feature of your team? 3. Anticipate some of the things that might go wrong when working on the project. What steps can you take to prevent these? 4. Use these to agree a list of ground rules that everyone in the team feels they can follow. Write these up on the A1 sheet. Advise that one person from each	Listen; ask questions if necessary.	Make it clear to students that they have achieved a *task*; now they are to think about the *process* of working together effectively.

	group will be asked to summarise to the large group.		
30 mins	Circulate and help if necessary.	Students use briefing to produce team rules, drawing on the group contract suggestions if they wish. Agree who will report to the large group.	It is important to keep the momentum going.
15 mins	Invite a spokesperson from each group to summarise briefly the group's 'rules' and the thinking that led to these. Invite comments from other groups but avoid contributing the bulk of the feedback yourself.	Each team reports.	The value of this session is that it extends the pool of ideas and allows teams to refine their contracts if they wish. (It is also good practice in succinct presentation.) It is essential that the tutor does not dominate—these have to be the students' ideas for them to experiment with them wholeheartedly.
5 mins	Explain the value of having a way of reflecting on how well the group is doing as a regular slot in their group meetings. Invite students to decide how they will do this and ask them to make a note on their group contract.	Teams decide a simple way of reviewing their performance at the end of each meeting and write this on their contract. (Contracts are subsequently typed up and everyone gets a copy.)	It is essential to get the students to commit themselves to following their 'rules'. The discipline of discussing 'How well did we do?' for a few minutes at the end of each meeting can help students to develop as team workers.
5 mins	Ask students for written feedback on the workshop: 'One thing I have	Students complete the written feedback on the workshop.	There are two reasons for this feedback: it reinforces what

	learned' and 'One question the workshop has raised in my mind'.		the students have learned; and it demonstrates to the tutors how effective the workshop has been in achieving its aims.

Back-up material

(A) COPY OF PAGE FROM AN ARCHITECT'S WORK DIARY, SHOWING NUMBERS OF TEAM MEETINGS

A week in the life of an architect—appointments and meetings

Day	Time	Event	Present
Monday	10 am–12 noon	Live project meeting (a weekly progress review)	2 directors, 3 architects, technician
	2 pm–2.30 pm	Kitchen design discussion	Architect, kitchen supplier/designer
Tuesday	9 am	Telephone hospital estates manager to discuss number of bathrooms in a proposed nursing home	Architect, estate manager
	9.30 am	Telephone manager of home to confirm her agreement to the previous discussion	Architect, nurse
Wednesday	1.45 pm–4.30 pm	Meet new client to discuss proposed residential home	Architect, 2 doctors, nurse, staff and residents of existing home
Thursday	9.30 am	Site meeting with engineer and builder to talk about complex foundation design on a site with mining subsidence	Architect, structural engineer, 2 builders (who are also the clients), JCB driver
	2.30 pm–4.30 pm	Meeting at health trust to discuss proposed new nursing home	1 architect, 1 health trust manager, estate manager, estate manager's assistant, 2 consultants in

			geriatric medicine, nurse manager of the new building, manager's deputy, representative of the relatives of the people who will move into the building, 2 directors of the company that is funding the project and who will manage it for the health trust, Quantity surveyor
Friday	2 pm	Meeting with client to discuss proposal for new golf club on open-cast mine site	Architect, clients—husband and wife, clients' financial advisor

The rest of the week is spent administering two jobs on site, working on the design of one major project (the health trust nursing home), and doing three quick initial sketch proposals for the golf club and two residential homes, which may turn into 'live' projects.

(B) DRAFTING A TEAM CONTRACT—BRIEFING FOR STUDENTS

- Discuss the experience of teamworking you have just had—in what ways did the team work well? What would you want to see done differently when the team works together again?
- Look back at the list of effective teamwork experiences you made earlier. What can you do to ensure these are a feature of your team?
- Anticipate some of the things that might go wrong in working on the project. What steps can you take to prevent them?
- Use these to agree a list of ground rules that everyone in the group feels they can follow.

(C) THINGS TO CONSIDER WHEN DEVELOPING A TEAM CONTRACT

- Agree the responsibilities of the 'chair' of the team. For example he or she should
  1 make sure there is a shared understanding of what is required from the project;
  2 make sure the team carries out all the necessary tasks;
  3 arrange the team meetings;
  4 ensure that notes are made of these meetings.

Team members should take it in turns to act as chair, from project to project.

- Responsibilities of the other team members:
  1 Agree to carry out specific tasks, as agreed with the team;
  2 Carry them out on time.
  3 Contribute ideas, information and opinions that advance the project
  4 Attend meetings—and be on time.
- Team behaviour: the team members should follow rules to help them work constructively together, for example
  1 Everyone should have a chance to speak in meetings. No interruptions or 'side meetings'.
  2 Listen constructively to each others' ideas.
  3 Devise a consensus approach to making decisions.
  4 Deal with any problems between team members openly and constructively.
- Learning from the team's experience: allow a few minutes at the end of each meeting to discuss what the team members have learned, both from the project and from working together. It can be helpful to keep a simple record of this in a file for future reference.

2 Developing ideas in teams (Timing: 1.5 hours)

Learning objectives

- To develop awareness that teams work more effectively when they have a range of working methods to draw on and are able to select the appropriate method for a particular situation.
- To introduce a process for teams to use to develop rapidly a pool of ideas and then select the ones they want to take further.
- To use this process to develop ideas for a particular stage of a design project.

Student output

Each team should produce a written list of possible ideas (to which everyone has contributed) to use for the given task and agree which ones the group will take forward.

Running order and script

Time	What the tutor does	What the students do	Notes
5 mins	Outline the session—aims, output, working methods. Explain that a process for generating ideas will be introduced. Students will use this to develop ideas for the project task.	Listen. Check understanding by asking questions.	Emphasise that the session is as much about developing a team skill as it is about getting the project task achieved. Check whether students are following by asking one or two of them to say what they understand the aims to be.
5 mins	Outline project task—e.g. to develop together questions to put to clients and users in a forthcoming meeting.	As above	Make sure the task you choose is appropriate for the use of this technique—i.e., The task is one that can be achieved in lots of ways.
5 mins	Introduce the first part of the process: generation of ideas—a variant of brainstorming. Explain why this approach helps. In brief: we tend to look for what is wrong in ideas, thereby censoring many that could have potential. Letting ideas flow uncriticised results in a lot of ideas from which to select later. (Ask students how they feel when their ideas are criticised.) Outline the rules: 1 Everybody contributes.	Listen, ask questions if necessary. Respond to tutor's questions	It is important to get students to think about the idea—suppressing the 'inner censor', becoming aware of their own self-censoring devices and how they protect themselves when offering ideas in public: 'I haven't had time to think this through.' 'I'm not sure if this will work but . . .' This enables them to see the value of letting go of the inner censor in order to develop a lot of ideas quickly. Point out that the whole

	2 Switch off the censor—no criticism of your own ideas or anyone else's. 3 Go for quantity. 4 Give ideas as 'headlines'. 5 Scribe records verbatim.		process does not exclude analysis of ideas, it merely defers it until there are enough ideas to evaluate.

10 mins	Brief students to use rules on a quick warm-up exercise—for example how to deal with 20 000 unsold toothbrushes. They have 5 minutes for this.
	    Keep students to time. Take one idea from each group. Ask for any comments on what the exercise feels like and whether they followed the rules.
		Teams appoint a scribe who can write quickly and legibly. They have 5 minutes to generate as many ideas as they can for how to solve the problem. Scribe records ideas verbatim and numbers them.	Brainstorming should be done with speed, the scribe dashing ideas down and asking for more. Encourage the students to be playful—ideas often come from silly beginnings.
			    The scribe's record sheets should be visible to all members of the group so they can see what has been suggested and use each other's ideas as prompts. Make sure that each idea is numbered—this helps later selection.
			    Take one idea from each team— this acknowledges their effort and makes them laugh, which is a way of raising energy levels.
			    It is important to make some comments on what this technique feels like together, with observations about whether the teams followed the rules and whether they will do it

			differently when they get on to the real project
2 mins	Brief students on the real task. Remind them to use the rules and that the purpose is to generate lots of ideas from which they will select later.	Listen, check anything they do not understand.	Use the 'headline' and 'background' in the briefing, i.e., make your points succinctly. This models the process for the students.
15 mins	Circulate, make sure the teams are keeping to the rules. Otherwise do not intervene. Act as timekeeper.	Student teams generate ideas for 15 mins. Scribes record them verbatim and number them.	It is important to keep this energetic.
10 mins	Introduce the idea-selection technique, as follows. Each student chooses his or her favoured ideas from the team's list. Each student is allowed 5 ticks, which can be allocated as he or she chooses, for example he or she can allocate all the ticks to one idea, or one tick each of the five ideas. This quickly shows which ideas are most popular.	Listen, check they understand. Each team selects its top ideas, using the technique.	Use the 'headline' and 'background' when briefing the students. An important role for the tutor is to convey good communication skills.
5 mins brief, 20 mins work	Brief the students to go through the chosen ideas in turn, using the following approach: for each idea they should first say what they like about it and then what concerns they have about whether it will work (on the	Students discuss and develop their ideas using the technique outlined. (Teams should appoint a chair to run this process as it requires some discipline from the group.)	It is important for the teams to stick to the recommended technique at this stage. It can be tempting to drop back into criticism and unprofitable debate. The process as outlined allows everyone to contribute and

	projector). On the basis of this discussion the students should then refine the ideas to the point where the group reaches a consensus on their value, although some may need more work. Demonstrate this approach by taking the 'top idea' from a sample team and asking the team members to respond and develop it as outlined.		leads to the development of ideas that team members feel happy about adopting because they have contributed to their development.
8 mins	Review the session with the students. Ask first about the value of the ideas generated. Invite each team to select one idea and give an account of how it was developed. Then ask for comments from each team on the value of the process and what their experience has been in trying it out.	One student reports from each team, using headline and background format to keep the report concise.	It is valuable to do this as it shares the pool of ideas beyond the initiating teams.
5 mins	Asks students for brief written comments on the value of the process used, their suggestions for where the team will use it subsequently and any recommendations for rerunning the workshop.	Students write feedback.	Useful as a means of reinforcing what the students have learned. Also provides hints for subsequent reruns.

Issue students with brief summary of process they have tried out.		

Back-up material

(A) IDEA-GENERATION RULES

- Everybody contributes.
- Switch off the censor No criticism—of your own ideas or anyone else's
- Be playful
- Give ideas as 'headlines' (scribe notes headlines verbatim).

(B) STAGES OF THE PROCESS

- Getting the ideas together:
  1 People contribute as many ideas as possible. Do not discuss them!
  2 Note down all ideas in large and legible handwriting. Number each one.
- Selecting the ideas to work on:
  1 Idea selection—everybody has five ticks to distribute amongst the list of ideas. No discussion.
  2 The top ideas are those with the most ticks.
- Working up the ideas into a useful form:
  1 Discuss what team likes about these ideas, then outline any problems with them.
  2 Generate some more ideas for ways of getting round the problems.

3   Reviewing teamwork (Timing: 45 minutes)

Learning objectives

- Students reflect on a recent team project in order to improve their understanding of team processes and develop their effectiveness as teamworkers.
- Students derive some lessons to take forward.

Student output

- Personal action plans to work on during the next teamwork project.

- A set of notes to remind the students what they said they would do differently (if the team remains the same for the next project).

Running order and script

Time	What the tutor does	What the students do	Notes
3 mins	Outline the aims of the session: to reflect on what has been learned from the experience of teamwork in order to take that forward into subsequent teams. Focus is on learning from the process of teamworking rather than the task achieved.	Listen, check understanding.	The first time you and the students do this there are likely to be some misunderstandings. Make sure that all the students are clear about the purpose of the session before they start.
7 mins: 2 on brief, 5 on notes	Brief students to make short individual notes about their experience of this recent teamwork in preparation for discussion with the other team members: 1 What did you do well as a team? 2 What could you have done differently?	Listen. Make individual notes under the suggested headings.	This reflection is simple and allows many different things to emerge (see back-up notes). Asking them to write their own notes first is a way of encouraging everyone to participate.
15 mins	Ask the students to share and discuss their individual experiences. Everyone must contribute to this. Remind the students that useful feedback is specific feedback. If necessary, point out that the aim of this review is to	Students work in teams to share and discuss their individual experiences of the teamwork.	Depending on how well the teamwork has gone in the project, you may want to introduce an approach that prevents students from blaming each other for perceived failures. Offering specific feedback on where you would like

	learn, not to allocate blame or settle scores.		improvement—'I found it difficult when you didn't get your work done in time'—is easier to do something about than 'You messed up the whole project'.
10 mins	Ask the students to synthesise from this discussion three things the team has learned from the experience and be prepared to report on these.	Students pick out three things they think the team has learned from its experience.	Asking for a limited number of things learned makes this an achievable task.
10 mins: 2 for brief, 8 for discussion	Take one thing learned from each team and note on a flip chart. If time allows, go round a second time. Lead the students into a short discussion of how they will take these forward in subsequent teamwork. Suggest that the students individually note what changes to their own teamworking behaviour they would like to make.	Reporters from each team summarise key team learning as requested.	It may help to finish with a short homily on how working at being better at teamwork pays off in the long run. You may also want to alert them to the next piece of teamwork in the course.